Learning History in America

Learning History
in America

Schools, Cultures, and Politics

Lloyd Kramer, Donald Reid,
and William L. Barney, editors

University of Minnesota Press

Minneapolis

London

Published by the University of Minnesota Press
2037 University Avenue Southeast, Minneapolis, MN 55455-3092
Printed in the United States of America on acid-free paper

Library of Congress Cataloging-in-Publication Data
Learning history in America : schools, cultures, and politics / Lloyd
    Kramer, Donald Reid, and William L. Barney.
        p.   cm.
    Includes bibliographical references (p.) and index.
    ISBN 0-8166-2363-5 (alk. paper)
    ISBN 0-8166-2364-3 (pbk : alk. paper)
    1. United States—History—Study and teaching.   2. History—Study
and teaching—United States.   3. United States—History—Textbooks.
4. Political culture—United States.   I. Kramer, Lloyd S.
II. Reid, Donald.   III. Barney, William L.
E175.8.L43   1994
907'.2073—dc20   93-25489
                                                                          CIP

The University of Minnesota is an
equal-opportunity educator and employer.

Contents

Part III. Popular Films and Historical Memory

Part IV. Political Culture and Historical Interpretation

Acknowledgments

This volume began as a conference at the University of North Carolina at Chapel Hill in April 1991 that brought together a wide range of people concerned with historical understanding in the contemporary United States. The conference organizers — in their new guise as book editors — would like to thank all those who made this conference possible. Funding was provided by the Department of History, the Institute for the Arts and Humanities, and the Arts and Sciences Foundation, Inc., at the University of North Carolina at Chapel Hill (UNC); the North Carolina Humanities Council; and the Z. Smith Reynolds Foundation. This support was not only financial; it came in the form of valuable encouragement and advice as well. We especially thank Colin Palmer, former chair of the UNC history department; Gillian Cell, former dean of the College of Arts and Sciences at UNC; Barbara Hyde, former director of the Arts and Sciences Foundation, Inc.; Alice S. Barkley, executive director of the North Carolina Humanities Council; and Thomas W. Lambeth, executive director of the Z. Smith Reynolds Foundation. We would also like to thank the North Carolina Center for the Advancement of Teaching, and Christine Shea in particular, for providing financial support and intellectual community to two conference participants, Alice Garrett and Glenn Tetterton-Opheim, who prepared their essays at the center's facilities in Cullowhee, North Carolina.

In arranging the conference and the publication of this book, the editors have relied upon the unfailing support of a number of individuals at UNC. Pamela Fesmire, Yvonne Funk, Jane Lindley, Mattie Hackney, and Rosalie Radcliffe provided valuable clerical and administrative assistance; Don Young helped with computer technology. Helen Wilson and Harihar Bhattarai of the Institute for the Arts and Humanities helped in all facets of publicity and outreach.

The conference drew upon the talents and skills of a number of individuals who as moderators and commentators initiated lively and fruitful discussion from conference participants. We thank for their contributions to our collective project Judith Bennett, Craig Calhoun, Peter Filene, Barbara Harris, John Kasson, Colin Palmer, Ruel Tyson, and Joel Williamson of UNC; Linda Orr and William Reddy of Duke University; Steven Vincent of North Carolina State University; James Raths of the University of Vermont; and Jacquelyn Boykin of the North Carolina Department of Public Instruction.

There is one final group of individuals to whom we would like to offer our special thanks: the graduate students of the UNC Department of History. We particularly appreciated their enthusiasm and willingness to perform the hundreds of tasks that create a successful conference, but they added significantly to the intellectual debates as well as to the logistics of the event. Mark Meyers, a history department research assistant, and Michael McFalls of the UNC Institute for the Arts and Humanities played leading roles. They were ably assisted by Mary-Jane Aldrich-Moodie, Mason Barnett, Doris Bergen, Kristine Bradberry, Sandra Chaney, James Crawford, Richard Derderian, David Grier, Cindy Hahamovitch, Michaela Honicke, Claire Kirch, Tracy K'Meyer, Marybeth Lavrakas, Jennifer Lettieri, Timothy Long, Carolyn Marks, Daniel Mattern, Edison MacIntyre, Marla Miller, Joseph Mosnier, Kathyrn Nasstrom, Karen Paar, Scott Philyaw, Claire Sanders, David Shaw, Joel Sipress, Michael Sistrom, Gretchen Skidmore, and Janet Sorrentino. This book is dedicated to the graduate students and to all those preparing for careers that involve critical engagement with history as a means of understanding the world in which we live—and the world we will make in the future.

In transforming the essays from conference papers into a book, we have drawn on the enthusiasm and guidance of Janaki Bakhle and Robert Mosimann at the University of Minnesota Press, and the advice of Craig Calhoun. Rosalie Radcliffe provided outstanding assistance in organizing and preparing the manuscript for publication; we thank her warmly for the quality of her work and for the efficiency with which she completed it. Finally, we thank Gwynne Pomeroy, Holly Russell, and Elaine Barney for their interest, patience, and assistance during all phases of our work on this book.

The editors have directed all royalties from this volume to the Project for Historical Education in the UNC Department of History. This project sponsors workshops and other activities that bring together instructors from secondary schools, colleges, and universities in order to improve the teaching of history and to emphasize the value of new forms of historical knowledge and pedagogy.

Introduction: Historical Knowledge, Education, and Public Culture

Lloyd Kramer and Donald Reid

A well-publicized intellectual and emotional debate about cultural diversity and national unity has divided polemical opponents in the schools, the media, and the political parties of contemporary American society. Some of these debaters—including many advocates of non-European cultures, critics of traditional education, and historians—celebrate the expanding cultural emphasis on previously overlooked ethnic groups, women, and racial minorities. The new interest in diversity, however, has provoked others—including many advocates of European cultures, critics of educational reforms, and historians—to complain that recent trends in education are fragmenting America's cultural tradition and undermining the unity and coherence of American society. One prominent historian, for example, has issued strong warnings about the "disuniting of America" that will result from the teaching of particular ethnic and racial histories if this teaching is not also linked to an emphasis on shared political and cultural ideals.[1] These debates, which appear in all regions of America, have become known in simple terms as the debate over "multiculturalism." The controversy seems certain to continue into the next century because it is closely connected to social, economic, and cultural patterns that are creating a new, more diverse American society.

The editors of this book do not regret these debates or wish they would go away. On the contrary, we welcome this public discussion, and we would like to see it continue because we believe that critical debates about education and the future evolution of a multicultural society are essential for democratic political life in America. More specifically, we believe that the "multicultural debates" and the continuing development of America's political culture should include self-conscious, well-informed interpretations of the past. Indeed, we assume that present conflicts and power struggles in

1

schools, the media, and politics cannot be separated from conflicts over historical knowledge and historical interpretations. This book therefore carries the obvious influence of recent public arguments about America's multicultural society, education, politics, and history, and it sets out explicitly to explore both the practical and the theoretical implications of these arguments for people who learn and teach history in the United States.

Most of the essays in this collection were originally prepared for a public conference on the transmission of historical knowledge in American schools and popular culture. The conference took place in April 1991 at the University of North Carolina, Chapel Hill, where faculty and graduate students in the history department have been meeting in recent years to discuss the connections between teaching, research, and the structuring categories of historical understanding that enable us to talk about the past. We call these meetings Clio's Friday Club, and we regularly launch the informal discussions with some provocative comments on a particular thematic issue in the current study of history. Many of these themes raise questions about how our analytical categories (e.g., objectivity, politics, gender, revolution, nationality, race, Western culture) shape the teaching and writing of history, but we also consider how other forms of culture (e.g., literature, film) contribute to historical memory and education. Having explored such issues among ourselves for several years, we decided that it was time to expand the discussion with the help of others who have thought about the nature of historical knowledge in education, popular culture, and politics—all of which provide the historical information and interpretations that define America's national identity. This book is therefore the extension of a dialogue that began by crossing the normal boundaries of academic life (graduate students/faculty) and expanded by asking people to move outside their normal intellectual circuits (university professors/high school teachers/journalists). The diverse perspectives, methods, and professions that we have brought together here represent both our intentions and the differences between people who are thinking about the importance of history in various spheres of American society.

All of the authors in this volume are concerned with the problem of communicating historical knowledge and interpretations within a culture that often ignores or trivializes historical understanding. They differ, however, in their specific interests, in their explanations of the general indifference to historical analysis, and in their rationales or strategies for enhancing historical consciousness. The research historians who teach in universities tend to emphasize the importance of bringing new forms of knowledge and conceptualization into education and public culture, whereas the high school teachers and journalists highlight the difficulty of imparting basic or required historical information and perspectives to an unreceptive audience. Our conference thus exposed some of the significant differences that separate a graduate seminar from a high school classroom, a popular film, or a newspaper article. These differences inevitably created certain tensions as people tried to find (or deny) connections between their own concerns and the priorities of others. But the tensions that appeared within our conference also became the local expression of issues that surface constantly in contemporary America's cultural and political debates.

The Historical Context

The essays in this book, like all other texts, have been written in a historical context that shapes both the themes and the prose styles of the authors. A close reading of these texts would in fact lead to many overlapping contexts of politics, social hierarchies, modern communications, and international relations, but we want to focus briefly on two contextual influences that carry the most obvious connections to this book: the wide-ranging public debate about the proper curriculum for American schools and universities, and the more specific debate among historians about new trends in historical scholarship. Although the general trends in contemporary education receive far more public attention than the relatively obscure trends of research among professional historians, the debates in both spheres raise similar questions about the nature and function of knowledge. The passion of such debates suggests that the cultural meaning of knowledge, including knowledge about history, reaches deep into the social and psychological life of American society.

The most common critique of American education today stresses that the rising generation lacks even the most elementary knowledge of American history and the traditions of American culture. This situation is not new (complaints about the ignorance of youth appear in every generation), yet the typical media report on the factual knowledge of contemporary students describes a remarkable ignorance of virtually every important event in American history. Many students are unable to give the dates or name the key leaders of the American Revolution or Civil War or World War I, and the more complex aspects of such influential events are almost surely less well known than the dates and names.[2] A comprehensive historical explanation for this kind of historical ignorance would expand the analysis of education into economic changes and financial problems, the mass media and advertising, popular films and music, social inequalities and racial conflicts, immigration patterns and family life—but the most popular explanation blames the ignorance of history mainly on the curriculum of schools and universities. According to this curricular explanation, students lack essential knowledge because they no longer learn the facts of history that were taught to earlier generations. The public schools (in this view) have fallen into chaos by teaching skills over content or by choosing entertainment over hard work or by caving in to the political pressures of vocal minorities. Meanwhile, the universities (in this view) have abandoned the teaching of basic information and turned instead to either specialized research or the cultural agendas of special interests and tenured radicals.[3] To place this curricular critique of education in its most general terms, many critics believe American schools and universities have been taken over by theorists and theories that emerged in various cultural or political movements of the 1960s.

This concern about the legacy of the 1960s appears prominently in the widespread arguments about a "multicultural" challenge to the "canon" of "great books" in Western culture. As even a casual reader of newspapers and magazines must now know, many teachers and students have sought to expand the canon of traditional books (mostly written by white males) to include works by women and non-European authors. This challenge to the canon, in turn, has elicited ardent defenses of the traditional curriculum from those who see the critique of great books as a profound threat to cultural coherence and national unity.[4] Although debates about the canon developed their polemical tone and urgency in the field of literary studies, the issue clearly carries an equal significance for the study of history. The central question in both cases refers to the social implications of education: Is there a core body of texts or knowledge that every educated person should study? Most teachers have probably assumed that such a core of knowledge exists, though their definitions of its contents have varied. For teachers of literature, this core has traditionally been constituted by the major works of great authors; for teachers of history, this core has traditionally been constituted by the major public events of great nations. The emergence of multicultural history (stressing women, minorities, non-Western cultures, etc.) has thus challenged the historical canon of great events in ways that resemble the multicultural challenge to the literary canon of great books, though historians have been less inclined to discuss their work in the language of a canonical tradition. One purpose of this book is to make issues of the canon as explicit for historians as they have become for literary theorists.

The desire for an expanded canon of historical reality nevertheless raises political questions that may be more acute for historians than for literary scholars, because history has generally played a more fundamental role than literature in the creation and maintenance of national identities. A democratic public culture cannot survive without broad commitments to democratic ideas, traditions, and freedoms that come in part from a knowledge of history. Public debate requires a shared vocabulary that emerges from the historical experience and language of people who acknowledge some common values or principles or founding events. Historians in modern nations have thus helped to sustain the collective identity with stories of important past events (e.g., describing the origins of the nation) and stories of important past leaders (e.g., describing the heroic Founding Fathers). At the present time, however, this traditional social function of historians has given way increasingly to another social function: the rediscovery of lost or ignored or excluded people who never entered the "canon" of events that constituted the collective national history and identity. The trends of recent historiography therefore raise another organizing question for this book: Can the new knowledge and concerns of historians be brought into the teaching of history without losing the shared vocabulary and knowledge that are needed for public debate, informed citizens, and democratic societies? Or, to pose the question another way, can historians provide a new shared vocabulary and knowledge that can encompass the fruits of their new research?

These questions necessarily take us into the more specific context of contemporary historical scholarship, much of which focuses on the social and cultural history of people or problems that received little attention from earlier generations of historians. The "new" social history has emphasized the history and experiences of workers, women, slaves, racial and ethnic minorities, colonized societies, unknown members of the middle class, homosexuals, students, criminals, and other groups who seemingly had little or no influence on the political, diplomatic, and military events that formed the traditional object of historical studies.[5] Contemporary social historians tend to deemphasize or ignore the leaders and policies of political elites (except as they affect or were affected by excluded social groups) and to stress the prevalence of various forms of oppression and resistance in all past societies. Yet even the most radical new social histories often share some deep similarities with traditional political histories insofar as they describe historical processes in terms of a struggle for freedom, and insofar as they stress the exemplary roles of various leaders in that struggle. The strong desire to include more people in recent accounts of the past thus extends a well-established American tendency to foster democratic aspirations and commitments through historical commentaries, though the story of democracy moves here from Founding Fathers and famous political leaders into that great majority of people who never attended a political convention or held public office or even voted in an election. To put it simply, the former heroes of political history lose some of their democratic status in the new social history, and Whiggish interpretations of history (tracing the progress of freedom) take on new negative or positive meanings in the histories of excluded people struggling to be free.

The evolution of meanings in a term such as "freedom" suggests one of the connections between contemporary social history and the "new" cultural history. Social historians who set out to explain the structures of power or the struggles for freedom in past eras (sometimes with Marxist categories of analysis) increasingly recognized that the exercise of power in social, economic, and political systems cannot be separated from the languages, symbols, and cultural traditions through which people shape or define themselves and are shaped or defined by others in every society. This expanding appreciation for the complex influence of cultural traditions was given impetus by the concurrent development of a "new" cultural history in the 1980s. The new cultural historians, for their part, drew on literary criticism and cultural anthropology to stress that both the events of history and the writing about history are embedded in deep structures of linguistic and symbolic meaning that enable people to describe and organize the world.[6] Indeed, the experiences of daily life and the creation of historical understanding can be compared (in this view) to the writing of literary texts in that all descriptions of reality or meaning depend on some kind of linguistic narrative. But the language that explains and organizes our daily lives, the meaning of history, and also great works of literature evolves through its own dynamic history of change, conflict, and social relationships, so that the history of the world (as we know it) is inextricably linked to a complex history of contending narratives and linguistic systems. The new cultural historians thus make the recurring and central points that historical writing depends on specific forms of cultural meaning (e.g., narrative traditions) and that historical knowledge carries the unavoidable traces of the cultural context in which it appears (i.e., its own historicity).

The imaginative recent research of social and cultural historians has helped to expand and revitalize American historiography, but it has also attracted criticism from persons who defend other forms of history inside and outside the university.[7] Significantly enough, a common criticism of current trends in both social and cultural history charges that the new approaches and methods undermine the objectivity of historical knowledge and hence represent a clear danger to the identification of what is true in history. Critics of the new social history, for example, often contend that it serves the political agenda of aggrieved groups rather than the criteria of dispassionate, careful scholarship, and critics of the new cultural history often argue that it leads to hopeless relativism rather than to rigorous, verifiable truths. The basic complaint in both cases suggests that critiques of earlier historical research are fostering ahistorical or unhistorical forms of writing, teaching, and research. Debates about the implications of new historical approaches will surely continue, fueled partly by the work of some of the contributors to this volume of essays. We therefore want to stress that none of the authors in this book deny the possibility of historical knowledge. It should also be stressed, however, that many of the authors draw attention to the structuring categories upon which knowledge depends, and many emphasize that historical truths can never lie outside history. Contrary to charges that such thinking is ahistorical, this conception of historical knowledge places knowledge itself firmly within history and historical processes.

The emphasis on the historicity of historical knowledge becomes especially disorienting in the works of contemporary historians because it poses major challenges to the desire for objective historical understanding. The call for more study of women, racial minorities, and workers may disturb someone who thinks that history is simply past politics (if such a person actually exists), but it does not necessarily pose questions about how these new categories of historical analysis are also part of the historical process. In fact, the truly complex historical project for "old" and "new" historians alike is to think about how our historical knowledge is shaped by the explicit or implicit categories that we use to describe the past. This frank admission of our own historicity does not mean that we can say whatever we want to say about the past, that all narratives of history are equally valid, or that we can have no knowledge. It does suggest, however, that we need to think about how our own categories necessarily enter into accounts of other cultures or into accounts of our own national history; and we can assume, moreover, that recognition of those structuring categories ultimately helps historians listen more carefully to voices from the past (or present) that might not otherwise be heard.

An explicit analysis of the various categories of modern historical understanding does not therefore condemn historians to their own relativistic obsessions. Indeed, the critical examination of our own categories of knowledge can lead to more insight into the autonomy and differences of past cultures. Historians cannot really avoid the use of their own categories as they study or describe the past because they are situated like everyone else within a culture that continually develops new ways of understanding its own society, and these new perspectives inevitably enter into the ways that historians interpret the past. Given this context for all historical studies, the real question concerns the historian's interaction with the culture's evolving conceptual categories: How can historians self-consciously use or extend the cultural assumptions of their own era? In answering this question, historians have the advantage of sustained contact with people who (though they are often dead) pose constant questions to our own culture and our own categories of analysis. Historians use the past to express their own concerns, but the past also challenges, defies, and transforms the meaning of all historical research. As Dominick LaCapra notes in his theoretical account of this "dialogic" process, we can never know the past simply on its own terms (history constantly changes meanings), and yet we should also never assume that our own terms stand free from the language or problems of the past (history constantly connects meanings across time). Our task as historians — and not just as historians — is to accept the autonomy of others without denying ourselves.

The essays in this book therefore give much attention to the categories of historical understanding that have structured modern American and European narratives of past societies and people. There can be no escape from analytical categories, but a key purpose of this book is to stimulate more discussion about how we use them and which ones are important when we learn history or write textbooks or watch a film or debate politics. The book is organized in four thematic sections that examine three broad spheres of historical education in American society: classrooms and textbooks, historical films, and political culture. All of these spheres are linked, however, through a common reliance on certain deep structures or categories of historical meaning and interpretation, some of which receive their most explicit thematic analysis in the essays of Part II ("Rethinking Categories of Historical Meaning"). This section of the book forms a bridge between the specific concerns that shape the learning of history in schools and the wider cultural patterns that shape the learning of history in films and politics.

Textbooks, Survey Courses, and Historical Education

Every day our families, neighbors, churches, politicians, and mass media offer us interpretations of historical events and narrative structures to make sense of the past. Most people, however, receive the most complete, systematic presentation of history in the survey courses that are taught at schools and universities. Most history teachers in the United States regularly confront the challenges of teaching these broad courses to large numbers of distracted students, so it is not surprising that the essays in this section of the book refer often to personal experience with classrooms and textbooks. The two pedagogical structures are closely connected because, as Mary Beth Norton stresses in her essay, the textbook plays a crucial role in the codification of historical knowledge in this arena: students often believe that information is not important if it does not appear in a textbook.

Norton, whose own textbook on American history has been widely adopted in American colleges, gives us a personal look at the often faceless textbook author. She brings out the interplay between personal and professional identity and the construction of a historical narrative, which is a recurring theme in this volume. Reading historical fiction as a youth sparked Norton's interest in history, and writing a textbook that incorporates some of this idea of history as stories has brought her full circle. The process of writing and revising a textbook, she explains, has helped her integrate her roles as a researcher and a teacher in new and unexpected ways.

Norton chronicles the growing inclusion of social history in American history surveys and shows convincingly how it transforms older categories of analysis that have been used to construct narratives of the nation's past. She concludes that the much-lamented fragmentation in American history is the result of too little rather than too much reliance on recent scholarship. If, for instance, women's history is inserted into the survey simply as a "compensatory" gesture, the result will be fragmentation. Real engagement with recent research in women's history, however, opens a way to rethink analytical categories such as "politics" and to provide greater coherence for the study of American history.

Norton is optimistic that the dissonance between older political narratives and new research in social history can be resolved. She sees no reason to challenge the necessity or validity of the American history survey itself, and she expresses considerable confidence that the new social history enables the author, the teachers of historical surveys, and the American citizen to clarify their own identities and histories through a more comprehensive narrative.

Lynn Hunt also draws on her experience as the author of a textbook, but she offers a more problematic picture of the Western civilization survey. Academic politics, scholarship, and systems of professional prestige often seem to suggest that the course be jettisoned, not reworked in Norton's terms. Hunt responds by asking us to take a different look at the "Western civ" survey. Rather than focus on charges of sexism and racism in the content of the course, she discusses the people who commonly teach or take the course. While conservatives have often been most concerned with defending Western civ courses at prestigious institutions as a means of transmitting cultural values and norms to future elites, Hunt discerns a democratizing element in such courses. She notes that they are most often taught by instructors at the bottom or the margins of the professional hierarchy to students at nonelite institutions who are eager to attain the "cultural capital" they consider necessary to climb the social hierarchy. (This, incidentally, is one of the few references in these essays to class, a subject that would have functioned until recently as a crucial category of historical analysis or revision.)

Hunt does not seem deterred by her own recognition that Western civ has a clear historical and political genealogy, that it is peculiarly American, or that it requires the historian to fashion a narrative, with the necessary hierarchies, exclusions, and deformations this implies. On the contrary, she offers a strong defense of the teaching of Western civ as the "obligation [of] historians to the community at large—to the American public and its collective memory—to provide some sense of how we came to where we are in the world community today."

Hunt provocatively suggests that the very questioning that emerges in current thinking about the Western civ course can forward this goal. Why, she asks, does the United States occupy such a marginal place in the typical

Western civ survey? Such questions about these courses may challenge the many proponents of Western civ who assume that in 1776 the United States inherited a tradition spanning from the ancients to Adam Smith and remained true to this timeless legacy while the Western Europe of Marx, Nietzsche, Freud, and Foucault wandered paths antithetic to this definition of Western civilization. Or, as Hunt asks bluntly, "What is distinctively Western in Western civ?"

Daniel Gordon also writes about Western civilization courses, drawing upon his experiences as a student and graduate student instructor in "great books" courses at Columbia University and at the University of Chicago, and as an instructor in the Cultures, Ideas, and Values (CIV) course at Stanford University. While Gordon shares Hunt's belief in the importance of such courses, he is less concerned with academic criticisms of Western civ than with external criticisms of the attempt to rethink the topics or texts that are taught in these classes. Gordon cogently criticizes commentators who draw sweeping conclusions from a quick glance at the reading lists for CIV courses. His own careful explanations challenge these superficial reactions by suggesting that the major difference between the Stanford curriculum and its Columbia and Chicago counterparts is less in the titles of assigned texts than in the ways the books are read and analyzed in class.

According to Gordon, traditional courses on the great books mostly teach students to interpret texts in terms of their place in ahistorical conversations about allegedly unchanging philosophical questions. The largest track of the CIV program at Stanford, by contrast, approaches texts as historical documents rather than as elements in a canon of great books; in other words, Gordon and his colleagues stressed the connections between books and the specific historical contexts in which they were written. On the particular question that has attracted the most controversy—the inclusion of works by women and men of non-European ancestry—Gordon argues that the course at Stanford does not serve the purpose of promoting gender or racial quotas. Instead, the inclusion of new texts in the curriculum encourages discussions about the historical processes that generate cultural identity and about the ways in which these processes have shaped societies in the past as well as in the present. Gordon notes that debates about the meaning of "Western culture" are almost as old as the concept itself, and he joins with Hunt in proposing that we need to ask about the multiple meanings of the term "Western" in courses that teach the history of Western civilization.

Richard Roberts poses the question of cultural meaning somewhat differently in his essay about designing a course entitled The World outside the West: What is distinctively Western in the term "civilization"? Lynn Hunt recognizes that the move from history to the more normative concept of "civilization" places many contemporary historians of Western culture in an uncomfortable position, and Roberts wants to make them even more uncomfortable when they turn their analysis to societies outside the West. Responding to the same debates over Western culture that Gordon observed at Stanford (a well-publicized example of the wider arguments about "multiculturalism" and "canons"), Roberts contends that Western civilization textbooks present a definition of the apparently universal category "civilization," which is, in fact, extrapolated from a certain conceptualization of "high culture" in ancient Greece. The point is not to pursue a variant of what Norton labels the "compensatory" project and show that this form of civilization is to be found in non-Western societies. Instead, Roberts argues, scholars and students must develop less hierarchical categories of analysis suitable for understanding other societies in terms that do not rest solely on their similarity to or difference from Western civilization. The conceptual approach to such societies, for example, should "sensitize students to the distortions of complex social realities that arise with the use of terms like 'non-Western world' and 'Third World,' which are residual categories indicating not what various cultures are, but what they are not."

Through his World outside the West course at Stanford, Roberts hopes students learn about different cultures through the internal perspectives of those cultures as well as the perspectives of outsiders: "We expected that students would come to see that the Western tradition is just one possibility among many. As a result, students would come to adopt a more detached perspective on their own culture." This broadening of historical attitudes complements Hunt's view of Western civ as a course that should help students discover the "debate about the fundamental values of our culture."

Alice Garrett and Glenn Tetterton-Opheim conclude this section of the book with essays that address the specific problems of teaching history in American high schools, including the problem of bureaucratic constraints that are imposed on most teachers in secondary schools. Garrett argues for an approach to the coherence of history that stresses its comparative, apparently cyclical nature, and she advocates a form of pedagogy in which students constantly intervene personally in a past they have reconstructed. Garrett is especially concerned with history and historical personages as moral exemplars (but which, to anticipate Dominick LaCapra, could be open to dialogic exchanges between past and present).

One element of Garrett's essay deserves particular attention. While Hunt, Gordon, and Roberts use the term "canon" in its traditional sense, Garrett adapts the term to fit her classroom experience. North Carolina high school teachers, like the teachers in many states, are given a tightly prescribed body of facts, skills, and texts that they are required to teach students. Labeling this material a canon may, at first glance, seem to parody recent debates on the subject. After all, as a representative of the North Carolina State Department of Public Instruction explained at the conference, required materials in the state education system come not solely from some carefully transmitted body of traditions, but also from well-funded campaigns of chambers of commerce (for a required course on free enterprise), the National Geographic Society (for geography), and even from an individual textile magnate (for legislation requiring that the *Federalist Papers* be taught in all North Carolina high schools).

Despite the evident role of powerful interests in setting secondary school curricula, Garrett is right to say that state-mandated materials are transmitted to teachers as though they were a secularized canon. From here, she goes on to suggest that such materials seem to require an authoritarian, "canonical" form of instruction. Garrett argues, however, that truly creative teachers do not limit themselves either to canonical materials or to canonical forms of instruction. Nor should extracanonical materials and teaching methods necessarily follow, like poor cousins, canonical methods and modes of instruction; on the contrary, her examples suggest that nontraditional materials and pedagogy are often most effective when they precede the standarized curriculum. And in teaching "outside the canon," teachers may well point to some of the ways that people in past and present societies have made history by stepping outside the officially sanctioned ways of doing things. She conceives of the classroom not simply as a place where a cultural tradition is transmitted to promote good citizenship, but also as a site where the student acquires skills that are needed to become an active citizen.

Although Tetterton-Opheim shares this goal, he takes a different approach, arguing that the limiting category of analysis is "history" itself; unlike Hunt's university colleagues, he would prefer to teach courses in "civilization," which would offer him greater latitude to explore science and literature. Tetterton-Opheim's approach to teaching resembles Garrett's in two ways. First, he breaks with many demands of the advanced placement history examination (for which he is preparing his students) because the extensive attention he gives to science and literature is not warranted by the few questions about these subjects on the test. Second, although Tetterton-Opheim teaches students whose academic expectations may differ significantly from those in Garrett's classes, both make student interest and input the focal points of their teaching.

Tetterton-Opheim recognizes that the students themselves want to reject the fragmentation of their academic experience and make a coherent whole of their studies. He responds to this desire with the claim that history should not be viewed as a discrete discipline, but as an approach to knowledge that can provide meaning and coherence to the diversity of high school curricula. Tetterton-Opheim joins Hunt in emphasizing the importance of coherence and in using the history of science as an example of knowledge that is too often separated from the other themes of historical surveys. He pursues this insight to argue that students who grasp Heisenberg's uncertainty principle will be better able to see that history itself involves subjective choices on the part of historians. This in turn recalls his basic premise that the student's own desire to give meaning and coherence to the world is the basis of successful historical synthesis. Tetterton-Opheim concludes that history is best conceived as a body of literature, but that academic historians' efforts to retain the veneer of scientific objectivity often render it far less engaging than fiction and films.

Norton, Hunt, Gordon, Roberts, Garrett, and Tetterton-Opheim therefore address the important pedagogical issues of attracting student interest, introducing new forms of knowledge, providing synthesis as well as details, and making students think about their own relation to the history that is presented in textbooks and classrooms. Their thoughtful commentaries on their work in the classroom show that teachers of history care far more about teaching than one would ever expect after reading the recent condemnations of American schools and universities. They all propose new themes or methods to enhance historical education, and, equally important, they all agree that the attempt to teach new ways of knowing history requires new ways of conceptualizing historical reality.

Rethinking Categories of Historical Meaning

James Anderson, Bonnie Smith, and Dominick LaCapra address similar problems in their discussions of how historical knowledge depends on underlying or unexamined assumptions about reality and the uncritical use of categories such as race, gender, and context. Each seeks to introduce greater critical consciousness into historical analysis by showing that such categories are not natural, but historically constructed. All three emphasize the importance of reading critically the founding or canonical texts of a discipline or mode of analysis to discover its implicit assumptions. They remind us, in short, that the writing of history can never be separated from the theories of history.

Anderson analyzes various narratives of American history and the themes of secondary school textbooks to show how they communicate the assumption that "race" is a natural category rather than a historically created ideology of human cultures. Arguing against the tendency to explain complex historical interactions in the simple terms of "racial" identities and differences, he urges teachers to counter the everyday notion of race as a fixed biological fact that naturally generates solidarities among those of the same "race" and conflicts with those who are different. Past and present claims about irreducible racial difference or racial essence therefore reflect for Anderson the unfortunate consequences of ahistorical thinking. The truly historical discussion of race, as he explains with some persuasive examples, should describe its emergence as an ideological system that is derived from and sustained by specific historical experiences. Teaching with this historical perspective clearly in view, the well-informed instructor would help students see that "race and ethnicity are, above all else, products of history, that they are not created by nature but by men and women, and that men and women can change them." Indeed, the shifting meaning of "race" in modern history offers one of the best examples of how unexamined analytical categories shape our understanding of both past and present realities.

Anderson's critique of textbooks relies upon recent scholarship that has been transforming the significance of race in American history. Bonnie Smith recognizes that gender has also received new, revisionist attention from historians, but she questions the structuring assumptions of most contemporary historical scholarship, including much of the work in genres such as the histories of race and gender. She argues that academic historiography (whether practiced by men or by women) has conceptualized itself since its origins in the nineteenth century from the position of the male historian seeking to ravish and subjugate a feminine-coded historical object. If the language through which historians conceptualize the past preserves gendered hierarchies and sexist practices, then the reconceptualizations of historical understanding attendant on the inclusion of women in the historical survey will not be accomplished as readily as Norton suggests. Although Smith offers alternatives to traditional history in Lucy Salmon's distinctly "unprofessional" language and in her own narrative of reproduction as a historical rather than a natural experience, she concludes on a pessimistic note. Academic history continues to parade its claim to be "about objective Reality and universal truth when in fact it is partial and so filled with fantasies of masculinity. . . . As long as we try to fit a few women into a narrative that assigns primacy to the details of political struggle and great men, learning history will remain a far from benign enterprise." Her essay thus suggests that the first step in a fundamental transformation of modern scholarship would come with the recognition that our implicit conceptions of gender shape and reflect an identifiable historical process.

Dominick LaCapra extends the argument about the historical construction of race and gender into the realm of great books, which he also situates in culture rather than in some sphere of natural or transcendent reality. Yet, much as Anderson and Smith use the categories of race and gender even as they question the assumptions on which they rest, LaCapra defends certain methods of reading canonical texts even as he questions obsessive affirmations of the faith in canonicity. His openness to critiques of the canon and his affirmation that some texts are in fact better to think with than others are reminiscent of Hunt's recognition of validity in the critiques of master narratives and her defense of the Western civilization survey; both LaCapra and

Hunt emphasize the importance of shared reference points for the continuation of cultural and historical debates.

LaCapra encourages a dialogue between two basic ways of reading texts, arguing that neither is sufficient unto itself: he accepts the traditional, historical project of placing texts within the specific contexts in which they were produced and received (Gordon's approach at Stanford), but he also strongly advocates a dialogic exchange between past texts and "the performative and creative way in which we rewrite the past in terms of present interests, needs, and values." Dialogic exchange with certain texts may "make claims on us and may even disrupt the explanatory or interpretive molds in which we try to contain them" for "we are always implicated in the things we analyze and try to understand." Dialogic exchange, then, is not simply a method one might choose; it enters more or less consciously into any serious historical analysis, though some historians may want to deny that their own concerns shape their approach to history or that history constantly escapes their own analytical categories. This account of historical research might be seen to fit with Tetterton-Opheim's understanding of subjectivity in historical literature, and it provides a theoretical underpinning for Roberts's suggestion that "Western" students' study of (or dialogue with) cultures outside the West will ultimately lead them to view their own historical context (Western civilization) with broader and somewhat different perspectives. More generally, some form of dialogic exchange is the way in which most students naturally confront the past; instead of repressing this, LaCapra suggests that scholars and students recognize it and think directly about its consequences in order to receive maximum benefit from it.

Popular Films and Historical Memory

Most Americans learn more history from films and television than from books—a fact of modern cultural life that history teachers are gradually learning to accept. It is significant, for example, that Alice Garrett uses the film *Glory* to criticize the limits of a fixed secondary school curriculum and that James Anderson makes his points about race by recounting scenes from the television show "All in the Family" and from the popular film *Norma Rae*. While some academicians may resent the importance of such artifacts in American culture, Robert Rosenstone and Ariel Dorfman embrace the challenge they present and offer assessments of their importance and meaning. The cultural influence of film in the United States (and throughout the world) raises important questions about the medium as a means of conveying historical knowledge and about the historical messages that most successful films send to their audiences. Rosenstone and Dorfman address these issues in essays that deliberately depart from the conventions of academic essay writing, just as films depart from the standards of academic written history.

Rosenstone places this difference between academic history and mainstream Hollywood films at the center of his essay. Instead of judging filmed history by the standards of written history, we should recognize that both are narrative constructions with their own rules and conventions. Thinking dialogically about the similarities and differences in filmed and written history can bring out the limitations and possibilities of both mediums. As Rosenstone notes, "The world on the screen brings together things that, for analytic or structural purposes, written history often has to split apart." This fusion of images and historical relationships challenges the conventions of written history, but it also attracts large audiences, offers new opportunities for the transmission of historical knowledge, and evokes emotional responses to historical events. Rosenstone points out that a good historical film "will always include images that are at once invented and true; true in that they symbolize, condense, or summarize larger amounts of data; true in that they impart an overall meaning of the past that can be verified, documented, or reasonably argued." Although the "inventions" in Hollywood films should not cause undue alarm among historians, Rosenstone stresses that films should lead them to think about ways to judge the "truth" or "falsity" of such inventions in relation to ongoing discussions about history. (This will become increasingly necessary in our evolving "postliterate" culture.) His own discussion of the representations of race in *Mississippi Burning* and *Glory*, for example, connects with Anderson's analysis of how race has been examined in recent professional historiography.

Ariel Dorfman develops a similar approach to films by focusing on how they rework and reshape the past in order to permit Americans collectively to unlearn or to deny a troubling history. The problem is not so much that films offer false "facts" (Dorfman is all for the imagination); instead, the main flaw lies in their tendency to tell stories that erase conflict from the past and, by extension, from the present and future. This is in keeping with the simplifying, optimistic message that Rosenstone sees in all mainstream films, where the "solution of . . . personal problems tends to substitute itself for the solution of historical problems."

Dorfman pursues his themes via a commentary and his own video script (from a video directed by Jonathan Beller) on *Field of Dreams*, a popular Hollywood film that he analyzes with what LaCapra might call contextual and dialogic readings. Dorfman emphasizes the need to contextualize the production and commercial success of films in order to engage in dialogue with those who approach them only as entertainment—thereby ignoring their more subtle lessons of history. Yet Dorfman's inclination toward dramatic dialogues also allows him to intervene in the way Americans construe their past in order to interrogate his personal concerns about the ways in which his own Chilean culture is deflecting direct confrontation with its past (an important theme in the recent Broadway production of his play *Death and the Maiden*). In spite of his efforts to delineate difference and distance from American audiences, Dorfman is not an untainted outsider who finds American mass culture alien or something to be avoided; on the contrary, he suggests that the ability both to immerse oneself in this culture and to see it as other than it asks to be seen are crucial to the historically minded critic.

Rosenstone's and Dorfman's explorations of the popular films *Glory* and *Field of Dreams* reiterate LaCapra's desire to address the past for critical perspectives on our own problems; in other words, the historical value of specific films might be measured by the extent to which they help us ask questions about the present as well as the past. Rosenstone and Dorfman also return us to public issues that Norton and Hunt raise in their discussions of textbooks. Historians and critics concerned with the transmission of historical knowledge should acknowledge the importance of commenting on mainstream films in the same way that they should accept the importance of writing textbooks.

Political Culture and Historical Interpretations

Historical knowledge and interpretations may carry their most tangible public consequences in the structuring of political debates and the formulation of government policies. In any case, many Americans learn their views of history from political leaders, and this aspect of historical understanding receives particular attention in the essays of Frances FitzGerald and Edwin Yoder. FitzGerald, like Dorfman, is concerned with the ways in which history creates a consensus in public policy and a conception of the nation's identity, especially in its dealings with other nations. Stressing the influence of a rhetorical tradition that links Ronald Reagan and George Bush to a long line of predecessors, FitzGerald shows how religious conceptions of good and evil and a belief in American exceptionalism have consistently shaped the way public culture teaches Americans about their history. No momentous event, most notably a war, can ever be represented in historical terms that do not repeat this basic evangelical conception of the world. She suggests that such historical narratives help reduce internal conflicts by creating internal consensus in the battle against an outside force, but the demise of Soviet communism as a viable enemy has exposed at least some of the tensions in this rhetoric and practice of American foreign policy. The transformation of national enemies may thus open stories about the past to closer scrutiny and lead to new analysis of conflicts within American history. Indeed, following the implications of FitzGerald's argument, one might describe the interest in multicultural history and especially the opposition to it as examples of the historical transitions and anxieties that may result from the disappearance of America's most visible modern enemy.

Edwin Yoder is also interested in the links between history and politics, but he expresses more concern about the influence of current political rhetoric on historical scholarship than with the effects of historical rhetoric on public policy. He draws some provocative comparisons between Ronald Reagan's loose interpretation of historical facts and the "new historicism" in literary studies, both of which raise questions about the use of history to promote present interpretations of past realities. Yoder's discussion of the "new historicist" interpretation of Shakespeare's play *The Tempest* challenges LaCapra's idea of a dialogic exchange by arguing that the introduction of present concerns and categories (e.g., colonialism) may distort rather than enhance our understanding of the past on its own terms. (There is an interesting parallel here with Roberts's call for an approach to non–Western cultures on their own terms.) His warnings about presentist perspectives takes us back into the continuing debate about objectivity and historical knowledge, though Yoder acknowledges that historians can never know the whole truth about past societies.

Yoder's concluding commentary surveys the thematic direction of the essays in this collection and points to several areas of concern: the importance of contemporary political preoccupations may relegate historical facts to a secondary status in historical studies; the emphasis on previously excluded or marginalized groups threatens the coherence that the United States requires to maintain its national unity; the present generation needs to be as sensitive to its own blind spots as it is to the blindness of earlier generations; and the attention to historical particularities should not prevent historians from also addressing the universal issues that history has traditionally explored. In short, drawing on his own perspectives as a student of history and a journalist, Yoder concludes this volume with examples of the critical dialogue that must continue.

Extending the Dialogue

The aim of this volume is to encourage a rethinking of the categories of analysis and narrative that enabled historical actors to understand their world and enable us to discuss them today. This rethinking of analytical categories has its social analogue in the very structure of a conference that brought together a diverse group of individuals who are engaged in the production, interpretation, and dissemination of historical knowledge. Among the speakers and commentators were a novelist and playwright, a representative from the North Carolina Department of Public Instruction, journalists, high school teachers, and university professors. The audience was even more diverse, with a large contingent of high school teachers, several news-paper reporters, university undergraduate and graduate students, commu-nity college faculty, and other people in North Carolina who have an inter-est in history. The effort to bring such diverse groups of people into a shared public discussion and to question, even tentatively, the boundaries and hi-erarchies that keep them apart may have been as challenging as anything that was actually said.

If the past can be questioned by the reexamination of analytical categories such as race and gender, and if our own understanding of historical experi-ence can be questioned by the past, could we not apply this same dialogic process to the sociology of the historical profession? The professionalization of historical study since the nineteenth century has accentuated the differen-tiation of historians engaged in academic research from other historians. Strong forces in the culture serve to keep people with historical interests in separate intellectual and professional spheres: journalists often consider aca-demics to be out of touch with real-world motives and policies; university historians have a guild mentality about their training and credentials; high school teachers are often isolated from research scholars (and vice versa); teachers at all levels must work hard to resist a view of their students as be-nighted; education officials are usually inclined to emphasize only those ele-ments of instruction they can evaluate; and politicians clearly prefer histor-ical accounts that justify their own power or policies.

Ironically, the current interest of many academic historians in the origins, functions, and hierarchies of historical analysis has acted to divide and sep-arate them from others who make history their business or vocation or both. At the conference where the essays in this book were first presented, for example, many secondary school teachers were frustrated by the tension between abstract calls to open the teaching of history to new ways of un-derstanding the past and the state supervisor's announcement that more standardized examinations would be introduced. Some teachers in the au-dience wanted more concrete pedagogical information and less theorizing than the conference provided; others demanded the same right to philoso-phize about history as the university faculty arrogated to themselves. And the newspaper reporters followed the discussions in a constant search for concise, comprehensible story lines! Yet despite the professional, political, and bureaucratic pressures that separate the various advocates of historical understanding in American society, this conference pointed toward real pos-sibilities for bringing together individuals who share broad commitments to historical knowledge.

College teachers and graduate students should establish more relation-ships with secondary school and community college teachers based on a common recognition that conflicts over historical understanding are crucial for the future of the discipline and of the nation. The point of these contacts should not be for professors to assume a magisterial position as imparters of knowledge, but instead to approach other history teachers as different but equal partners in a wider project. We have no illusions about the difficulty of such a proposal. Most university faculty are no different from other professionals in the ways they define professional boundaries. They find it easier to accept abstract equality with a fellow professor of another race, sex, or sexual orientation than to interact as peers with secondary school teachers. We hope that this book and the conference from which it emerged will lead to further exchanges among the many scattered individuals who seek to explain diverse forms of historical knowledge and analysis. (We also note that such interactions are already part of intellectual life in many places across the nation.)[8]

Several of the authors represented in this book complain about the relative absence of academic history from public discussion. In criticizing academic history's "deadening style," for example, Tetterton-Opheim recalls the nineteenth-century debates between amateurs and professionals analyzed by Smith (and evoked by Rosenstone in his comparison of makers of historical films and historians). There may be ways out of this problem. The experiences of Norton and Hunt suggest the role that textbooks can play in presenting the fruits of recent research to students in a clear narrative fashion, and there is no reason why lively, well-written textbooks could not be edited to become mass-market paperbacks that would provide a wider public with readily available general syntheses of contemporary historical knowledge.

Yet readability is not the only problem facing university historians. As FitzGerald argues in her discussion of American politicians, there is a deep Manichaean strain in American culture that describes history, politics, international events, and other nations in the language of moral dichotomies. This moral and narrative tradition is clearly at odds with the multicultural perspectives, ambiguous lessons, and complex empirical data of most contemporary historical scholarship. Historians who draw on the past to develop critical dialogues with the dominant historical and cultural assumptions of our own time are not likely to reach a mass audience in American society. James Anderson's discussion of race provides a typical example of the problem. The historical analysis of race (stressing its social construction rather than biology or nature) will enter American textbooks only when Americans decide they are willing to "face our past squarely"—a task that few nations or cultures fully accept.

This book does not provide a definitive study of the problems of historical understanding in the United States. It seeks to examine some inherited categories of historical analysis, expand them with some present perspectives, and allow history to open or challenge our conceptions of the world rather than to close the meaning of past and present societies. This dialogic process (which leads us into the structuring categories of historical commentary) can be the basis of critical thinking about the past (including great books) and the present (including politics and the mass media), but it requires a strong historicity among historians themselves. The following essays therefore contribute to an expanding public debate about the structures of historical understanding, the nature of historical education, and the role of history in the popular culture and political culture of contemporary American society.

NOTES

1. See Arthur M. Schlesinger, Jr., *The Disuniting of America: Reflections on a Multicultural Society* (New York, 1992). Debates about national coherence and cultural diversity are by no means uniquely American; similar issues have become prominent in the political and cultural disputes of multicultural nations in every part of the world.

2. The most systematic survey of historical knowledge among contemporary American students appears in Diane Ravitch and Chester E. Finn, Jr., *What Do Our 17-Year-Olds Know?* (New York, 1987). The authors propose specific curricular reforms to close the gaps in knowledge that they document in detail. Similar assessments of the flaws in historical education inform the recent report of the Bradley Commission on History in the Schools. See the commission's report, "Building a History Curriculum: Guidelines for Teaching History in Schools," and the commentary of notable historians in Paul Gagnon and the Bradley Commission on History in Schools, eds., *Historical Literacy: The Case for History in American Education* (Boston, 1989). The report of the Bradley Commission also receives detailed commentary in a special issue of *History Teacher* 23 (1989). The discussions of pedagogy in *History Teacher* often provide a helpful guide to recent trends in historical education. Finally, for a more radical analysis of the problems in America's historical knowledge, see Susan Porter Benson, Stephen Brier, and Roy Rosenzweig, eds., *Presenting the Past: Essays on History and the Public* (Philadelphia, 1986).

3. The popular contemporary critiques of American education come mostly (though not exclusively) from cultural conservatives and focus especially on the humanities and social sciences. See, for example, E. D. Hirsch, Jr., *Cultural Literacy: What Every American Needs to Know* (New York, 1987); Allan Bloom, *The Closing of the American Mind* (New York, 1987); Roger Kimball, *Tenured Radicals: How Politics Has Corrupted Our Higher Education* (New York, 1990); Page Smith, *Killing the Spirit: Higher Education in America* (New York, 1990); Martin Anderson, *Imposters in the Temple* (New York, 1992); Charles J. Sykes, *Profscam: Professors and the Demise of Higher Education* (New York, 1988); Dinesh D'Souza, *Illiberal Education: The Politics of Race and Sex on Campus* (New York, 1991); James Atlas, *Battle of the Books: The Curriculum Debate in America* (New York, 1992). For some alternative views (and some responses to this literature of denunciation), see Darryl J. Gless and Barbara Herrnstein Smith, eds., *The Politics of Liberal Education* (Durham, N.C., 1992); Francis Oakley, *Community of Learning: The American College and the Liberal Arts Tradition* (New York, 1992); Peter N. Stearns, *Meaning over Memory: Recasting the Teaching of Culture and History* (Chapel Hill, N.C., 1993); and the important analysis in Gerald Graff, *Beyond the Culture Wars: How Teaching the Conflicts Can Revitalize American Education* (New York, 1992).

4. The polemical exchange over "multiculturalism" and the "canon" has become a cover story for the American media and has become linked to other debates about "political correctness" (the claim that a new form of leftist repression and "thought control" has descended on

American campuses). For two examples among many in the major media, see *Newsweek*, December 24, 1990, and *Time*, July 8, 1991. A useful summary of the debate appears in John Searle, "The Storm over the University," *New York Review of Books* 37 (December 6, 1990): 34–42. Arthur Schlesinger offers his views of these controversies in *The Disuniting of America*, especially pp. 101–18. Other responses to the "storm" can be found in Charles Taylor, *Multiculturalism and the "Politics of Recognition"* (Princeton, N.J., 1992); Paul Berman, ed., *Debating PC: The Controversy over Political Correctness on College Campuses* (New York, 1992); Patricia Aufderheide, ed., *Beyond PC: Toward a Politics of Understanding* (St. Paul, Minn., 1992); and Henry Louis Gates, Jr., *Loose Canons: Notes on the Culture Wars* (New York, 1992). See, also, the discussion of the multicultural debate in the special issue of *Radical History Review* 54 (Fall 1992), which includes an important commentary by Joan Wallach Scott, "The Campaign against Political Correctness: What's Really at Stake," pp. 59–79.

5. The variety of works in contemporary social history precludes any brief list of relevant examples, but a convenient introduction to the thematic directions and research in this growing literature is available in various scholarly journals. See, for example, *Journal of Social History*, *History Workshop Journal*, *Signs*, and *Social History*.

6. For an introduction to the conceptual themes in recent cultural and intellectual history, see Lynn Hunt, ed., *The New Cultural History* (Berkeley, 1989), and Dominick LaCapra and Steven L. Kaplan, eds., *Modern European Intellectual History: Reappraisals and New Perspectives* (Ithaca, N.Y., 1982). Other surveys of new trends in recent historiography appear in Michael Kammen, ed., *The Past Before Us: Contemporary Historical Writing in the United States* (Ithaca, N.Y., 1980), and in Peter Burke, ed., *New Perspectives on Historical Writing* (University Park, Pa., 1992).

7. The *American Historical Review* has given much attention in recent years to conceptual debates among historians. See, for example, the articles in "AHR Forum: The Old History and the New," *American Historical Review* 94 (1989): 654–98; all of the essays in this collection are informative, but the key issues emerge most acutely in the contrasting perspectives of Gertrude Himmelfarb ("Some Reflections on the New History," pp. 661–70) and Joan Wallach Scott ("History in Crisis? The Others' Side of the Story," pp. 680–92). See, also, the criticisms of the "new" history in Gertrude Himmelfarb, *The New History and the Old* (Cambridge, Mass., 1987), and in Theodore S. Hamerow, *Reflections on History and Historians* (Madison, Wis., 1987). For a detailed, well-informed description of the American historical profession's debates about the nature of historical knowledge from the end of the nineteenth century to the end of the 1980s, see Peter Novick, *That Noble Dream: The "Objectivity Question" and the American Historical Profession* (Cambridge and New York, 1988).

8. Following up on the conversations at the conference in Chapel Hill, history faculty at the University of North Carolina and at secondary schools in the area launched the Project for Historical Education. The project sponsors regular workshops on recent historical research with a strong emphasis on strategies for bringing new forms of knowledge into college and high school teaching. Each workshop focuses on a specific theme, includes graduate students and future teachers as well as people who presently teach at either secondary schools or colleges, and stresses informal dialogue on shared problems.

Part I
Textbooks, Survey Courses, and Historical Education

Rethinking American History Textbooks

Mary Beth Norton

This essay begins with two observations, one historical and one personal. They will initially seem quite different, but will turn out to be closely interrelated.

First, the historical remark. As recently as twenty-five years ago, or about the time I entered graduate school, a debate about how we learn history would not have been conceived of, for the simple reason that the learning of history—aside, perhaps, from a discussion of methods—was then regarded as unproblematic. The shape of history appeared to be clearly defined. Scholars, everyone knew, could be expected to disagree over interpretations of facts, but the body of knowledge that was subject to such interpretation was generally agreed upon. Almost by definition, history was the narrative of "public" life—of politics, economics, diplomacy, and war. Some persons, it was true, occasionally wrote about other topics—like family life, women's status, or material culture—but those subjects were recognized as having only marginal importance to "real" history. Most of the authors who considered them had not had formal historical training in graduate schools, and their works were widely regarded as being of purely antiquarian interest. Such books might have been read with pleasure by the general public, but professional historians ignored and denigrated them. In that context, there was little or no disagreement about what we now term "the social implications of historical knowledge."

Let me leave that general point hanging while I make my personal comment. As I began to think about writing this article, I asked myself, How did *I* learn history? Or, to recast the question slightly, Why did I decide to become a historian? The answer is not that I once had an especially inspiring teacher in a survey (or any other) course; or that I had been turned on by any particular book—certainly not a textbook(!); or that I had seen an excellent

25

historical documentary film. In high school in Indiana my history teacher was the track coach, hardworking to be sure, but someone who knew little more about the subject than what he read in the text. Even so, I went to the University of Michigan knowing before my arrival on campus that I wanted to major in history. Why? In retrospect, I realize that it was because of the reading I had done outside of school, because of the many biographies and, especially, historical novels that I had been consuming avidly for as long as I could remember. From those books I had learned that history was full of *wonderful stories*, stories I wanted to know more about, stories I thought it would be fun to learn how to tell to others.

Looking back, I am somewhat puzzled that my love for historical story-telling led me to history rather than to the study of literature. Certainly no textbook I was assigned to read ever treated history as more than a miscellaneous collection of names, dates, and facts about public events; and although collateral course readings were often eclectic and enlightening, they too never stimulated my imagination the way that novels did. Yet my interest in history was sustained through undergraduate and graduate school, until in 1969 I started to teach and began to put together my own courses, assigning a survey textbook very much like the one I had used as a sophomore history student.

My relationship to survey texts might have remained no more than that—a casual user—had it not been for two subsequent events. First, in the late sixties and early seventies the first articles and books on the history of American women began to be published. I started to read them with growing interest, until in 1972 I decided to embark on my own contribution to that field, a piece of research that became my book *Liberty's Daughters: The Revolutionary Experience of American Women*, which finally appeared in 1980. Second, while I was working on *Liberty's Daughters* I was approached by a former colleague, Tom Paterson of the University of Connecticut, to join him and others on a team that would write a new survey textbook for the Houghton Mifflin Company.

Paterson's letter arrived on my desk in late November 1975. For months I stalled, not giving him a definitive answer. Researching my monograph on women in the Revolution intrigued me greatly; writing a clone of the many survey texts then on the market did not, despite the promise of a considerable financial reward. Old files of correspondence show that he continued to push; I continued to resist. What made me change my mind was a review I conducted of several of the textbooks available in the mid-seventies.

Armed with my new knowledge of and commitment to studying the history of women in particular and social history in general, I approached those texts quite differently than I ever had before. How, I asked, had they incorporated the new scholarship of the last five to ten years into their narratives? What I discovered appalled me.

Without mentioning titles or authors, let me cite a few egregious examples. One text had added a stunning color portfolio on "The African Heritage," but discussed the founding of South Carolina without mentioning blacks (who constituted a majority of the population as early as 1710) and treated the history of colonial slavery entirely as the history of white attitudes toward blacks. Another—the updated version of the very text I had been assigned at the University of Michigan—included a portrait of Abigail Adams with a caption identifying her as "one of the few women in the eighteenth century who commanded respect from her male contemporaries." The fullest treatment of women came in one text that devoted two-thirds of a page to the topic and in another that inserted a two-and-a-half-page essay on women *between* two chapters, making women literally as well as figuratively peripheral to the main narrative. In every book then on the market, American Indians were discussed (if at all) only in the first few pages, thereafter disappearing from view, only to reemerge fitfully to fight European settlers in such conflicts as the Pequot War, King Philip's War, and (inescapably) the French and Indian War.

Once I completed this review and ascertained that the other members of the team Paterson was assembling were also committed to producing not just another text but rather a book very different in content from those available at the time, I was hooked. *A People and a Nation*, the book our team produced, is now going into its fourth edition.[1] Writing this textbook has changed my life in three significant ways.

First, working on a textbook has put an end to whatever bifurcation between teaching and research might have existed in my life. I should observe first that I have always been skeptical of that supposed "great divide." I have never understood how one could teach without doing research, or do research without teaching: in my experience, each activity directly informs the other. I introduce a new seminar topic because it interests me as a possible research subject, and teaching the seminar gives me a chance to review the existing literature systematically with a class. Or I bring material from my research into my lectures by revising or extending my treatment of different subjects. Yet even so, before I became a textbook author there was one major distinction between teaching and research: I regularly changed individual lectures or even developed new courses, but once I had written something, that work sat there in print, never to be revised.

A textbook, on the other hand, is constantly changing. My team currently operates on a four-year revision cycle, which works out in practice to two years on, two years off. It takes the authors a year (more or less) to produce the manuscript of each new edition; and then it takes Houghton Mifflin a year to turn that manuscript into a published volume. The authors are involved continually during the revision year, sporadically during the next. Like a course and like women's work, in other words, a textbook is literally never done. Cynics would say that the frequent revising is aimed only at rendering used books obsolete so as to keep the sales figures of new copies high, but I find that revising the text offers me an unparalleled opportunity to change my mind in print—to alter emphases, to bring in new topics derived from the latest scholarship, or even to change interpretations in whole or in part.

As I have become more adept at solving the uniquely difficult problems of textbook writing, I have also been able to accomplish in subsequent editions what I could not figure out how to do previously. Readers who compared the first and third chapters of my first edition with the same chapters in the second, for example, were undoubtedly surprised at the differences between them. Those differences arose from the simple fact that under the time constraints of producing the first edition I could not implement some of the ambitious plans described in my early outlines; when the second edition was prepared, I had both the experience and the time I needed to carry out my ideas. A textbook, then, does not represent an intellectual challenge to be surmounted and then forgotten, but rather an ongoing process of refinement, in which each version should be better honed and more clearly argued than the last.

Second, writing a textbook has made me a better writer and a clearer thinker. Like every other textbook writer, I have to assume an audience that knows little about my subject. Concepts have to be explained succinctly and without the use of jargon. Sentences must be crisp and unambiguous. I am not talking here about the "dumbing down" of prose that has been so properly criticized when it has occurred in texts aimed at elementary and secondary school students. Rather, I am referring to an emphasis on clarity above all else, to the creation of a vivid (if sparse) prose style. The process of producing such prose for the textbook has unquestionably affected my writing style in other works as well.

Furthermore, if textbook authors want to accomplish what we did—that is, to break emphatically with established norms—they must have sharply defined goals and cling resolutely to a firm vision of what they intend the final product to be. For us, at least, that vision evolved over time. The core was present from the outset—our book would incorporate social history into the narrative of a "traditional" text to an extent never before attempted—but its details emerged only after years of correspondence and meetings, after many (sometimes heated) exchanges among ourselves and with Houghton Mifflin editors over the relative importance of different themes, possible modes of presentation, and appropriate emphases. What became clearer as time passed was one guiding principle: emphasis on the experiences of ordinary people and a focus, as much as possible, on telling stories about individual lives. The traditional discussions of politics, economics, and the like would not be omitted, but rather placed in a very different perspective by putting them within the framework of the new social history.

Third, writing a textbook has made me far more sensitive to the questions that underlie the debates about historical education than I would ever have been had I not undertaken such a task: How do we learn history? How *should* we learn history? What should be included in, and excluded from, the standard narrative of American history? What are the social, political, and cultural implications of additions to or subtractions from that narrative?

A textbook author is continually confronted by those questions in ways that even teachers of survey courses are not. Professors can choose to emphasize in class the topics of most interest to them, but a narrative text's role is to fill in the gaps, to supply continuity among lectures and collateral reading assignments in other volumes. A good textbook should provide the framework within which students can learn about those aspects of history their teacher deems most important. (The difference between the function of the text and the role of lectures explains why, contrary to popular belief, textbook authors cannot simply transform their survey-course oral presentations into chapters with only a few minor changes. Adopting that technique leads to disaster, as I discovered when I attempted it while producing my first draft chapter for our book. It was so bad I threw it out immediately and started fresh.)

This observation about the proper function of a text brings me back to my first subject, the one I abandoned without further discussion: the once-unquestioned focus of American history textbooks on "public" life as embodied in formal institutions and its relationship to the way that students learn history. When our team first conceptualized a new textbook in the mid-1970s, a disjunction had developed in the American historical profession between the traditional narrative of survey texts and the thrust of current scholarship. The latter emphasized social history—the study of ordinary people and their lives. The former emphasized political, military, diplomatic, and economic history at the highest levels of government. Teachers who wanted to draw on the new work in their survey courses dealt with their dilemma as I did at the time: by assigning collateral readings representative of "the new social history" while still employing traditional textbooks to provide the background narrative.

But for two reasons that solution was not very satisfactory. One, unimportant in theoretical terms but of immediate practical significance for all teachers of introductory courses, arises from the common student attitude that *if it's not in the textbook, it's not important*. I and others like me found it very difficult to convince students that topics *not* covered in the text were of equal significance to those that were discussed therein.

Let me cite just one example from my own experience. Convinced by new scholarship that the impact of smallpox and other diseases on the native populations of the Americas was critical in explaining Europeans' success in gaining a rapid foothold in the New World, I nevertheless found it nearly impossible to persuade my students to adopt that interpretation. Lecturing on the topic and even assigning Alfred Crosby's brilliant work *The Columbian Exchange* made little dent in their mindset, which—thanks to the text I was using and the books they had read in high school—gave much greater weight to such factors as superior European technology, the invaders' use of horses, and Indian "superstitions." Readers familiar with *A People and a Nation* will now probably realize why the first chapter draws heavily on an eyewitness Aztec account of the smallpox epidemic that ravaged Tenochtitlán while the Spaniards were besieging the city.

The second reason why combining a traditional text with new-style readings was unworkable in the long run is both more important and more relevant here. I observed earlier that the proper role of a textbook is to supply the context for the learning that takes place in a classroom. But a text that focused on formal political and economic history could not serve that function for anyone interested in the new social history. The different parts of the course did not fit together: the narrative text said one thing, the lectures and collateral readings another. The latter, which emphasized social history, appeared to be extraneous to the "seamless web" of the former, which paid little attention to such issues as women's status, the daily lives of enslaved persons, or the work experiences of recent immigrants. The result was extraordinary fragmentation. No wonder students were confused about what was important and what was not.

This brings me to the central irony of the current debate in the humanities, in which many lament the breakdown of a former conceptual unity and the lack of coherence in historical curricula, all supposedly the result of the attempt to integrate new scholarship on women and ethnic minorities into our teaching and research agendas. Precisely the opposite is true, in my opinion: if there is a loss of coherence in our college and high school history courses today, it is because *not enough* is being done to reorient our thinking along the lines suggested by new scholarship, rather than because *too much* is being attempted.

A course, or an entire curriculum, will appear to be fragmented and incoherent if it merely adopts what in women's history has come to be called the "compensatory" or "contributory" method of encompassing new work.[2] Such a mode does not alter a book's—or a course's—original conceptualization while it nevertheless incorporates novel topics. The material added will seem anomalous, out of place: it will be marginal to the central narrative and it will indeed break up any previously existing conceptual unity. That result derives not from the effort to integrate new findings into the course, but rather from the incomplete manner in which that goal is usually pursued. *When new materials do not fit the narrative, it is time to change the narrative*. Keeping current scholarship out of basic courses, which is what many of today's critics of trends in the humanities seem to want to do, will solve nothing. It will only increase the cognitive dissonance for students and drive them away from "confusing" humanities courses.

Let me illustrate what happens when the narrative is changed by referring to an example from nineteenth-century American women's history.

Traditional political history in the United States has primarily encompassed the study of electoral politics. Thus the preferred narrative has been one that emphasizes the gradual expansion of voting rights and the consequences thereof. Textbooks have long told a story that describes, first, the definition of colonial voters as (white male) property-holders; second, a trend toward loosening restrictions, until in the Jacksonian period nearly universal (white male) suffrage was achieved; third, the nominal inclusion of black males via the Fifteenth Amendment after the Civil War; fourth, the extension of the vote to women in 1920; and fifth, the passage of the Voting Rights Act of 1965, which finally brought African-American men and women fully into the system.

In the standard narrative of nineteenth-century American political life, therefore, if women were considered at all it was only with respect to their quest for the vote; that is, women's only relevant "political" role was as members of the woman suffrage movement. Yet, since that movement remained quite small and isolated and did not achieve success until the decade between 1910 and 1920 — though it had begun at the Seneca Falls convention in 1848 — textbook writers discussing nineteenth-century American politics could, and did, largely ignore women. One or two paragraphs identifying Elizabeth Cady Stanton and Susan B. Anthony, and perhaps describing their major ideas, seemed more than adequate to handle such a peripheral topic. Any more extensive treatment of women would appear to be compensatory special pleading, added to the text not because it was intellectually justifiable but rather because of "political" pressure from feminists.

But if the narrative of "politics" is reconceived to encompass a variety of *nonelectoral* public roles, then nineteenth-century American women stood at the center of political life. As far back as the 1830s, Alexis de Tocqueville pointed to the importance of voluntary associations in American society. What he did not say, and what most historians have joined him in ignoring, was that many, if not most, of those voluntary associations — especially those with reform agendas — were composed exclusively of women, both whites and free blacks, each of whom had their own organizations.

I refer here not just to the relatively well known temperance and antislavery societies, which had a national presence, but also to the scores of local associations that supported widows and educated their children; that founded and ran hospitals, orphanages, libraries, and homes for unwed mothers; that aided young working women living alone in the cities; and that pressed for more city parks, cleaner air, purer food, improved water and sewage systems, and so forth long before the environmental activism of the 1970s. Indeed, if one carefully examines the history of much of today's social-service infrastructure in the United States, one finds that its origins lie not in programs initiated by elected male politicians, but instead in institutions founded and supported by women's voluntary associations for many years before they were incorporated into the nation's formal political structure.[3]

Therefore, the overall narrative of American political history needs to be changed in order to make electoral politics merely one of a number of aspects of "public" life. Once that change has occurred, women are no longer marginal to the story, persons who are by definition peripheral because they obtained the vote only in 1920 and until very recently rarely held public office. By contrast, attention to their public-service activities is required in order to tell the complete tale of how the contemporary welfare state evolved and why it took its current form. Moreover, women's great success in accomplishing their reform agenda *before* they acquired the vote raises a question that renders the entire standard narrative problematic: If women achieved so much without the vote, why are electoral politics of such crucial importance?

Incorporating a description of women's political roles in nineteenth-century America into a general narrative of political history in the period does not in any sense introduce chaotic or inexplicable elements into the story, nor does it produce an incoherent narrative. Quite the contrary: only if women's activities are included in the description of events can a textbook author tell a coherent, fully comprehensible tale.

Thus far I have been discussing what should be included in textbooks rather than the closely related (and occasionally more difficult) problem of what should—or can—be omitted. The bane of a textbook author's existence is the page and word limits within which all of us must work. Those limits affect not only the first edition, in which the initial conceptualization is presumably worked out, but also each subsequent revision. Books cannot grow exponentially; for every word that is added, another usually must be removed. Sometimes simply compressing one's prose will solve space problems. At other times, whole paragraphs must be dropped. The process is agonizing, but it is also useful. One must constantly reassess what is important and continually rethink the structure of one's arguments, paring them down to essentials.

What makes a successful textbook is an author's ability to set up clear criteria for what is to be included and what excluded from the narrative. What is to be emphasized, what merely mentioned in passing, what omitted entirely? The team that produced *A People and a Nation* decided that our narrative would revolve around the lives and experiences of ordinary Americans, and that discussions of developments or trends that did not affect our subjects directly would be attenuated or excluded. Accordingly, persons who want a detailed description of "high literary culture" will not find it in our book; they will, however, find in its place a more extensive treatment of popular culture—ranging from novels to sports to contemporary television—than in most other textbooks. Likewise, someone searching for a detailed description of the internal structure and politics of the joint-stock companies that founded the first English colonies in America will not find it in my early chapters; they will, on the other hand, find lengthy discussions of the relationships among white settlers and their Indian neighbors, a topic that I think better helps to explain the survival of the early settlements.

I like to think that our solution to the inclusion/exclusion dilemma was the right one, at least in terms of contemporary scholarly trends. The fact that most of the textbooks that have appeared since our first edition was published in 1982 have adopted a similar approach suggests that other authors and publishers agree with us on the importance of basing a text firmly in "the new social history." Indeed, if I take pride in anything apart from our text itself, it is in the fact that we pioneered a trend that offers professors and secondary school teachers today a far greater range of choice in textbooks than was available when I started teaching in 1969. That can only work to the benefit of students, whose need to learn history is, in the end, the motivation that lies behind all of our endeavors.

NOTES

1. Mary Beth Norton, David Katzman, Paul Escott, Howard Chudacoff, Thomas Paterson, and William Tuttle, *A People and a Nation* (Boston, 1982, 1986, 1990, 1994).

2. One of the first scholars to identify this mode of historical writing about women was Gerda Lerner; see her *The Majority Finds Its Past: Placing Women in History* (New York, 1979).

3. Such topics have been examined in detail by many scholars in recent years. For just a small sampling of book-length studies, see, for example, Paula Giddings, *When and Where I Enter: The Impact of Black Women on Race and Sex in America* (New York, 1984); Nancy Hewitt, *Women's Activism and Social Change: Rochester, New York, 1822-1872* (Ithaca, N.Y., 1984); Mary P. Ryan, *Cradle of the Middle Class: The Family in Oneida County, New York, 1780-1865* (New York, 1981); Peggy Pascoe, *Relations of Rescue: The Search for Female Moral Authority in the American West, 1874-1939* (New York, 1990); and Kathryn Kish Sklar's forthcoming biography of Florence Kelley.

Reports of Its Death Were Premature: Why "Western Civ" Endures

Lynn Hunt

In 1967, a report on education at Stanford University concluded with this warning:

> General education, as epitomized by the Chicago curriculum of the Hutchins era and the Columbia two-year sequences in Humanities and Contemporary Civilization, is dead or dying. . . . The general education ideal is totally impraticable as a dominant curricular pattern in the modern university.[1]

A short time later, the Western civilization course, first instituted at Stanford in 1935, was abolished. Reports of its demise, however, proved premature, for efforts to revive it began almost immediately. A new year-long course was instituted in 1980 and required of all incoming students. Suggestions for the revision of this course in 1988 helped quicken the debate that is now raging around the teaching of Western civilization.[2]

I begin with this brief reminder of the history of the conflicts over the teaching of Western civilization at Stanford not so much because the Stanford case is paradigmatic—though for various reasons it has had far-reaching echoes—as because it reminds us that even the most recent debates have come out of a longer history that is intimately connected to American ideas and ideals of national cultural identity. The Western civ course in history is apparently, at least by historians' standards, a relatively recent development, since it first took shape during the professionalization of the universities between 1870 and 1910 and then got a distinct push in the aftermath of World War I.

In a useful article, Gilbert Allardyce has traced what he calls "the rise and fall of the Western civilization course." Although he is too quick to celebrate the "fall" of the course, he is no doubt right to emphasize that it first developed as a way of reaffirming the United States' allegiance to the Atlantic democracies. The contemporary civilization course at Columbia, for example, grew out of the war issues course that was taught to the Students Army Training Corps (SATC) on the campus in 1918. The aim of the war issues course was to teach students what they were going over to Europe to defend. In 1919, the new contemporary civ course was described by a dean at Columbia as creating "a citizen who shall be safe for democracy."[3] Such courses began to disappear from the elite institutions in the 1960s as part of the attack on general requirements and the loss of faith in general education (and in the midst of another, much less successful, war). The course has returned, albeit in different forms, with a renewed stress on the need for core requirements and in the midst of debates about the politics of higher education.[4]

The American academic wars on the subject of Western culture and Western civilization have focused recently on two main possibilities: is the subject or the course based on a hopelessly ethnocentric, outdated concept that promotes bigotry and exclusion of minorities and hence is politically dangerous, or is it the essential common ground of cultural literacy for any mass democracy in the West and hence politically salutary? I will admit that the political dimension of the pro-Western civ side is not always this clearly articulated. But I take William McNeill's anguished cry of 1976 as typical. In place of the old surveys, he insisted, it was essential to "find something worth teaching to undergraduates en masse: something all educated persons should know; something every active citizen ought to be familiar with in order to conduct his life well and perform his public duties effectively."[5]

This debate is typically, and perhaps exclusively, American. The French, for instance, do not worry about Western civilization or culture; they do not teach it, and they do not debate its present-day meanings. French schoolchildren, whether they are Moroccan, Senegalese, Martiniquais, or "hexagonal" in origin all still study Joan of Arc and Baudelaire—that is, French civilization—to the exclusion of much else in Europe, not to mention the world. The situation is much the same in Britain, Germany, and Russia: nationalist, rather than "Western," concerns lead the way. It may well be that the integration of Western Europe will promote a more Eurocentric and less nationalist approach. A comparative study of this question in European countries might lead to some interesting, perhaps even surprising, results.

In contrast to Europeans, we Americans specifically debate the merits of "Western" civilization and not American civilization. We are either too humble about our national contributions to "civilization" or too uncertain about the central values of our own culture to focus exclusively on American civilization. Am civ, as we call it at the University of Pennsylvania, has long been in a marginal position as a discipline in the American university, sometimes attached to literature departments and sometimes standing alone, but often in a state of legitimacy crisis.[6] It is certainly not at the center of the current debates.

The Western culture debate in its most recent incarnation began as a struggle over core requirements, course readings, and course syllabi. It has brought to public attention a term that used to be considered esoteric, "the canon." Something is canonical, according to the *Oxford English Dictionary*, when it is of "admitted authority, excellence, or supremacy; authoritative, orthodox, accepted, standard." The debate over the canon seems to have generated much more heat, if not light, in literary than in historical circles. The special issue of the *South Atlantic Quarterly* of 1990 that was devoted to "The Politics of Liberal Education" included only one historian (and I only know he is a historian because he is my colleague, for he is listed there as a professor of the humanities), along with eight professors of literature and three of philosophy. There is a good reason for this greater intensity of interest among professors of literature and philosophy; historically, they have been the ones most responsible in American higher education for teaching the canonical great texts, for determining which texts were canonical, and for determining what the standards of canonicity should be.

As a consequence, the very raison d'être of professors of literature, in particular, is at issue in the debate over the canon. The professional study of English literature, as distinct from the classics, is a relatively recent phenomenon, as Terry Eagleton has argued. Not surprisingly, but very significantly, it came into being in English universities at the same time that Western civ courses were appearing in American colleges. As Eagleton tells the story, English lit made its way from the dingy Mechanics Institutes for workers and the lowly training of women teachers into the hallowed halls of Oxford and Cambridge thanks to the efforts of such sons and daughters of the provincial bourgeoisie as F. R. Leavis. Critics like Leavis insisted that it was possible to develop a discipline of reading that would train students to rigorously discriminate works of some enduring value from those that lacked such value.[7]

Although Eagleton's purpose is to uncover the ideological and historical meaning of this "rise of English," and thus in some sense to debunk it, he must implicitly accept its premises if English is to continue as a discipline. Thus he concludes his discussion of Leavis by claiming that "some of [Leavis's] own published work ranks with the most subtle, pioneering English criticism that the century has seen."[8] What is the meaning of those adjectives *subtle* and *pioneering* if not admittedly authoritative and excellent, that is, canonical? In fact, if the notion of the great work is entirely eroded, if the idea of a canon is thrown out altogether, then the distinctiveness of the study of literature as a discipline is also in doubt. Why shouldn't all the humanities disciplines disappear into one giant cultural studies unit, in which comic strips compete for equal attention with Flaubert?[9]

This is an interesting question, but not one that I will try to answer here. I want to focus instead on the relative reticence of historians about these matters. Historians have been involved in their own institutions in the debates over the teaching of Western culture, since they have often been doing the brunt of that teaching. But the debates have only become really acrimonious when others have been involved, and historians have not been known for their comments in the national debates on Western culture. As long as Western civ is strictly a history department undertaking and not a general requirement, it usually arouses little criticism or even interest elsewhere in the university. No one ever asks me why I teach History 2: Europe in a Wider World from the Reformation to the Present in the way I do, not even the TAs! Presumably they might, however, if History 2 became a kind of general requirement, as it did in some places. Then the Western civ course might become a site of cultural contestation and a source of cultural legitimation. I will return to this point in a moment.

Historians have been relatively quiet on the subject of Western civilization because they feel confused as citizens and especially as professionals about the meaning of Western culture. Like many people since World War II, historians have lost their confidence that the history leading up to the present has been a story of increasing freedom and progress. The confident teleologies about Western values, with their reliance on science, technology, and mass political participation, disintegrated in the aftermath of fascist rallies, death camps, and the atom bomb. The Vietnam War, the threat of ecological disaster, AIDS, and the new forms of state torture and terrorism have deepened further the doubts about the meaning of modern Western history. By the 1980s, it was clear that Auschwitz and Hiroshima could not be dismissed as aberrations in an upward curve toward progress in human rights. The result of this recognition has not been the replacement of the history of freedom and progress with another paradigm. Instead, historians have lost faith, along with their colleagues in other fields in the humanities, in any form of "master narrative," by which I mean a unifying teleological thread of interpretation.

There are several reasons for the decline of master narratives. The master narrative of Western hegemony has been found guilty by association with elitism, sexism, and racism. Too often the history of freedom was equated with the course of parliamentary democracy in England, the United States, and continental Europe. Colonialism, slavery, the immigrant working classes, and women's rights hardly appeared at all, or appeared entirely subordinate to the agendas set by white men. Moreover, the course itself seemed to foster attitudes of Western "superiority," since it was the story of the West's rise to hegemony and in some sense a commemoration of that rise.

Some critics have denounced all master narratives as totalitarian by nature; just telling one overall story, such as the history of freedom, promotes, they maintain, the authority of a single voice, one sex, a single culture, class, or race and closes the way to inclusion of other groups, other classes, other races, other cultures. Master narratives inherently oppose diversity by the very way that they function.

An important strand in poststructuralist and postmodernist thought has taken the challenge to master narratives even further and attacked history and narrativity more generally. As Hayden White summarizes these views (of Foucault, Althusser, Barthes, Derrida, and Kristeva), "history in general and narrativity specifically were merely representational practices by which society produced a human subject peculiarly adapted to the conditions of life in the modern *Rechtsstaat* [government by law]."[10] In this view, narrative itself was ideological, and presumably intimately connected to capitalism and modernity. This position is taken to its logical conclusion by Sande Cohen, who argues that when historians write for the ordinary educated public, they inevitably suppress all the contradictions and tensions in history and therefore promote only "disthought," or a lack of critical awareness. In his view, narrative itself is guilty for discouraging criticism.[11] It is no wonder, then, that historians might be reluctant to trumpet their views on Western culture.

The decline of master narratives has also been facilitated by the increasing specialization of history as a discipline. It is not easy to teach Western civ if, as I have, you have been trained as a specialist in eighteenth-century French social and political history. If you write books, if you want to get ahead in the profession, if you want to be a professional leader, you only have time to read books and articles about eighteenth-century French social and political history. Graduate history education is taught within the confines of national traditions of historiography; the need to master one of them inevitably discourages comparison and hence model building or rethinking of broader Western paradigms. Moreover, one of the central topics in the history of Western civilization—the rise of Western science and technology—has been hived off from many history departments; because the study of the history of science and technology is conceived as a separate discipline, it no longer figures in the training of most history graduate students and rarely rates prominence in a Western civ course.

Thus the history of the post–World War II world, the political attack on Eurocentrism and narrative itself, and the imperatives of disciplinary specialization all came together to undermine the very notion of teaching about Western civilization. This has created a puzzling and disturbing situation with some surprising political consequences. The first of these is a paradoxical class division. Eagleton traced the "rise of English" to the entrance of critics from the lower middle classes into the elite universities; English was designed to teach a method to everyone who wanted to exercise discrimination in taste. It was thus a kind of democratization of the matter of taste, though at the same time it was also a way of reintroducing social distinctions. Any educated person might learn to make rigorous aesthetic judgments, but not everyone was educated. The rise of English provided a new form of cultural capital available for accumulation by more but not all classes of society.

Similarly, it might be argued that Western civ was invented just at the time when young men—and women—from the lower or at least lower middle classes began to enter American universities. Like the rise of English, Western civ consequently had a double, and sometimes contradictory, function. In the most "common" schools—especially the community colleges and state schools founded after World War II—Western civ was required as an entrance exam to citizenship, to cultural belonging. In the most elite schools, on the other hand, it served as a foundation for elite education; it was what everyone who was anyone needed to know, as certified by Columbia, Chicago, Stanford, and so forth. Western civ was thus either the basis of common citizenship and cultural assimilation or the grounds for renewed social distinction, depending on where you learned it.

The difference between elite and nonelite versions of Western civ can be seen in the roles of the teachers. Western civ in the nonelite schools is often the only or almost the only teaching done by historians of Europe. Their training for this course comes on the job, for the last time they studied Western civ was the moment when they took the course themselves as beginning students. It is a sign of their low professional status that they have to teach section after section of Western civ; Western civ for the masses is taught by the most proletarianized sector of the intellectual work force. With few exceptions, they will never see an article or attend a conference on the conceptualization of Western civ because this has not been considered an area of disciplinary interest for serious scholars.

The picture in elite schools is more mixed, but in some ways no less depressing. Some elite schools have reinstituted a Western culture requirement in the name of standards and values. In most of these places, Western culture is now a source of great contention and has often been so diluted as to lose any real significance, except as a general requirement that still signals social distinction and cultural legitimacy. Where Western civ is not required, it often has very large enrollments but arouses no faculty interest. Some elite schools refuse to teach anything resembling Western civ on the grounds that it is too superficial to encourage real historical analysis. Others teach it only for nonmajors or majors who don't know enough to know better. In other words, the charge that Western civ courses are politically incorrect (Eurocentric, sexist, racist) has another, perhaps more surprising side: in history the teaching of Western civ is treated with contempt, even in many elite schools; it is often assigned to the deadwood in the department; and it is completely unrelated to professional training. Needless to say, the writing of Western civ textbooks suffers from the same disfavor. People write Western civ textbooks, it is thought, for opportunistic reasons: to make money. No one could be imagined to be writing one for moral or political reasons because the subject is so morally and politically fraught. Everyone I know who writes a Western civ textbook distinguishes between textbook writing and "their own work," that is, specialized, scholarly research. They apologize for the way the first detracts from the second; the textbook is holding up their professional progress.

You will notice that I have tried to stay away from abstract arguments about the virtues of Western civ and have tried instead to use the history of the debates over Western civ and the canon and the actual practice of teaching Western civ to get at some of the issues involved. These suggest that, for all their defects, the Western civ course and textbook can be vehicles of democratization and that the attack on—just as much as the defense of—Western civ might be a sign of elitism. This is confirmed for me on the most immediate practical level—that of someone actually trying to write a new Western civ textbook, which has been without question the single most daunting of all my professional experiences.

It is our obligation as historians to the community at large—to the American public and its collective memory—to provide some sense of how we came to where we are in the world community today. The survival of a successful democratic national community depends on some sense of its distinctive identity and a feeling of collective participation, which depends in turn on a living relationship for all members to its cultural past and future prospects. Because modern cultural identity is always caught up in webs of time that span past, present, and future, modern history will always be in some sense teleological, a story with a direction. To refuse to take this on is simply to refuse the role of educator in our society, to refuse the role of constructing narratives about how we came to be as a culture. To tell the story of where we fit in the world does not necessarily mean that we have to tell the story in the same old ways. I see three major questions that have to be confronted by any narrative of Western civilization: why tell the story of Western civilization as opposed to world history?; where does the United States fit into this story?; and how are the new methods and topics in history—social history, cultural history, the history of women and minorities—going to fit into this old framework? The issues of present-day debates about Western culture are made more pressing by the simple fact that you cannot just make the textbooks longer and thus incorporate new trends and ideas. Something has to be exchanged, just as in a fourteen- or fifteen-week syllabus.

Western civilization, as opposed to world history, is still an important focus for our teaching because America's cultural identity was and still is dependent on the development of distinctively Western cultural values and on the rise of the West in world geopolitics. Although the implicit frame of the narrative is familiar — the emergence of distinctive notions about the individual and the rise of participatory democracy, the development of science, industrialization, and world hegemony — most opportunities for fresh thinking on the question of Western identity have been ignored. Guilt and avoidance of conflict have been strong deterrents along with the decline of faith in progress and the specialization of the discipline. To emphasize what is distinctive about the West seems to celebrate its hegemony, but this need not necessarily be true, especially at a time when the West is no longer so hegemonic. It would be well worth our while to begin rethinking the question of what is distinctively Western in Western civilization.[12]

Similarly, it would be worth reconsidering the place of the United States in the story of Western civilization. In recent years, the place of America has been surprisingly minimal, no doubt because most students also take an entire course on American history proper. In Western civ textbooks, the United States appears very little before the eighteenth century and only becomes prominent at the end of the nineteenth century. Better integration of America should go hand in hand with more integration of Europe's relationship to the rest of the world. Progress is being made in this direction in recent textbooks. The world outside the West is steadily growing in importance in Western civ textbooks because the world outside the West is steadily growing in political, economic, and cultural importance in our lives.

These slow but real changes in coverage and emphasis serve to underline the ways in which changes in the geopolitical and cultural balance of power are reflected eventually in the textbooks. The textbook is a kind of record of ongoing cultural conflict and struggle. It is a forum for working out subtle and not-so-subtle changes in our national and international identity. Textbooks are also, very eventually, a record of changes in our professional methods. In the last decade or so, Western civ textbooks have given much more prominence to social history, especially women's history, and they are beginning to incorporate the methods of cultural history as well. Women's history and the histories of the Jews, of slavery, and of immigrant populations are being integrated into the narrative of Western civilization and not simply appended as additional, useful material. Such integration has not been easy or immediate, but authors are out there trying their best. I believe that these efforts produce a better history of freedom — to put it most schematically — because they give due weight to the struggles of women and minorities to gain representation.

I do not mean to give the impression that everyone is writing in the same kind of direction, that everyone agrees on both the virtues of pluralist democracy and the virtues of an ever more capacious definition of it. At the same time that some textbooks aim for integration of social and cultural history, others resolutely refuse it. The market is now quite disparate and filled with all kinds of special niches. Some instructors want to emphasize the ancient Near East, others skip over it altogether; some want to emphasize great books and political leaders, others want to focus on history from below and the struggle of repressed groups. Still others want a satisfactory balance, whatever that might mean. There are many different perspectives on how best to achieve cultural and political integration.

I hope to have been able to convince readers that Western civ courses and textbooks are something more than an antediluvian embarrassment. They provide us with an excellent arena for ongoing discussion and debate about the fundamental values of our culture. In my view, the area in which we have been least successful in the teaching and writing of Western civilization is in conveying a sense of that discussion and debate. Integration of the United States, the world, and new historical methods and topics is not enough: the writing of grand narrative does tend toward homogenization and the effacement of all gaps, question marks, and controversies. But we can never solve this problem—the creation of an effect of enduring truth and inescapable reality through the very structure of presentation of the course and the textbook—if we simply turn our backs on the entire project or, worse yet, leave it to those who are not embarrassed to be interested in defending their sense of our fundamental political and cultural values. Why should we leave the entire terrain to the traditionalists who reject social history and every other new historical approach or perspective?

Historians could and should play more of a role in the debates over Western culture. As historians in a democratic society, we have a responsibility to explain, debate, and reformulate our roles in the ever-continuing discussion of our national values. The public wants to hear from us, and we cannot always use the excuse of the next books to be written on our scholarly specialties as a way of avoiding this engagement. As we become a more and more diverse society, we may move away from the distinctly Western values that shaped the United States in earlier times, or we may not, but how would we know one way or the other if we never discuss it in public? Teaching Western civ, for many historians, is still the point of contact with the largest public of students. It is time that we engaged the larger public of interested readers on these issues.

NOTES

1. From "The Study of Education at Stanford," as quoted in Gilbert Allardyce, "The Rise and Fall of the Western Civilization Course," *American Historical Review* 87 (1982): 724.

2. See the useful overview by Mary Louise Pratt, "Humanities for the Future: Reflections on the Western Culture Debate at Stanford," *South Atlantic Quarterly* 89 (1990): 7-26.

3. Allardyce, "Rise and Fall," p. 707.

4. Ibid., pp. 695-96.

5. Quoted in ibid., p. 696.

6. As Barbara Herrnstein Smith argues in her attack on E. D. Hirsch, "The existence of an American 'national culture' is by no means self-evident" ("Cult-Lit: Hirsch, Literacy, and the 'National Culture,' " *South Atlantic Quarterly* 89 [1990]: 71).

7. Terry Eagleton, *Literary Theory: An Introduction* (Minneapolis, 1983), pp. 17–53.

8. Ibid., p. 43.

9. For some suggestive remarks on the current debate on the canon, see John Searle, "The Storm over the University," *New York Review of Books* 37 (December 6, 1990): 34–42.

10. Hayden White, *The Content of the Form: Narrative Discourse and Historical Representation* (Baltimore and London, 1987), p. 35.

11. Sande Cohen, *Historical Culture: On the Recoding of An Academic Discipline* (Berkeley and Los Angeles, 1986), p. 326. I have rendered Cohen's position into clear and distinct terms that fail to do justice to the impenetrability of his prose. The passage that I have in mind reads: "When historians synthesize so that their narrations are readable by an 'ordinary educated public,' such syntheses restabilize semanticizied, logicized, and especially cognized markers and sign forms of discourse already riddled with semantic contraries, status, ideology, modals, symmetry, 'appropriate' contradictions, disthought."

12. I made an initial, all too brief foray in this direction in Lynn Hunt, "What Is Western about Western History," in *What Americans Should Know: Western Civilization or World History?* ed. Josef W. Konvitz (East Lansing, Mich., 1985), pp. 155–65.

Teaching Western History at Stanford
Daniel Gordon

In 1989, Stanford retired its requirement in Western Culture and introduced freshmen to a new requirement in Cultures, Ideas, and Values (known as CIV). That same year, I arrived at Stanford to be an instructor in the new program. I had a B.A. degree from Columbia and was about to receive a Ph.D. in history from the University of Chicago. As a result of my experience at these two institutions, I was (and still am) a strong believer in required courses in Western civilization. My interest in history began in a Columbia course, An Introduction to Contemporary Civilization in the West. Founded in 1919, CC, as it is called at Columbia, is the oldest required course in Western civilization in America. CC pioneered the Great Books approach to Western civilization and was the model for Stanford's old Western Culture program. But if Columbia has the oldest, Chicago has the most extensive set of undergraduate requirements in Western history and thought. In 1987, when Allan Bloom published *The Closing of the American Mind* and offered the spirit of Chicago as a solution to the failures of higher education, I was a graduate student teaching The History of Western Civilization to Chicago undergraduates.

My move from Chicago to Stanford was accompanied, I admit, by a certain amount of anxiety. I had been immersed in traditions of European thought and emerged as a specialist in Enlightenment philosophy. Would I now be required to teach rap music and Rastafarian poetry? It did not take long for me to discover that this fear was unfounded. There is no question that the Stanford program is different from the traditional Great Books course. Yet in terms of a number of important criteria, such as the coherence of the course and the range of sophisticated issues to which students are subjected, there is also no question, in my mind, that it compares well with the older model.

Since Edmund Burke, one of the key aspects of conservative philosophy has been the belief that one cannot responsibly criticize an institution unless one participates in it enough to have an intimate sense of how it works. Burke developed this point in response to the Voltairean method of criticism, a method based on the presentation of decontextualized examples of institutional failure. The shortcoming in current debates about the curriculum is that too many of the ardent participants, on both the left and the right, have no concrete experience, either as student or as teacher, with the types of courses that are in question; for the fact is, most universities do not have, and never have had, required courses in Western civilization, Great Books, or multicultural studies. Hence, most academics, not to mention most journalists, face a severe difficulty as they try to participate in the debate. The easy way is to adopt the Voltairean style: to take a position and defend it by means of caricature.

In denouncing Stanford's CIV program, authors such as Bloom and Dinesh D'Souza have done little more than publish snippets from atypical reading lists. It is important to have a fuller sense of what students read. It is important, as well, to recognize that CIV is more than a reading list; it is a process, a year-long rite of initiation marking the transition from high school to college. Ideally, an outsider wishing to portray the program to other outsiders would adopt the method of the anthropologists and reside within the CIV tribe for a year. Yet even that would be insufficient. For in the end, we want to know not merely what the Stanford program is like but also how it compares to some of the more traditional programs at other universities. Advertisers often show us people comparing the flavor of different drinks, but there is no easy taste test for university courses. Fortunately, the itinerant lifestyle of young academics can produce people with inside experience of the main competitors — and as such a person, I would like to offer my opinion of CIV.

In the debate over the canon, defenders of traditional courses have taken the offensive by pointing out examples of what appear to be absurd readings on the Stanford syllabus. Frantz Fanon's *The Wretched of the Earth* is a case in point. Born in 1925 in Martinique, Fanon studied medicine in France, specializing in psychiatry. During the French-Algerian war, he was assigned to hospitals in Algeria, where he observed Algerian patients who had been tortured by French forces. *The Wretched of the Earth*, published in 1961, is an impassioned denunciation of European colonialism and a call for violence against Europeans. Fanon's critique of colonialism has both Marxian and Freudian elements. The condition of being a native, he argues, is not only one of economic exploitation, it is also a "nervous condition" brought about by the imposition of European repression upon the natural urges of the Algerians.

Writing in the *Wall Street Journal*, Allan Bloom declared that Fanon is a "demonstrably inferior and derivative thinker to whom no one would pay any attention if he were not the ideologue of currently popular movements,

and did not, as a black Algerian, fit Stanford's job description." In the fact
that Stanford freshmen read this text, Bloom finds "a stunning confirma-
tion of my thesis [about the closing of the American mind]." In the chapter
on Stanford in *Illiberal Education*, D'Souza has also pointed to Fanon as an
example of Stanford's "affirmative action in books."

These critics argue that Fanon is assigned simply because he was black.
Having taught this text, I can deny their assertion. There are no rules requiring that the courses (or "tracks," as they are called) in the CIV program
assign minority authors. The only specific rule is that the issue of the treatment of minorities in Western societies be raised at least once per term. In
fact, *The Wretched of the Earth* serves very well as the basis for discussing not
only the treatment of minorities but also general philosophical issues. As I
prepared to teach this text, I was encouraged by more experienced members
of the faculty to organize discussion around a series of questions proceeding
from the factual to the ethical: What is colonialism? In what ways can one
argue that colonialism benefited the colonies? Even if we assume that colonialism was a highly exploitative enterprise, is that enough to justify terrorism on the part of the natives? What particular arguments does Fanon make
to justify violence? What problems are there in his perspective? In this way,
one can raise the classic issue of might versus right, but with specific reference to colonialism.

D'Souza has stated that the inclusion of Fanon on the syllabus reflects "a
primitive romanticism of the Third World" among Stanford faculty. But the
purpose of teaching Fanon is not to imbue students with the resentments of
intellectuals who hate Europe. The main reason Fanon is included is that one
of the goals of CIV is to focus on the interaction between Western polities
and non-Western ones, and to study the cross-cultural perceptions that have
emerged from this interaction. Students learn what Columbus, Cortés,
Montaigne, Rousseau, and Marx thought about the relation of Europe to
the outside world. Why shouldn't they critically evaluate what some non-
Western "ideologues" have written on the same theme? The fact is, systematic attacks on the West are a part of the world we now inhabit. Students
should be aware of the content of these attacks and the historical situations
in which they have developed.

I have dwelt on Fanon in order to show how critics of Stanford misrep-
resent the study of minority issues. But it is also important to demonstrate
what place minority issues and writers have in the syllabus as a whole.
D'Souza has claimed that the European classics are taboo at Stanford. In *Illiberal Education*, he presented a short extract from the syllabus for the Europe and the Americas track in the CIV program to prove his point. Europe
and the Americas is an experimental course within CIV that is open to a
small number of freshmen each year. Unlike the other tracks, Europe and
the Americas tries to focus systematically on the contributions of minorities

to American civilization. But it also tries to instill appreciation for the European classics. In fact, the course is based on the "juxtaposition of texts," a method devised by Renato Rosaldo, the Stanford anthropologist who directs the course. Something interesting happened when he assigned Augustine's *Confessions* along with *Old Man Hat*, the life history of a Navajo man: "Both texts got better," Rosaldo says. This course pays more attention to genres of writing (e.g., autobiography) than to any linear version of the history of ideas. It does not provide a chronological account of the development of European civilization, but it does try to reveal some of the distinctive features of the European classics by comparing them to non–European works that are similar in form.

But let us put Europe and the Americas aside and look at part of a more typical Stanford reading list. What follows is the set of topics and authors assigned for the period between the Protestant Reformation and the French Revolution in the track entitled Europe from Late Antiquity to the Present. This is the track in which I taught from 1989 to 1991. The course has about 350 freshmen each year and is not radically different from the other CIV tracks. For purposes of comparison, I have also reproduced a typical syllabus for the same period as studied in Columbia's CC course in 1991.

Stanford	*Columbia*
The Reformation	**The Reformation**
Luther	Luther
Calvin	Calvin
	Mornay
New Worlds and Old	
Montaigne	
Shakespeare	
Documents illustrating debates	
about nature of American	
Indians	
Documents from witch trials	
Towards Cosmopolis	**The New Science and Polity**
Documents illustrating Jesuit	Bacon
missions	Descartes
Galileo	Hobbes
Descartes	Locke
Absolutism and its Critics	
Loyseau	
Hobbes	
Locke	

The Enlightenment
Montesquieu
Newton
Locke
Diderot
Turgot

The Costs of Civilization
Rousseau
Wollstonecraft
Raynal
Equiano

French and American Revolutions
Rousseau (again)
Sièyes
Documents from French
  Revolution
Madison
Adams

The Enlightenment
Rousseau
Hume
Kant
Wollstonecraft

French and American Revolutions
Documents from French
  Revolution
Madison

Stanford students take fewer courses per term than Columbia students do. Hence, they do more reading in their required courses—and so they read more Great Books. At the same time, Stanford has not limited its course by overinvesting in the notion of Great Books as Columbia has. At Columbia, greatness is the main standard that candidates for the syllabus must meet in order to be included. As one instructor explained to me recently, CC is "much more a Great Books course than a history course. Second-rate texts that might illuminate aspects of a historical epoch are generally not included." But if the course is not about the historical development of Western civilization, what makes it coherent?

According to Columbia instructors, not historical context but the very greatness of the texts provides the course with thematic continuity. This is an argument I remember very well from my days as a student at Columbia. What makes a "Great Book" great is that it contributes to the ongoing conversation about important questions: What is the method by which we attain knowledge? What is morality? What is political justice? Texts are selected in such a way that students can see the process of argument and counterargument among authors.

My own opinion about the notion of a conversation among great authors is that very formal and precise exchanges about faith, human nature, politics, and other subjects do indeed take place over long periods of time. But if one wishes to describe Western civilization as an ongoing intellectual conversation, one should at least recognize that part of the conversation is about what the conversation should be about, and who should be allowed to participate in it. (I borrow this formulation from Professor James Sheehan, who made this point in his final lecture to students in Europe from Late Antiquity.) The consideration of important questions often breaks up into intellectually and socially differentiated dialogues. There is not one all-inclusive conversation. The great minds speak to each other selectively, not in one vast salon but often tête-à-tête. As a result, some debates among great minds occur independently of others, and some even evaporate for want of participants.

The fundamental problem with the idea of a Great Books course is that there are too many dialogues and too many great authors to include in one course. Hence, some criterion other than greatness is needed as a principle of selection and organization. The traditional Great Books programs, however, have no tradition of admitting any other criteria. My recollection of being a CC student is that the books were fascinating and were sufficient to kindle my desire to learn more, but the course itself did not greatly enhance the experience of reading the texts because it offered neither a profound definition of the essence of Western civilization nor a complex account of the dynamics of change within Western civilization. These shortcomings, I believe, are inherent in a course in which textual greatness, rather than a specific set of thematic concerns, is the main principle for selecting the readings.

At Stanford, the CIV program is not committed to assigning only Great Books, though it does draw on the classics liberally, as the syllabus suggests. The principle for choosing from the Great Books is determined differently by each of the tracks in the program. Values, Technology, Science, and Society, a track that is popular with students in engineering and the hard sciences, places more emphasis than the other tracks on the role of science and technology in Western societies. The Europe from Late Antiquity track in which I taught emphasizes the development of democracy and the inescapable dilemmas facing people who are committed to the principles of individualism and equality. In the old Western Culture program at Stanford, a single canon existed for all the tracks, just as a single canon existed for all the CC sections at Columbia. One of the reasons for abolishing the canon in 1989 was not to do away with Great Books but to allow the tracks to choose more freely so that they could improve the inner coherence of their courses.

Comparison of the two syllabi shows that the Stanford course includes two units that the Columbia course does not: New Worlds and Old, and The Costs of Civilization. Keith Baker, a professor of history at Stanford and the author of the syllabus for the early modern period (1500-1800), devised New Worlds and Old so that students could see how debates about European claims to cultural supremacy began not in the 1980s or even in the 1960s but in the sixteenth century, in response to problems raised by the

Reformation and the discovery of the New World. The Costs of Civilization presents a series of arguments within the Enlightenment about the status of women, slaves, and colonial peoples. Baker states that it is important for students to appreciate that the philosophers of the Enlightenment defined the essential categories of modern political culture. In the process of formulating such ideas as "natural rights," "progress," and "civilization," Enlightenment authors were inevitably drawn into discussions about the nature and rights of women, slaves, and colonies. Issues concerning the status of these groups are thus part of our intellectual heritage. "These issues have not been invented by people who hate the Enlightenment and Western civilization; they lie at the very heart of Western political discourse," Baker says.

Among the books in the two units just discussed, the one that is most foreign to the traditional canon is the autobiography of Olaudah Equiano. Equiano was born in 1745 in what is now eastern Nigeria. He was kidnapped as a boy and forced to work as a slave on British merchant vessels. Eventually, he bought his own freedom, converted to Christianity, and became an adventurer who embarked on two voyages to the Arctic. Equiano was also an abolitionist, and in 1789 he published *The Interesting Narrative of the Life of Olaudah Equiano; or, Gustavus Vassa the African*—one of the first books to appear in a European language by an African author. Equiano portrays vividly what it was like to be a slave. He refers not only to acts of brutality he suffered but also to the laws that made these acts possible, such as the 329th Act of the Assembly of Barbados. According to this law, a master who killed his slave was subject to no prosecution if the slave had run away or committed "any other crime or misdemeanour toward his said master." But if a master killed a slave "out of wantonness or only bloodymindedness, or cruel intention," then the master was liable to be punished—with a fine of fifteen pounds sterling!

Equiano helps students to see that the concept of human rights in the Age of Enlightenment was limited to those who were deemed human—and who qualified as human was a matter of debate. Although Equiano reveals the underside of European civilization, the purpose of assigning his book is not to generate hostility toward Europe. In fact, Equiano clearly shows that Africans were also practicing slavery as part of their indigenous culture. In his critique of slavery, Equiano is moderate, amiable, and very English. His proposals for reform are much less radical in tone and substance than those demanded by Raynal in his *History of the Europeans in the East and West Indies* (also on the Stanford reading list), first published in 1770 and the most popular work of the late Enlightenment.

Defenders of the old canon sometimes assume that the addition of minority writers in the syllabus will entail an influx of radical values into the curriculum, as if any argument by a minority writer is ipso facto more radical than any argument by a nonminority writer. Readers of Equiano quickly discover the absurdity of this assumption. Equiano appears on the cover of his book, very dark skinned and dressed like an English gentleman. Students must deal with the questions, Who is this man who remembers his African tribe with nostalgia and who believes that the Indians of North America should be converted to Christianity? Is he an African or a European? It all depends on how you define "African" and "European," and, above all, it depends on what you consider to be the essential feature in the identity of humans in general—is it their color, their place of origin, their religion, their memories, their fears about how others will define them? These are the issues that Stanford students must confront in Europe from Late Antiquity and that are often excluded in the traditional curriculum.

The purpose of the course is not to suggest that these issues have easy answers. The purpose, rather, is to get students to appreciate the importance of the questions themselves. As an instructor in the program, I was encouraged by the architects of the course to make connections between past debates and present situations, but I was not given a political agenda. Although critics have suggested that Stanford professors are brainwashing their students, the students themselves do not feel that they are being pressured to adopt a "correct" ideology. One need only read student evaluations (a neglected source of information in debates about "political correctness" and required courses) to see that this is the case. "The discussions required a good knowledge of the texts and listening to varying viewpoints was stimulating," one student wrote. "Homogeneous thought is not what this class is all about. We were expected to challenge ourselves and others." Another student wrote, "I feel the course made the works very understandable and even the most dry writings enjoyable. The instructor never emphasized, or even made known, his own views and I think that was good. This year I came to determine some of my own values and some of the things that I really believe."

I could cite many other such comments. But it should be clear by now that the critics of Stanford do not always understand the CIV program. I have compared Stanford's program to Columbia's not in order to devalue the latter but in order to validate the former by showing that it stands up well in comparison to a program that is widely respected. We should always bear in mind that most universities do not have required courses in Great Books or Western civilization. Columbia and Stanford share something that is far more important than the differences between their reading lists: a commitment to a highly structured core curriculum that immerses students, for at least a year, in rigorous discussion of some of the most general problems in our culture. I believe that those universities that have abandoned required courses are the ones that most deserve critical scrutiny today. I also believe that those universities are the ones that are experiencing the most severe onslaughts against academic freedom.

At Stanford, I often formulated arguments in class in favor of absolute monarchy, aristocracy, male dominance, and slavery. I was never harassed by students because they knew that I was doing my job, which was to harass them intellectually. But for most students this Socratic spirit does not come naturally. It can only be fostered in a special type of course—a course that is so philosophical that common sense gets lost, a course that is so panoramic in viewpoint that our deepest values show their historical specificity. Students with no such training who find themselves in specialized history courses may not be able to understand why the instructors adopt a sympathetic attitude (in Herder's sense of *Einfühlung*) toward kings, aristocrats, and other creatures who are inherently repulsive to the modern American mind. Students have even been known to launch protests against a professor's right to discuss the values of these antiquated beings. But students who have been properly introduced to Western civilization will know that inequality has been not only a fact but also a norm throughout most of history. Already accustomed to counterintuitive speculation, these students may even be disappointed if the professor does not make a strong effort to portray the beliefs of people who think differently from themselves.

I am suggesting that a required course in Western civilization is the best, perhaps the only, opportunity for a university to make it clear to all students that part of a professor's role is to delineate unsavory ideas and that part of a student's role is to learn about them. I have also tried to suggest that Stanford has done a reasonably good job of creating a distinctive program in which this Socratic enterprise is enhanced by the addition of minority authors to the syllabus. Now that I am no longer at Stanford, I may perhaps be allowed to say that more universities should look to its CIV program as a model for their own programs.

Teaching Non-Western History at Stanford

Richard Roberts

The universities are in the midst of a profound struggle over the nature of knowledge and the shape of its transmission. There is no one struggle, nor is there a coherent vision of the future. Instead, there are overlapping trends, practices, debates, and decisions, which, when taken together, suggest that academics and teachers, students and professors, administrators and legislators are staking out positions in a public debate about the future of the university. These debates are going on everywhere: from departments revising their graduate and undergraduate curricula to university senates debating the shape of undergraduate requirements; from the panels of foundations deciding fellowship applications to the pages of the *Chronicle of Higher Education*; from the floors of state legislatures to the tables in school cafeterias. These discussions and the policies that are adopted as a result of them will profoundly affect how we teach, what we teach, and what we aim for when we teach.

My concern here is not with the debate about the future of the university as a whole, but a small part of it: I see the debate about multiculturalism as a challenge to the categories of historical interpretation. Framed primarily in terms of American history, the challenge of multiculturalism also goes to the heart of the ways we teach about the non-West. In this essay, I will argue that multiculturalism's challenge to Western culture for an inclusion of minority representation has been paralleled in the shift from Western civilization to world history in some widely used college textbooks. In both cases, the result has been a more inclusive unit of analysis: instead of one Western culture, we now have many Western cultures; instead of one Western civilization, we have many world civilizations. Although the units of analysis in both projects have been broadened, the historical and analytical ordering concepts remain largely the same. I will conclude that the challenge of mul-

53

ticulturalism for the teaching of non-Western history—as well as Western culture—is not resolved merely by including those who are not represented. The challenge must be to rethink the categories of analysis.

My specific reference point is the multiculturalism debate at Stanford University and the ways in which this debate has influenced the university-mandated undergraduate "liberal arts" curriculum. One of the recently adopted changes (1990) in the Stanford undergraduate curriculum is the requirement that all students take a world cultures course. The issues of the debate at Stanford will lead me to examine several popular world history textbooks in order to assess how well these texts satisfy the challenge of multiculturalism. In particular, I will examine the legacy of the concept of "civilization" that undergirds the textbooks—if not always the teaching—about both Western culture and world history. In the final section of this essay, I will describe the World Outside the West course sequence at Stanford. This course began in 1983-84 as a conscious effort to engage in a debate with Stanford's Western Culture program about the categories of "civilization." The issues raised here may also provide an agenda for a more thoroughgoing discussion of the teaching of world history and non-Western history.

Multiculturalism

Multiculturalism is, like the critique of Western Culture, a large and loose category, filled with many claims and claimants. When Stanford students in January 1988 marched outside the meeting of the University Senate, which was debating the composition of the mandated freshman year-long Western Culture requirement, they chanted "Hey hey, ho ho. Western Culture's got to go."[1] These students were protesting the "canon" of the "great books" around which the freshman core courses were organized.

In their critique, these students drew inspiration from various forms of postmodernism and literary criticism, which maintain that the canon is a political statement made by self-styled white male academic guardians of an intellectual tradition over whose persistence they draw their own intellectual (and professorial) authority.[2] Protesters demanded that the canon be opened, allowing representation from those groups hitherto excluded: people of color, women, subaltern classes, gays, and so forth. The students were not attacking the notion of a canon per se, but the composition of the canon and control over election to it.

The 1988 demonstration at Stanford had its roots in at least two other trends. First, there had been a relatively quiet, but sustained, debate among African-American students at Stanford concerning the failure to recognize the important contribution of Eastern Mediterranean, and in particular "black" Egyptian, civilizations to Greece and, hence, to Western civilization. Many Western civilization textbooks now acknowledge the "Asian" roots of civilization, including Mesopotamia and ancient Egypt, but they do not satisfy these students' demands for an emphasis on the wide influence of Egyptian culture on Greek civilization.[3]

Representatives of the Chicano and Asian-American student organizations argued that "Stanford can no longer freely silence the voices of minorities and women in the classroom. It is time for Stanford to recognize that people of color outside of Europe have made intellectual and artistic contributions to the world we live in." Moreover, inclusion of minority voices in the Western culture canon would offer Stanford students a "better appreciation of our fellow students' heritage and would promote tolerance and help dispel racism."[4]

Second, the composition of the student body at Stanford was changing dramatically during the 1980s, yielding student populations that were far less white, middle class, and male. In 1988-89, for example, women composed 43.5 percent, African-Americans 8.4 percent, and Chicanos 8.6 percent of the total undergraduate student population. Asian-Americans accounted for 16 percent of the student body. Demographic changes at the University of California were greater still. With the shifting ethnic and gender composition of undergraduates, multiculturalism has become a shorthand term for demanding more attention to the histories of minorities and those not represented in the standard political and cultural narratives of Western civilization. These students also argued for a shift in the focus of Western culture courses from Western Europe toward the peculiar conditions of America, and in particular the ways in which race, class, and gender shaped American history.

Responding to this evolving social and cultural context at Stanford, the University Senate in 1987 and 1988 debated changes in the orientation of its Western culture requirement. It would be wrong to suggest that it was student agitation that prompted the changes in the requirements of the freshman course in 1988. Faculty had taken the lead in criticizing the Western culture requirement and the form it took. By 1984-85, an interdisciplinary group of Stanford faculty were collaborating in an experimental course under the Western Culture program called Conflict and Change. Although this experimental course was still bound to the "list" of great books, it sought to provide alternatives to the Western European-centered narrative. Using the latitude already provided in the list of core books, which allowed instructors to tailor their courses by choosing some books in addition to the required ones, these instructors examined Islam, the Iberian peninsula, the conquest of the New World, and the underside of European culture. Instructors from this course eventually led the faculty's own call for reforms, which focused on a formally mandated review of the Western culture requirement scheduled to begin in 1986–87. The debate on the Western culture requirement took place throughout the university over two academic years, 1986–87 and 1987–88. The debate in the University Senate was condensed into three months, from January through March 1988. Reading the arguments presented at the Senate and those published in both the student and administration newspapers, I am struck with how impassioned, yet thoughtful, the debate was. Those supporting the opening of the canon prevailed in an overwhelming vote on March 31.[5]

The critique of the canon has been an important step in rethinking the categories of teaching and scholarship. At Stanford, and at other universities, the canon has been widened to include minority voices.[6] This has been, however, only a partial victory. If the ordering concepts remain intact—a canon, regardless of its composition—then the cultural architecture of "great" (and perhaps not so great) books continues unchallenged. Moreover, these ordering concepts sustain (just as before) the authority of those who determine the now-more-open selection process.

As I shall argue, merely opening the canon to new voices and applying "civilization" as used in Western culture to world history textbooks permits the organizing concepts (and their cultural and political implications) to remain unchallenged. If we are to take the challenge of multiculturalism seriously, then we need to design courses that challenge the prevailing intellectual paradigms.

The Concept of Civilization in the Teaching of World History

In many textbooks dealing with Western culture—and more recently those dealing with world history—the development of what most authors unproblematically call "civilization" lies at the heart of the narrative that constitutes the meaning of the past. I will argue that the peculiar ways in which "civilization" has been used has impoverished the study of the past by narrowing the range of human experiences studied. Just as the concept of a canon has narrowed the range of literatures studied, so too has the concept of civilization narrowed the topics and the issues studied historically.

In the popular *Western Heritage to 1715*, Kagan, Ozment, and Turner argue that "civilization, then, is a form of human culture in which many people live in urban centers, have mastered the art of smelting metals, and have developed a method of writing."[7] This seems reasonable and is not ethnocentric. The authors recognize the historical importance of Mesopotamia and ancient Egypt, and, indeed, this concept of civilization could be applied with some modifications to the civilizations of Asia and Africa, although it would not fit those of pre-Columbian America. The concept of civilization employed by Kagan, Ozment, and Turner, however, entails a further narrowing:

> The roots of Western Civilization may be found in the experience and the culture of the Greeks, but Greek civilization itself was richly nourished by the older, magnificent civilizations of the south and east, especially in Mesopotamia and Egypt. In the valley of the Tigris and Euphrates rivers (Mesopotamia) and soon in the valley of the Nile in Egypt, human beings moved from a life in agricultural villages, using tools of wood, bone, shell, and stone, into a much richer and more varied social organization that we call *civilization*. . . . The need for organizing this new and varied activity and for keeping records led to the invention of writing. The wealth acquired through more effective agriculture, better tools, the specialization of function, commerce, and conquest permitted the development of unprecedented skills. Great advances took place in the arts and sciences, in literature, and in the development of complex religious ideas and organizations.
>
> The new style of life required firm, efficient management and soon produced governments that were centralized and powerful. The kings' power rested on their capacity to manage the economy and to collect taxes.[8]

Although the authors derive their concept of civilization from non-Western examples, the histories of these non-Western cases are subordinated to the narrative of classical Greece. The characteristics of civilization are thus no longer culturally neutral, but are chosen because they find their flowering in "Western" civilization, with the Greeks serving as the takeoff phase. This is, after all, the authors' objective. I do not find fault with their objective as much as with the implications this narrowing has for the use of the concept "civilization" for a study of the past. In its use here and in the textbook by Lerner, Meacham, and Burns, we can begin to see not only a narrowing of the ordering concept, but also a kind of teleological bias, which presupposes the rise of the West out of the myriad roots of the "ancient" world.

In their widely popular (now in its eleventh edition) *Western Civilizations: Their History and Their Culture*, Lerner, Meacham, and Burns begin with a brief overview of the paleolithic era, but—much like Kagan, Ozment, and Turner—see "civilizations" only as the outcome of urbanization:

> Discussing the origins of cities is really the same as discussing the origins of *civilization*, which may be defined as the stage in human organization when governmental, social, and economic institutions developed sufficiently to manage (however imperfectly) the problems of order, security, and efficiency in a complex society. Around 3,200 B.C. Mesopotamia was "civilized." That is, at least five cities existed, which all included among their inhabitants warrior-rulers, administrators, and priests,

which all encompassed several monumental temples, and which all boasted in addition elaborate private residences, communal workshops, public storage facilities, and large marketplaces. Rudimentary forms of record-keeping were mastered, and writing was on its way. Herewith the story of civilization in the West begins.[9]

But the story of the West really begins, as the authors indicate eighty pages later, with the Greeks.

> Among all the peoples of the ancient world, the one whose culture most clearly exemplified the spirit of Western society was the Greek or Hellenic. No one of these peoples had so strong a devotion to liberty or so firm a belief in the nobility of human achievement. The Greeks glorified humanity as the most important creation in the universe and refused to submit to the dictation of priests and despots. Their attitude was essentially secular and rationalistic; they exalted the spirit of free inquiry and made knowledge supreme over faith. Largely for these reasons their culture advanced to the highest stage that the ancient world was destined to reach.[10]

Civilization has narrowed here even further. It has become essentially a narrative history of Western cultural elites and their ideas, propelled through time by the vagaries of politics and the decline of empires. Simply stated, civilization is "high culture," and this means written works of philosophy, politics, religion; written forms of literature and poetics; works of plastic and painted art, enduring architecture; and so on.

Although these two textbooks recognize the influence of non-Western ideas and institutions on Greece, to what extent has this concept of "civilization" become indelibly imprinted with the stamp of the "Western" culture? The cold war, the decolonization of Africa, the war in Vietnam all contributed to a growing awareness of the interdependence of the "West" and the rest of the world. This growing awareness ushered in a wave of new (and continuously revised) world history textbooks. Does a study of world history, however, demand a new categorization of the past, or can the concept of civilization be refurbished and reapplied?

In 1955, Edward McNall Burns launched what has become a widely used text for world history. In the preface to the original, he states:

> The time has long since passed when modern man could think of the world as consisting of Europe and the United States. Western culture is, of course, primarily a product of European origins. But it has never been that exclusively. Its original foundations were in Southwestern Asia and North Africa. These were supplemented by influences seeping in from India and eventually from China. . . . The exhaustion of Europe by two World Wars,

the revolt of the colored races against Caucasian domination, and the struggle for the world between Communist powers and the United States have made every part of the earth of vital importance to every other. If peace is indivisible, so are prosperity, justice, and freedom; so, in fact, is civilization, itself.[11]

Burns, Ralph, Lerner, and Meacham's *World Civilizations: Their History and Their Culture* attempts to survey "the struggle for civilization" throughout the world. "No major area or country has been omitted. . . . The aim throughout has been to give the student an appreciation of the distinctive achievements and limitations of the principal human societies and cultures past and present, and an awareness of their relevance for contemporary problems."[12] These laudatory objectives are somewhat clouded by the very organization of the book: "Each edition [of *World Civilizations*] has included the whole of Edward McNall Burns's *Western Civilizations*, except for sections on the non-Western world, which are more fully covered in this work."[13] World history is not a distinctive undertaking, but one that operates under the hegemony of the historical category of "civilization" as it was invented for courses in Western civilization. The world, then, is merely a larger field to play out the teleological tendencies in the historical development of Western "civilization."

This same tendency to see world history through the narrow lens of the cultural and political categories of Western civilization is also evident in Palmer and Colton's *A History of the Modern World*, first published in 1950 and revised most recently in 1992. In a section entitled "The Civilized World," (which deals with the period 1871 to 1914), the authors narrowly define the "civilized world":

With the extension of the nation-state system Europe was politically more divided than ever. Its unity lay in the sharing by all Europeans of a similar way of life and outlook, which existed also in such "European" countries as the United States, Australia, and New Zealand. Europe and its offshoots constituted the "civilized world." Other regions—Africa, China, India, the up-country of Peru—were said to be "backward." (They are today referred to as "less developed.") Europeans were extremely conscious and inordinately proud of their civilization in the half-century before 1914. They believed it to be the well-deserved outcome of centuries of progress. Feeling themselves to be the most advanced branch of mankind in the important areas of human endeavor, they assumed that all peoples should respect the same social ideals—that so far as they were unwilling or unable to adopt them they were backward, and that so far as they did adopt them they became civilized in their turn. . . .
    Even if we apply quantitative or sociological indices alone, we can say that after 1870 there was in fact, and not merely in the opinion of Europeans, a civilized world of which Europe was the center.[14]

Perhaps more blatantly than others, Palmer and Colton began with a Western civilization core and merely appended bits and pieces of the non-West to provide a "world history."[15]

Not all textbooks on world history are so narrowly construed. William McNeill's *A World History* is organized around the notion of precarious balances among "civilizations," where a series of shocks or disturbances to those balances constitute the "major historical benchmarks of world history." For McNeill, although civilization remains purposely vague, it is still a fairly familiar concept:

> Civilizations are unusually massive societies, weaving the lives of millions of persons into a loose yet coherent life style across hundreds or even thousands of miles and for periods of time that are very long when measured by the spans of an individual human life. Being both massive and long-lived, civilizations must perforce also be few. Indeed, from the time when human societies first attained civilized complexity and size, no more than four different major civilized traditions ever co-existed in the Old World; and in the New, where Amerindian development remained always weak and retarded, no more than three distinct civilizations ever emerged.[16]

McNeill's "civilization" is somewhat broader, but it too imposes an ordering on human societies, deeming some worthy of study and others not.[17]

Two other world history textbooks are cut from a different cloth. Eric Wolf's, *Europe and the People without History* and L. S. Stavrianos's *The World Since 1500: A Global History* differ from other world history texts in that they are concerned above all with explaining the patterns of European dominance over the world in the period after 1500.[18] Wolf's book is theoretically rich, but it is idiosyncratic, petulant in tone, and uneven in coverage. It is the kind of book area experts love to hate, precisely because the theoretical sophistication is greater than the author's knowledge of the component regional histories. It is also a difficult book and one that assumes a certain facility with Marxist theory. Undergraduates, and quite often instructors, have a hard time understanding it.

Stavrianos's *The World Since 1500* is perhaps the most successful of the world history texts available because it begins with the assumption that a world history perspective requires "a fresh start":

> Too often, the Modern World History course retains these traditional topics [of the modern European history course] and adds others concerning developments in non-European regions. The net result is an overburdened course that is neither European nor world history. It is essential, therefore,

to start fresh and to organize the course on a new and genuinely global basis.[19]

Indeed, Stavrianos takes his global perspective to an otherworldly direction when he begins his study with how the world would have looked to a Martian observer in 1500. From that perspective, Europe was only one of "four Eurasian centers of civilization, and by no means the most prominent." By the end of the eighteenth century, however, Europe had gained control over the oceans, conquered vast areas in the Americas and in Siberia, and had organized a system of global commerce.

Stavrianos's reference to "civilization" is merely descriptive; it plays no analytical or organizing role in his history. Stavrianos does not see Western culture as a bundle of traits ever more refined: "During most of the pre-1500 period, Western Europe would be termed an underdeveloped area. Its peoples were on the periphery — on the outside looking in. They were quite conscious of being isolated and vulnerable."[20] The text is organized around explaining why Europe emerged from regional isolation, why and how it exerted its dominance over the world, and what led to decline of the Western world's hegemony.

Global history is not, however, the only way to teach about the non-Western world. Indeed, one of the liabilities of Wolf's and Stavrianos's texts is that the global perspective gets in the way of explaining the historical dynamics of regional cultures and societies. Instead of learning about different cultures in their own terms and thus trying to see how their societies changed in response to regional influences, they are presented as part of a whole tapestry. As I will argue, the World outside the West course sequence at Stanford purposely departed from both the high-culture framework of Western civilization courses and from the totalizing approach of world history.

The World outside the West Course Sequence

Since 1980, when Stanford undergraduates were again required to take a year-long course in Western culture, they have also been required to take one course on some aspect of non-Western culture, society, or politics.[21] In 1988, the Western culture requirement was modified in response to the protests and reforms I outlined earlier to be more inclusive of the varied cultural traditions that make up the West and America in particular. A series of structural changes in the canon were made and the Western Culture sequence became CIV (Cultures, Ideas, and Values). In 1990, the University Senate changed its undergraduate liberal arts requirements yet again: in addition to the three-quarter CIV sequence, Stanford undergraduates are required to take a one-quarter self-standing course on non-Western culture,[22] one course on American societies (which was a compromise wording for a required course on race and class), and an "asterisked" course on gender.

The World outside the West course was a faculty response to the 1980 Western Culture requirement. A small group of area studies faculty shared a common grievance: compared with the three-quarter Western Culture requirement, an unspecified one quarter, non-Western culture course would not adequately portray the tremendous cultural and social diversity in the non-Western world. Moreover, this group was dissatisfied with the "high" cultural emphasis implicit in the teaching of the Western Culture requirement. We proposed, instead, a comparative study of three non-Western cultures over a two-quarter sequence, focusing on a broader definition of "culture." In this course, "culture" was conceived as lived experience,[23] thus emphasizing social history. Since there were no ready-made models for such a course, we spent considerable time exploring alternative ways of conceptualizing and organizing the material we hoped to include in the course and in developing a model of culture that could be used as part of a debate with the proponents of Western "culture" as commonly conceived. We found Fernand Braudel's division of time into natural, social, and eventful time, as developed in his *The Mediterranean and the Mediterranean World of Philip II*, provocative and helpful in organizing course materials. Our agenda was to find alternative categories for the study of culture and civilization that would allow us to apply to teaching the conceptual advances in social history that had transformed the practice of historical scholarship.

As our thinking evolved, the course came to concentrate on aspects of selected cultures in Asia (China), Africa (Nigeria), and the Americas (Mexico), and was to have a threefold objective: to introduce students to a select number of non-Western cultures before and after extensive contact with the West; to help students better understand the values, attitudes, and institutions of non-Western peoples in the modern world; and to furnish students with a framework for comparing and contrasting all cultures, including that of the West, thereby heightening their sensitivity to and appreciation of the varieties of human experience.

Students would not be the only beneficiaries. The process of course development would present opportunities for enhanced dialogue among faculty who specialize in the study of non-Western societies. We expected this dialogue to encourage greater sensitivity to the comparative dimension in courses taught in our own fields of specialization and to generate insights into further innovation in the curriculum in regard to introductory courses in specific non-Western areas.

Teaching The World outside the West began in the autumn of 1984-85.[24] From the outset, the faculty team, comprising two anthropologists, three historians, and a political scientist, had to confront and resolve two critical intellectual problems. One was to see how the various parts of each of the cultures with which they dealt could be presented in such a fashion as to make them into an interrelated, coherent, and apprehensible whole. The second problem was to shape the elements of the course—the peoples, societies, and cultures of China, Nigeria, and Mexico—into a common and shared discourse. Tackling the first problem required development of intracultural understanding; handling the second necessitated transcultural comparison.

The faculty involved were convinced that the best way to confront the basic epistemological difficulties was to present an overall and unifying analytic framework that stressed how men and women in different cultural areas responded to common problems relating to human efforts to control both nature and cosmic forces, and how these efforts shaped the society, economy, and polity. Particularly in the first quarter, when we study these three cultures prior to their sustained contact with the "West," we wanted to portray the cultures as dynamic and changing in order to avoid the stereotype of the "changeless" non-Western world. We paid special attention to the social, economic, political, and intellectual feedback between natural time and social time. Although we began with detailed discussions of physical and human geography, we spent considerable time examining the indigenous worldview—the bodies of philosophical, social, and religious thought—in each of the three cultures. The course came to be structured around an examination of what, explicitly, these indigenous bodies of thought express and how they are linked to social, economic, and political organization and change.

The professors' pedagogic goals were to analyze, mediate, and compare these bodies of thought; and to specify how peoples use these bodies of thought to inform, shape, and construct their various cultures. Central to our comparative approach was the idea that these very different cultures were alternative responses to problems all human societies seek to resolve.

This comparative concept—different responses to common problems—helped organize the syllabus, lectures, and reading assignments. The goal here was to get students to appreciate that the great diversity of human cultures reflects the enormous creativity of human beings in their responses to problems and opportunities. We expected that students would come to see that the Western tradition is just one possibility among many. As a result, students would come to adopt a more detached perspective on their own culture.

While none of the faculty agreed on a common definition of culture, there was general concurrence that it should include the schemes of perception, conception, and social action shared by members of a society in their quest to relate to each other and to make sense out of the universe in which they live. The concept of culture emphasized in the course would include the "great traditions" of art, literature, religion, and philosophy, dealing with them not as eternal and immutable verities, but as part of the everyday structures of life—including birth, rites of passage, marriage, and death. The course depicted culture as a fluid phenomenon and solidly rejected the usual assumption that non-Western cultures, once established, remain essentially unchanged.

Teachers presented both exogenous and endogenous views of the Chinese, Nigerian, and Mexican societies. Ethnographies, travelers' accounts, and similar documents imparted a sense of how these societies were viewed by outsiders, while the cultures' own written and oral traditions imparted a sense of how members of the societies perceived themselves. Faculty considered this emphasis on a dual perspective one of the main tasks of the course, for it would encourage students in the idea that any society can be regarded from a number of viewpoints and that truth is relative to the social and cultural position of the actor and the observer.

The faculty believed it imperative to stress in their teaching the immense variety of non-Western societies and cultural traditions. They wanted to sensitize students to the distortions of complex social realities that arise with the use of terms like "non-Western world" and "Third World," which are residual categories indicating not what various cultures are, but what they are not. Such terms not only incorrectly suggest that the world outside the West is homogeneous, they have also come to imply backwardness, poverty, and inscrutability. Emphasizing the heterogeneity of the non-Western world would indicate the falsification involved in indiscriminate use of all-encompassing terms such as "Third World" and would suggest further why the responses of non-Western peoples to Western intrusion have varied enormously from place to place.

The World outside the West is a two-quarter sequence. The initial segment of the course originally dealt with the societies of China, Mexico, and Nigeria before their enduring contact with an aggressive and interventionist West. The instructors' main objective during the opening quarter of the course is to challenge stereotypical notions of presumably dormant and stagnant non-Western societies that became dynamic only after being energized through contact with the West. The lessons here are that many non-Western societies have traditions as complex as, and in some cases with a longer history than, those of the West, that there are no societies without their own sense of time, and that all societies have traditions of challenge and change that persist in their dealings with the West.

For the instructors involved in the presentation of Chinese society and culture before extensive contact with the West, teaching focuses on some of the major elements that characterized the Chinese outlook, illustrating the ways in which a widely shared, specifically Chinese worldview was manifested in social, economic, and political arenas. Elements that are stressed include the absence of a creation myth (while the emergence of civilized, humane society may need explaining, the world itself simply is and cosmogony is not a serious issue); the view that the cosmos, the human/social realm, and the ordinary world around the Chinese are part of one holistic entity; the closely related idea that this differentiated and hierarchical whole functions organically, so that conditions in one realm affect the others; the emphasis in Chinese thought upon eclecticism, complementarity, and harmony rather than exclusivity, contradiction, and struggle; the predilection among Chinese people not to divide what one thinks or knows from what one does (knowledge and action are but two sides of the same coin); and the absence of a self-conscious science, which did not prevent the Chinese from developing a rich tradition of scientific and technological discovery.

Religion is stressed in the examination of the central Mexican Aztec civilization. Teaching centers on the ways in which all aspects of what have been traditionally considered the religious aspects of culture—cosmology, pantheon, priesthood, ritualism, sacrifice, symbolism, sacred sites, architecture, pilgrimages, mythology, divination, magic, and theological and philosophical speculation—were elaborately developed and closely integrated with social and political organization, ethics, art aesthetics, literacy, and daily life. Partly through original documents, students are introduced to the central Mexican worldview: they read Aztec philosophical poetry and confront the rudiments of the complicated and sophisticated Aztec calendar. The intimate interweaving of religion with daily life is important for understanding the Spanish conquest of Mexico, for the Aztecs regarded Cortés as the fulfillment of a prophecy that foretold the end of a political-cosmological cycle. Thus the Aztec defeat cannot be comprehended without reference to Aztec religion and the interaction between Aztec and Spanish worldviews.

In Nigeria, with the exception of the Islamic tradition of the north, the relatively small scale of most societies hindered the development of a professional "intellectual" class. Lacking literacy, precolonial Nigerians did not bequeath to posterity a written corpus of philosophical traditions. The smallness of scale of many of the societies of Nigeria contributed to an intimacy of belief, analysis, and practice. Thus, it becomes extremely difficult, if not impossible, to separate religious thought from ethical behavior, philosophical traditions from political ideas. The Nigerians' complex cosmology, for example, demonstrates their understanding of causality and consequence. Problems of human survival demand a careful and continuous accounting to the spiritual world and the maintenance of balance within it. Examination of the Nigerian life cycle explores the closeness of the past, present, and future in the consciousness of Nigerians and in their religious thought. Throughout the Nigerian segment of the opening quarter, instruction hinges upon this critical sense of intimacy between thought and lived experience.

The first quarter ends and the second quarter begins with the interaction of the three non-Western cultures/societies with the aggressive, curious, expansionist, and interventionist West. As the first quarter ends, we have introduced Europeans onto the scene, exploring how, in the case of China and Nigeria, they were obliged to conform to local patterns of commerce and culture. In keeping with the religious, philosophical, and cosmological themes of the opening quarter, attention is directed toward the response of Christian Europeans (especially missionaries) to the religious ideas and values of the three societies and the responses of the peoples in these societies to the cosmology and ethical norms of the Christians in their midst. The course also addresses questions of how a society like China, with varying degrees of success, maintained its political independence in the face of Western pressure while at the same time it attempted to create new cultural syntheses between Western civilization and its own heritage. In its examination of the range of non-Western reactions to the West, the course reiterates its emphasis on the vast heterogeneity of the world outside the West. Discussion of the reactions of non-Western peoples to the West also reveals their deep ambivalence toward the West, an ambivalence that is an important, inescapable fact about the contemporary world. The ambivalence can be seen in the alacrity with which some social groups gravitated toward Christianity, Western literacy and numeracy, and Western technologies combined with their unwillingness to take Western culture in its prefabricated totality. The proliferation of syncretic or breakaway Christian churches provides an excellent example of these ambivalences.

The China portion of the second quarter addresses the issue of how Chinese social and religious thinking did or did not change in response to the intrusion of new modes and models of thought from the West. Lectures and readings cover the missionary movement in China and Chinese reaction to it, the confrontation of traditional ethical systems with rationalistic Western social theories, and the transformation of Marxism into a Maoist synthesis. In general, although the Chinese intelligentsia were exposed to Christianity, they found its message inadequate. They were more accepting of a wide variety of Western secular philosophies, materialist or positivist in character, ranging from Social Darwinism to Marxism-Leninism. Why there was a general embracing of Western secular thought is one of the principal questions of the second-quarter Chinese section. In seeking answers to this question, efforts are made to sensitize students to what is universal and what is parochial in Western thought.

The beginning of the second-quarter Mexico segment discusses the conquest and colonization of Mexico in terms of the philosophical debates about human nature that the New World inspired in Spanish conquistadores and missionaries. The main subject of debate was whether, and if so to what degree, the indigenous peoples of the New World were fully human, having intellectual capabilities of a level sufficient enough for them to become completely Christian. The enslavers and exploiters argued that Indians, although descendants of Adam and Eve, had devolved to such an extent that they were in essence beasts. Protectors of the Indians argued that they were just like Adam and Eve immediately after expulsion from paradise and that therefore Indians were ready for full-scale evangelization. From discussions of debates and policies in regard to the Indians, the segment concludes with an examination of the politics, policies, and challenges facing the various Mexican governments during the nineteenth and twentieth centuries.

Second-quarter lectures and readings on the peoples of Nigeria concentrate on the quite different responses to Christianity among followers of Islam and those adhering to "animist" beliefs. The argument presented in the segment is that the many similarities between Islam and Christianity, coupled with the long history of conflict between the two world religions, enabled Muslims to successfully resist the proselytizing efforts of Christian missionaries. The intense linkage of localized animist beliefs with the maintenance of a local small-scale political order, however, created special opportunities for Christian missionary efforts, particularly on the heels of European military conquest. The effects on small-scale Nigerian societies of the confrontation between Christianity and animism are graphically portrayed in Chinua Achebe's *Things Fall Apart*.[25] Although rejection and acceptance of Christianity were the most potent alternatives available to Nigerians in their encounter with this aspect of Western intrusion, they were not the only ones. The segment examines instances of syncretic responses to Christianity, such as the Cherubim and Seraphim movement and the efforts of Nigerians to establish an independent Nigerian Christian Church. Studying these syncretic movements accentuates the creativity and dynamism of Nigerian societies in their reactions to the West.

The World outside the West sequence was much neater and tidier on paper than it actually was in the classroom. China, Mexico, and Nigeria are very different cultures whose historiographical traditions differ considerably. Moreover, neither Mexico nor Nigeria was a recognized precolonial entity. This required that we redefine the units of study: for the first quarter, Mexico was essentially the valley of Mexico; for Nigeria, we had to balance two quite different narratives, one for the northern Muslim Hausa and the other for the acephalous Igbo of the southeast. While those who taught about China and Mexico presented more unitary views of their respective cultures and societies, those who taught about Nigeria tried to present the range of diversity in what was to become Nigeria. The Hausa and the Igbo were chosen because they were the principal players in the Nigerian civil war of the late 1960s.

Part of the problem for both teachers and students was the differences in the presentations of these regions and the unevenness in the quality of the literature available. Much more and much better introductory material was available for China and Mexico than for Nigeria, but the novels and other readings (including *Things Fall Apart* and the wonderful autobiography of a Hausa woman, *Baba of Karo*) more than favored the Nigeria side.[26] The course therefore avoided the problems of "equivalences" by acknowledging to students the very different historiographical traditions in the three regions.

Other forms of "equivalences"—including chronology—continued to plague the course. Events occurred at very different times in each of these areas, as did the beginning of sustained contact with the West, which was to serve as the transition from the first to the second quarter. Although it is somewhat awkward for students, we agreed to use what we call "conceptual" time. Thus, the establishment of the Aztec state could be compared to the Ming/Ch'ing transition in China, which was parallel to the consolidation of power by Muslim rulers in Hausaland. Similarly, the transition from the first to the second quarter also followed conceptual time, wherein the Spanish conquest of Mexico could be compared to the treaty port system in China and to the British abolition of the slave trade and the beginning of colonial conquest in Nigeria.

The World outside the West is not designed to be a "world history" course. It is meant to expose students to ranges of diversity in three deeply studied parts of the world, to challenge them to think critically about these areas in relationship to one another and in relationship to the West, and to propose an alternative way of presenting and integrating crucial parts of the history of the making of the modern world. The course has a reputation among students for being extremely demanding, but also quite rewarding.

Conclusion

Teaching non-Western history through the World outside the West course sequence has allowed faculty and students to explore different categories of historical analysis. The course was organized as a challenge to the concepts of "high culture" that undergird the study of Western culture, and it was designed to explode the concepts of "civilization" to permit students to appreciate the great diversity of human responses to common problems. If we are to take the challenge of multiculturalism seriously, then incorporating underrepresented minorities in a set of analytical categories that remain unchanged is to leave intact the cultural and political architecture of the study of the past, which privileges certain forms of cultural and intellectual expression over others and certain forms of history over others. As Stavrianos notes in regard to building a world history on the traditional topics of European history, the "net result is an overburdened course that is neither European nor world history." Our challenge is to rethink how we teach about the past and to use fresh ideas about how to make the past speak to today's students.

NOTES

1. This chant originated in January 1987 during an earlier Senate debate on this topic. Jesse Jackson, then a presidential candidate, participated in the march outside the Senate. In January 1988, the students also chanted "Vote now, we want change." See the *Stanford Daily*, January 20, 1988.

2. For two recent discussions of these issues, see John Searle, "The Storm over the University," *New York Review of Books*, December 6, 1990, a view from the liberal center, and Dinesh D'Souza, *Illiberal Education: The Politics of Race and Sex on Campus* (New York, 1991), a view from the right.

3. See, for example, the much-debated Martin Bernal, *Black Athena: The Afroasiatic Roots of Classical Civilization* (London, 1987) and the quite different but equally controversial Molefi Kete Asante, *Kemet, Afrocentricity and Knowledge* (Trenton, N.J., 1990).

4. "Minorities and ASSU [Association of Students at Stanford University] Laud Task Force Report," *Stanford Daily*, April 28, 1987.

5. An excellent compilation of documents relating to the Western Culture debate has been assembled by the office of the Cultures, Ideas, and Values program at Stanford University.

6. For a discussion of the new Cultures, Ideas, and Values program at Stanford and the new insights that can be derived from juxtaposing canonical and noncanonical texts, see Daniel Gordon's essay in this book.

7. Donald Kagan, Steven Ozment, and Frank M. Turner, *The Western Heritage to 1715*, 3rd ed. (New York, 1987), p. 7.

8. Ibid., p. 1.

9. Robert E. Lerner, Standish Meacham, Edward McNall Burns, *Western Civilizations: Their History and Their Culture*, 11th ed. (New York, 1988), p. 26.

10. Ibid., p. 105.

11. Cited in Edward McNall Burns, Philip Lee Ralph, Robert E. Lerner, Standish Meacham, *World Civilizations: Their History and Their Culture* (New York, 1986), vol. 1, p. xii.

12. Ibid., p. xiii

13. Ibid.

14. Robert R. Palmer and Joel Colton, *A History of the Modern World*, 6th ed. (New York, 1984), pp. 551, 554.

15. See their preface: "Since its first edition, the book has been designed to set forth the modern history of Europe and European civilization as a unit, and in its later chapters it attempts to tell the story of an integrated, or at least interconnected, world. Emphasis falls on situations and movements of international scope, or on what Europeans and their descendants have done and faced in common. National histories are therefore somewhat subordinated, and in each national history the points of contact with a larger civilization are treated most fully. Historic regional differences within Europe, as between eastern and western Europe, are brought out, and the history of the Americas is woven into the story at various points, as are developments of the last century in Asia and Africa" (Palmer and Colton, *History of the Modern World*, p. vii).

16. William H. McNeill, *A World History*, 2nd ed. (New York, 1971), p. v.

17. Jacques Maquet, a leading French anthropologist, wrote a fascinating little book that implicitly challenged the linkage between civilization and "high" culture. In this book, *The Civilizations of Black Africa* (New York, 1972), Maquet establishes a broadened typology of civilization by applying the concept to hunters and gatherers and to nomadic herders as well as to farmers and urban dwellers.

18. Eric Wolf, *Europe and the People without History* (Berkeley and Los Angeles, 1982), and L. S. Stavrianos, *The World Since 1500: A Global History* (Englewood Cliffs, N.J., 1966). See also L. S. Stavrianos, *The World to 1500* (Englewood Cliffs, N.J., 1974).

19. Stavrianos, *World Since 1500*, p. xiv.

20. Ibid., pp. 6–7.

21. An earlier version of this section, written with James Lance, appeared in the American Historical Association *Perspectives* 29, no. 3 (March 1991). In Stanford jargon, this requirement was an asterisk requirement, which meant that students could satisfy it by taking a course that also satisfied one of the other ten distribution requirements. It was, according to this system, a second-tier requirement.

22. The 1990 change, which took effect in the 1991-92 academic year, thus raised the non-Western culture requirement from a second-tier to a first-tier requirement.

23. The term is originally taken from James Henretta, "Social History as Lived and Written," *American Historical Review* 84 (1979): 1293-1333.

24. The National Endowment for the Humanities provided funds for the initial course development and the Andrew W. Mellon Foundation provided subsequent and ongoing support.

25. Chinua Achebe, *Things Fall Apart* (New York, 1988).

26. Mary Felice Smith, *Baba of Karo: A Woman of the Muslim Hausa* (New Haven, Conn., 1981).

Teaching High School History Inside and Outside the Historical Canon

Alice Garrett

Like the textbooks and guidelines of public school systems throughout the United States, the set of events and interpretations codified in the North Carolina State Department of Public Instruction's detailed guidelines for courses in American history serves the function of a "canon." Here I use *canon* in the sense of a select body of material rooted in a historical tradition that bears the imprimatur of the highest educational authority in the state. This canon in turn implies certain modes of instruction as most suitable for transmission of knowledge. The state guidelines have both advantages and disadvantages for the teacher and for the student. While such standard curricula offer a workable and necessary frame of reference, in many instances they leave much to be desired in the realm of real instruction. I believe that we learn history as a process rather than as a mass of miscellaneous facts. We also learn history more by way of sensitive, high-quality instruction than by quantity of material. A careful look at the state-mandated curricula in North Carolina, however, reveals an overwhelming amount of material to be covered in short periods of time.

The American history course is a lengthy survey that begins with the pre-Columbian cultures and takes one through the time tunnel to the present day. I believe that it could be better taught by the teacher and better understood by students over a span of two years rather than one. The history of our country is much too rich and important for fast-paced instruction. For example, it is virtually impossible to teach "the major events, their courses, and their effects on the foreign policy of the United States since 1945" in a matter of weeks. Time limitations sometimes pose a problem of dilution or omission of significant information because, as teachers, we constantly face the task of making required information as relevant as possible to students.

71

This is not always an easy task, given the wide range of student abilities and the mandated curriculum.

While the "official" curriculum helps in the process of course preparation, it does not offer much assistance in evaluating students apart from testing their knowledge of a specific body of information. Real evaluations of students take more time and planning than is presented or allowed in the state outline. As teachers provide supplementary materials to meet the needs of students, it becomes their responsibility to add objectives and evaluative activities outside the guidelines of the state curriculum. Yet extracanonical teaching materials and objectives must tie in with material as prescribed in the state canon. Consequently, exploring and making additions to the existing curriculum requires time-consuming research and planning. The real challenge, though, comes with the allotment of time and space for each subject and with decisions about what to add to or subtract from the curriculum. The teacher then becomes the evaluator of the canon and the judge of the value of each historical topic or piece of historical evidence. Teachers believe that such reworking of the curriculum is inevitable and even healthy in the sense that they, like other professionals, must apply their skills and experience to their work. Teachers too must realize that their task is to assist students to develop systems of beliefs that are meaningful and tenable. After all, for many students, the present course is the last time they will ever study history. Extending the official curriculum guidelines thus has important effects on students' understanding of themselves and their world.

Students react differently to canonical and extracanonical teaching. Their response to the standardized curriculum is usually a bit apprehensive, and it becomes even more so when the teacher begins to add more information to what is already thought to be a heavy load. Students understandably perceive the material required in one school year as a tremendous amount of work, and they express doubt about how well they will understand this material. Their anxiety can be alleviated in part by finding methods to modify the standardized curriculum outline. The purpose of this essay is to explore how a set body of historical information can be adapted to address students' needs.

Teaching outside the canon augments the creative side of teaching; it forces teachers and students alike to move past the seven straight rows of chairs and the quiet, teacher-centered classroom. Creative teaching employs themes and methods that will assist students in developing a more personal understanding of the past.

Like many teachers, I am fond of informal seminar instruction. In a seminar on the 1920s, for example, one might find the classroom set up as a speakeasy and students dressed as characters of the era. Each student must contribute the expertise that he or she has developed through research on the 1920s. The political, social, and economic events of the decade are put together as a news program, while movie clips, records, fads, and sports figures become the subjects of an entertainment segment. In a second seminar on the 1920s, the same "set" becomes the Cotton Club during the Harlem Renaissance for a revival of black music, art, and poetry. The class thus moves beyond the textbook and the politics of a historical era to develop personal identifications with figures and events in the past.

Another way I circumvent the traditional class format and textbook is to teach revolution and protest through the use of past and contemporary music. From the American Revolution to the civil rights and equal rights movements, the focus of the music seminar is largely developed by students. The seminar usually takes place after our study of the colonial protests that eventually led to the American Revolutionary War, thereby setting the stage for future discussion of the subsequent protest movements we study (including that against the Vietnam War) and suggesting a certain continuity in protest movements throughout American history. While none of the topics is covered in great depth, students begin to develop a working knowledge of each era and to see history as a process of recurring issues and problems. Eventually we move to a more detailed study of each topic. This seminar on music includes discussion of causes, events, and effects of protests, and it features sing-alongs with tapes that are made by students. Once again, the personal link to history becomes important. When students have volunteered to interpret songs of the 1970s, I have personally demonstrated dance steps—which makes for much fun!

There are many films that are entertaining and rich in historical imagination that may also be used in extracanonical teaching. *Glory*, an excellent example of such a film, chronicles the lives and struggles of black soldiers during the Civil War. Most textbooks make little reference to the valor of the all-black Fifty-fourth Regiment. What a lesson can therefore be learned from this Civil War movie (with parental permission, of course). Visual media bring back the human actor in history in a setting most students find more comfortable than books.

The canon represents to me, as a teacher, both form and content. A book can be either beautiful or plain, thick or thin, but it is useless if the pages are bare. Similarly, the history outline given to teachers is merely a frame. It is worthless to the teacher and to the students without substance, and the teacher has the responsibility to add less traditional materials—clothes from past eras, music, films—to the rigid curricular form.

Work done in the past twenty years has shed light on the textbooks and curricula we now use. As Mary Kay Thompson Tetreault has noted:

Curriculum analyses contribute the most illuminating ideas . . . when [these analyses] move beyond generalizations about the content of school books to question valuations, by which they mean the perception of one group's experience—for example, men's, whites' or management's—as legitimate, objective, and factual knowledge, while another group's experience—women, minorities, or laborers—is thought of as subjective and secondary knowledge.[1]

It is crucial for students to view history through both male and female eyes and eyes that center less on one group than on the whole range of contributors to our nation's rich history.

As an American history teacher, I am reminded of a statement made by Mary McLeod Bethune that best explains one of my reasons for departing from the canon: "It seems almost paradoxical, but nevertheless true, that the history of women and the history of Negroes are, in essential features of their struggle for status, quite parallel."[2] African-Americans and women are scarcely mentioned in most history texts: the names of Margaret Sanger, Abigail Duniway, Sojourner Truth, and Maria Mitchell "sound like answers from some historian's version of trivia to the majority of high school students."[3]

While today's textbooks have begun to make more reference to women and African-Americans, the experiences of both groups—and especially of African-American women—are still marginalized. I am proud to take the time to put designated texts and curricula aside to teach the worth, the contributions, and the empowerment of African-Americans and women, groups that have been and continue to be subject to omission and dilution in historical canons such as the official North Carolina curriculum. There is a lesson in integrity, character, determination, and self-worth to be learned from both groups' dignified resistance to oppression.

I do not think that the state curriculum fully addresses the needs of students in terms of their own interests and learning. For instance, in identifying primary sources or "masterpieces" in American history, the secondary school canon has been hard pressed to get beyond Washington's Farewell Address, Lincoln's Gettysburg Address, and Wilson's Quarantine Speech, to name a few. What a testament of strength and character, of patriotism and love for mankind and for peace, students find in a careful study of Martin Luther King's "Letter from a Birmingham Jail" or Mary McLeod Bethune's "Legacy" or the letters of Abigail Adams. While most students profess to know about Dr. King, few know the definition of nonviolence or civil disobedience. With many schools throughout the country in shambles and many school systems considering metal detectors to control violence, we can obviously benefit from more study of nonviolence and love. The lives of King, Bethune, and Adams were more than a dream: life by example is living personal history of the kind that high school students need to know and think about.

Many schools in North Carolina now have assistant principals for curriculum and instruction. It is common for teachers to submit long-range curriculum plans to these principals, detailing length of study, material to be covered, and methods to be used to achieve curriculum objectives. Since supervisors use these plans as part of the teacher evaluation process, extracanonical activities must be readily justifiable to the teacher's local administration. While I believe in teaching outside the canon, I also advocate a chronological sequence that carefully guides students into connecting topics. There should always be a careful link between the supplementary material and the state curriculum, in part because students need to know the canon to perform well on the tests that shape their future.

A break with the rigidity of the state's curriculum, however, allows me to escape from the traditional lecture, discussion, and activity mode of teaching. By moving away from the canon, I find it as easy to create an effective new teaching plan as to follow traditional and predictable methods. Extracanonical methods have the added benefit of allowing students to feel free to learn in a less stressful environment. I constantly remind myself and others that "proper planning precipitates participation," and students are more likely to meet my expectations for participation when they are relaxed.

Giving students an outline with objectives and traditional activities forces the class into a regimented and predictable routine. From one lesson to the next, students depend on the teacher always to be the leader and the facilitator. Cramming for tests and rote memorization become the norms, so that students play a game of jumping hurdles, forgetting the last barriers and then facing the next challenge. When students plan seminars and take active roles in activities, when they view a pertinent film or search for music from past eras, they learn as they plan and are less likely to forget the important questions: the whys and hows. Most students can and will accept responsibility for their learning when they are given the opportunity. The poor reader might just be the gifted graphic artist, or the shy and inhibited student may come alive through using music. The most verbally gifted might want to learn a dance step or to recite a poem by Langston Hughes.

In addition to the new knowledge that comes with active learning processes, teaching outside the canon almost always brings about different power relationships. The teacher becomes a learner; the student becomes a teacher. The parent becomes an expert consultant, and the most energetic individual student in the class emerges as a group organizer. Initially, the teacher may have to plan all extracanonical lessons and activities; once the class accepts the idea, however, students become more responsible and less reluctant to assume roles and to complete a project. Groups of students also plan to view films or organize seminars, debates, and discussions for the entire class. Groups may make their own home videos. In this less structured environment, teachers are more dependent on students to take the initiative and to complete needed assignments. In extracanonical teaching, the teacher must always bear in mind the motto Be Prepared.

It is perhaps more comfortable to teach solely within the state curriculum. There is less work and less worry about synchronizing material and planning relevant topics when one simply follows the designated form and content of the official guidelines. The best protection offered by the state curriculum is that it can serve as a calendar, especially since students are required to take the State Department of Public Instruction's End-of-Course Exam at the conclusion of the school year.

Teaching outside the curriculum, however, brings out some of the conflicts and exclusions inherent in most historical canons and also encourages students to look critically at information from the past and present, to learn to determine cause and effect, to compare events in different eras or places, and to apply what they have learned from history to analysis of the world in which they live. History, while it is a study of the past, also becomes a living subject. For almost every event from the past, there are contemporary analogues. How, for instance, did events leading up to the Persian Gulf War compare to various historical precedents?

Extracanonical teaching does not mean a complete deviation from the prescribed framework or body of traditional historical knowledge. It may consist simply of combining topics and events in new ways and using new media with the understanding that students will see much of the material in a different format later in the course. Comparisons across historical eras, for example, may give new meanings to well-known historical events. A good example of combining topics from one decade to another can be found in a discussion of Supreme Court rulings: *Plessy v. Ferguson* following Reconstruction, *Brown v. The Board of Education* in 1954, and the Bakke decision of the 1970s can be taught together to show past and recent rulings on constitutional law in the areas of civil rights. During the course of a single semester, students may explore seven and a half decades of constitutional law and see historical contrasts and similarities that would never appear in a strict chronological format. Persistence, tradition, and continuity are important in studying history, and such elements of historical experience often appear more clearly in a thematic approach that gives less attention to simple chronology.

I enjoy teaching and I take particular pleasure in teaching outside the official canon of historical events and personages. It not only gives me an opportunity to put my creative skills to work, it also creates the kind of atmosphere I seek in my classroom. Students are led to understand that the seminars are something special, and we all look forward to the presentations. Students learn firsthand that history involves similar processes at various times in the past, and they begin to look for comparisons between events or problems in different eras. Parents are encouraged to contribute their expertise by assisting students with assignments. I have seen many sack dresses, bell-bottom jeans, and dashikis come out of storage for class display—and, yes, many old military uniforms make their way into the classroom too. The historical canon of great events, wars, and famous persons does not disappear from my class, but it takes on new personal meanings, new appreciation for the diverse experiences of people of different races and genders, and new intellectual vitality when it is modified with new forms of classroom interaction, new subjects for student discussion, and new media to stimulate student interest.

NOTES

1. Mary Kay Thompson Tetreault, "The Treatment of Women in U.S.History High School Textbooks: A Decade of Progress," *Women's Studies Quarterly* 10, no. 3 (Fall 1982): 40.

2. Quoted in Tetreault, "The Treatment of Women," p. 40.

3. Tetreault, "The Treatment of Women," p. 40.

History, Science, and Literature: Integrating Knowledge and Involving Students in American High Schools

Glenn Tetterton-Opheim

Most secondary and beginning college students are just acquiring the knowledge and cultural breadth that will enable them to interpret the world in which they live, yet these students are expected to learn materials that are locked into rigid disciplinary categories. It should come as no surprise that students at the secondary and beginning college levels have scarcely made the connections necessary to view science as an integral component of modern culture, nor have they discovered the potential of literature for interpreting the past. Moreover, while high schools and universities have had some success in fostering the analytic skills that allow students to begin to quantify, disassemble, and scrutinize phenomena, they have had far less success in helping students construct meaningful relationships to and among the bits of disparate knowledge they have acquired. Too few students in our high schools consider what they learn to be of value unless it can be shown to have an immediate utility. Since, according to *Statistical Abstracts of North Carolina, 1991,* only 18.3 percent of North Carolina adults hold a bachelor's degree, the fragmentation of learning in high schools and colleges should be cause for concern. Is it possible that the low number is at least in part caused by the choices we make as instructors? Are there disciplines—history, literature, or foreign languages, for example—in which an integrated approach might help to promote synthesis, thus encouraging students to develop from rote learners into thinkers? Can history become the core of the curriculum, or will it face a future of continued retreat as other disciplines demand greater time and resources? In short, I am concerned with the social consequences of high school and general college education as well as intellectual content, and I believe that social consequences and content are closely related.

Two areas of study are appropriate candidates for the synthesizing core role in the secondary curriculum: foreign languages and history. Both offer a chance to explain the world in its complexity without being compelled to reduce the world to static models. On the college level there would be other candidates for this role, although they tend to implode into narrow, specialized topics—a tendency most readily seen in the other social sciences. Fields such as sociology, political science, and even philosophy seem to avoid answering the great questions that were their origins as they move into arcane languages of their own. While much of the research in academic history shows signs of moving in the fallacious, overly specialized direction of some of the other social sciences and the humanities, the history curriculum has fortunately retained the broad mandate to investigate and make meaningful interpretations of the past.

In this respect, foreign language studies can assume a comparable role at the core of the curriculum; in fact, the study of foreign languages should be considered a natural ally for history. From the start, language studies, like history, expand horizons, open new possibilities, and offer alternatives for comprehending the world. For example, those of my German students who plan careers in medicine find the articles they read on the contemporary science scene in Germany motivating and relevant to their needs. Others find texts in fields they plan to pursue of greater interest. They therefore have a stake in the materials they read. These students also discover, after several readings, that science in the German language is not quite the same as in English, and that the social and cultural context is different in Central Europe. They also cannot really avoid the need for historical context in interpreting these texts. Likewise, my history students have wide latitude in selecting books to read for reviews and class discussions; these choices reflect their concerns about the past. The challenge for teachers in foreign languages and history alike is to show students how the material they study can also become a part of their own lives. Knowledge does not consist of isolated fragments of information; it can and should add depth and richness to our lives both as teachers and as students.

In the past several years my involvement with history has focused on a high school advanced placement course in European history. This program allows students to pursue a more demanding study of modern history, from the Renaissance to the present, than is possible in the usual world history curriculum. The content of the course is driven to some extent by the end-of-course exam, which is designed and administered by the College Board. The free-response and document-based essay questions from previous years, as well as the entire 1984 exam, are available for preparation for the current exam. The breadth of the course is revealed in the variety of topics addressed by the exam. The 1984 exam includes one hundred multiple-choice questions that fall into nearly a dozen possible categories. Four of the multiple-choice questions concern literature; four are drawn from the history of science. One of the seven possible free-response topics addresses a history of science question, a practice that is regularly repeated with the essay questions. Since the document-based question refers only in part to specific content knowledge, and only one of the free-response questions must be answered, the College Board Advanced Placement Exam in European History is as fair an assessment of a student's ability to interpret modern history as can be found outside the individual classroom. Yet even this wide-ranging examination may foster the development of fragmentary knowledge rather than a broad, synthetic approach to history.

A student's success on the exam validates my competency as a teacher, while failure leads me to intensify the search for better means to motivate students. Subsequent student performance, especially continued study of history, is an even better indication of success. Statements from students that they learned a lot, sometimes more than in any other class, are also gratifying, as are the reports that what they learned in history helped them with their studies of English, physics, French, or art. In other words, no matter how my students perform on the standardized exams, I feel the greatest satisfaction for myself and for them when I see that their study of history has led them to apprehend the links among what they study in my class, what they study in other disciplines, and what they do in other parts of their lives.

The synthesizing themes that I try to develop in the European history course emphasize the roles of science and literature in the evolution of past societies. The history of science makes its initial appearance with an investigation of the scholastic worldview and the struggle to construct a meaningful synthesis of classical and Christian traditions. It reappears in discussions of Renaissance critical attitudes and the breakdown of the medieval models of the universe, of humanity, and of society. The increasing emphasis on evidence in science from the time of Bacon and Descartes and the widening application of empirical evidence in the scientific method leads students to see connections between science and society and to develop an understanding of the growing importance of science to Western culture. I find that student-designed reenactments of events such as Galileo's trial and witch trials before and after the scientific revolution allow students to experience and interpret different worldviews.

Recognition of the connections between an expanding role of science in the West, the institutionalization of science, and the application of science to social as well as technical problems is integral to understanding the eighteenth and nineteenth centuries. The rising status of science in the nineteenth century comes into our discussions of Marxism as well as of Ranke's attempt to achieve for history the objectivity that chemistry seemed to have reached at the time. The shift from a static Newtonian to a dynamic Darwininan worldview is comparable to the advent of Marx in the social sciences and philosophy. This kind of comparative view helps to further student abilities to understand major developments in nineteenth-century thinking and to see links among forms of knowledge that are often separated by the disciplinary lines of the curriculum.

The twentieth-century paradigms of Einstein and Heisenberg in physics as well as the shifts in thinking in biology and related natural sciences continue to affect society, law, and the contemporary worldview. For example, the subjective nature of scientific experimentation, obvious since Heisenberg's principle of uncertainty, means that one cannot know both the position "and" the momentum of a subatomic particle with absolute precision: physicists must predetermine the kind of data they intend to test before conducting an experiment. The inability of historians to set up experiments in the same manner as chemists and physicists do is therefore no longer such a disadvantage, and new post–Rankean approaches to history enter the realm of historical studies along with post–Newtonian conceptions of science. This is not to maintain that the methods of investigation developed in the social sciences should be discarded, but they should be recognized as subjective choices. Students thus gain a means of comprehending expressionism in painting, stream-of-consciousness literature, and existential philosophy, which no longer appear to be capricious or incomprehensible phenomena, since the influence of and the dramatic shifts in scientific thinking are understood as integral components of the culture. Helping students to learn to think developmentally, which the study of history does better than other disciplines, can then provide students with meaningful systems into which they can incorporate other knowledge, including the physical and biological sciences. Knowledge comes to be seen in terms of meaningful relationships rather than isolated facts.

Since Heisenberg's uncertainty principle so clearly demonstrates the subjectivity inherent in scientific research, Ranke's attempt to write history "wie es eigentlich gewesen ist" — that is, as it really was — can no longer be a tenable position. The attempt to recapture the past remains elusive: history can best be viewed as a body of literature about the past rather than as objective reports of past events. Literature therefore joins science as a second key theme in the development of a broader approach to history and historical understanding. It is, however, as a body of literature that history presents some rather somber problems to secondary and college students. While history lacks some of the esoteric jargon of the social sciences, too many of the texts are written in a deadening style that drives away students and general readers alike. Students are quick to call me to account for dull material, and poor communication is difficult to defend. Certainly the textbooks and supplemental readings for most courses are not always engaging, and much is quite dull. Sources are nevertheless essential for historical understanding. There are, of course, engaging, dynamic writers of history: Robert Darnton, Barbara Tuchman, Hugh Trevor-Roper, and Emmanuel

Le Roy Ladurie are now regularly featured on the class reading list largely because of their appeal to my students. These writers are good stylists and should be emulated more than they usually are. Unfortunately, relatively few historians are engaging writers, so student appreciation for the past is not easily evoked. How then does the history teacher engage students?

There are other ways to resolve this dilemma. Since the arts form a part of the culture of the past, they also reflect the values of their times and thus serve admirably to promote historical imagination. Music, the plastic arts, and architecture can all form part of the teacher's repertoire. I find novels can be extraordinary tools to entice students into involvement with the past. Literary works of the era under investigation are unique sources, and even historical novels can be used to show how the past can be variously interpreted. A novel cannot stand alone in an investigation of the past, of course, but it just might be more motivating than a badly written study by a lackluster historian. Students can also learn a great deal from poorly conceived novels and from carelessly researched and presented historical fiction. They come to see that reading critically is an essential skill. Moreover, once students are gripped by a topic through literature, they seem to tolerate less-stimulating sources—but only if they have already developed an interest in the topic by encountering more imaginative accounts of the era or problem under study.

Thus, we must find ways to combine different source materials. For example, when I teach about Nazi genocide, I read the passage on the train ride from Warsaw to Auschwitz in William Styron's novel *Sophie's Choice*; then I proceed to Claude Lanzmann's film *Shoah*, in which Lanzmann discusses with Raoul Hilberg the use of train records to demonstrate the vast extent of civilian involvement during the Holocaust. The literary passage, which focuses on one woman, engages the students. As a result, Hilberg's historical information subsequently gains greater importance to them as they realize that there are millions of such stories. Literature leads to history, and (as with science) encourages a deeper appreciation for the many connections among historical knowledge, personal experience, and the various subjects that enter into education.

As a final way of reaching a modicum of freedom for myself as well as for my students, I do what many teachers do; I provide options for students. For example, they have wide latitude in choosing which books they wish to read for the course, and they have a selection among possible essay questions on most tests. These are empowering activities for students. If other disciplines do not provide them with this kind of independence and emphasis on the overlapping content of knowledge, then they can look to history for broad understanding of their cultural heritage and for personal empowerment. At New Hanover High School in Wilmington, North Carolina, the European history course demands more time and mental acumen than most. It should help students learn to take responsibility for their own educations. Sometimes my students go outside the framework of the course in their reading selections. Although I usually advise them that other choices would be more appropriate or more helpful for the advanced placement exam, I do not feel compelled to forbid such explorations. The point is to stimulate active, creative learning and to connect what students learn on their own with what they learn in the classroom. My intention with this kind of active, integrated learning process is to motivate students to continue their educations.

As a teacher for talented, although inexperienced, young students, I see my mission as fourfold: to help students develop an integrated, meaningful knowledge of the past; to help them see history's relationship to other disciplines; to help them learn to think critically; and to help them become self-motivated learners. I am therefore a teacher of reading, a transmitter of the culture, an interpreter of difficult materials and topics, a counselor, and an editor. I hope that students leave my class every June with richer imaginations, keener minds, more sophistication in attacking texts, and greater finesse in communicating what they know and believe. I feel fortunate to teach a course that offers such a challenge. I bear in mind that this may be the last history course for some students, so this is the final chance they may have to develop the interpretive skills that history provides. I hope that the students who never again study history in the classroom will nevertheless be able to evaluate the world in which they live with greater awareness of its historical evolution and with an enhanced understanding of the connections among the various forms of knowledge and expression that constitute our modern cultural lives.

Part II
Rethinking Categories of Historical Meaning

How We Learn about Race
through History

James D. Anderson

A s a general rule, the category of race has been distorted or omitted in the writing and teaching of American history. Despite the fact that race has been a major ideology in American life and culture since the colonial era, there is little systematic effort to explain concepts of race and racism in the writing of standard textbooks and in the teaching of regular courses on American history. The inherent confusion generated by this process of omission is compounded by the fact that we tend to acquire meanings about race not out of conscious reflection based on scholarship, but through conventional wisdom that is deeply entrenched in our culture. We believe that we know race when we see it; white people, black people, yellow people, brown people, and even "red" people are held to be various subspecies of a multiracial society. We arrive at nothing short of confusion, however, when we are pressed to define race.

Let us consider the case of Susie Phipps, filed as *Jane Doe v. State of Louisiana* in 1983. As F. James Davis recounts in his book *Who is Black? One Nation's Definition*, the Phipps case goes back as far as 1770, when Jean Gregoire Guillory took his wife's slave as his mistress. More than two centuries later, their great-great-great-great granddaughter, Susie Guillory Phipps, asked the Louisiana courts to change the classification on her deceased parents' birth certificates from "colored" to "white" so she and her brothers and sisters could be designated "white" (they all had white skin, and some were blue-eyed blonds). Mrs. Phipps had been denied a passport because she had checked "white" on her application although her birth certificate designated her race as "colored." She claimed that the classification came as a shock, since she had always perceived herself as white, had lived as white, and had twice married as white. The Louisiana district court ruled that the Phipps family had a "traceable amount of black blood" and thus declared

Mrs. Phipps and her parents and siblings to be legally black. In October and December 1985, Louisiana's Fourth Circuit Court of Appeals upheld the district court's decision and affirmed the necessity of designating race on birth certificates for public health, affirmative action, and other important public programs. When this case was appealed to the Louisiana Supreme Court in 1986, that court declined to review the decision, saying only that it concurred in the denial of a passport for the reasons assigned by the court of appeals on rehearing. In December 1986 the U.S. Supreme Court dismissed Phipps's appeal "for want of a federal question." Hence, both the final court of appeals in Louisiana and the highest court of the United States saw no reason to disturb the application of the one-drop rule that defines as black any person with any African-American ancestry despite his or her physical characteristics (i.e., skin color, facial features, hair texture). This case proves that we do not always know race when we see it and that we do not know how to define it in any logically consistent or scientific way.

If we adopt the definition of race implied in the Phipps case, that a traceable African ancestry is the only requirement for being black, then all human beings are black. The provocative best-seller *Lucy: The Beginnings of Humankind* argued that an African female who lived about 3.5 million years ago is the mother of all humankind, and that one of her genes exists in all contemporary human beings.[1] Hence, if Phipps, who looks as white as any other person classified as white, was judged to be black because she had a traceable amount of (black) African ancestry, then how should we classify all other human beings who inherited the gene of a black African female? Are they also blacks passing as white? The very concept of passing as white confirms that "race" is not an obvious fact of life; the phenomenon known as passing is, like "race," predicated on the mythical one drop of blood rule. What scientific and folk beliefs underlie such a definition—a definition embraced by personnel officers, census takers, judges, school admissions committees, affirmative action officers, and the public at large? When did such a definition of race emerge in our society and how has it changed over time? Do definitions of race vary from country to country and across different cultures? Generally, these questions are not even raised in the history books that our young people read to learn about the evolution of their nation and the nature of contemporary society and culture. Hence, our citizens, as they progress through our formal educational system, acquire from textbooks a fragmented, incoherent, and superficial understanding of the role of race in American history.

Race, like class and gender, has been relegated to a specialized field of study. Although the existing historical scholarship on race is now very rich, diverse, and complex, it is nonetheless marked by its abstraction or exclusion from any general synthesis of the American experience. Attention to race in standard histories usually emerges when it is virtually impossible to ignore the question, such as in discussions of the constitutional convention, the defense of slavery, Civil War and Reconstruction, or, more recently, the civil rights movement of the 1960s and 1970s. It is conceived in these instances as the tragic flaw that temporarily derailed the American pageant's procession toward democracy and justice for all. This very approach abstracts race (whether as ideology or the alleged representation of biological distinctions among human groups) from the historical process, treats it as an aberration of the normal flow of history, and undermines its depth, persistence, pervasiveness, and centrality in social thought, culture, and politics throughout history.[2]

Because I am concerned here with the manner in which Americans are educated regarding race and racism, I will focus on two separate and distinct bodies of scholarship: that written by professionals for professional consumption, and that written by professionals to educate the average American high school student. I learned from an earlier study of the treatment of African-American experiences in secondary school history textbooks that what is often emphasized in professional scholarship finds little or no place in the textbooks.[3] I am convinced, however, that what is emphasized in the writing of history for the general public tells us how historians wish the nation to perceive itself, its future as well as its past. In vital respects, the teaching and writing of history for the general population reveal what we choose to transmit to future generations. Hence, even when professional historians and instructors are willing to consider a more balanced and comprehensive history among themselves, there remains the tendency to teach children a history that celebrates consensus, progress, assimilation, intergroup harmony, and democracy. Race (which is usually highlighted during discussions of slavery, genocide against Native Americans, the Mexican-American War, Jim Crow laws and practices, etc.) is viewed as the contradiction of this synthesis and incompatible with a story emphasizing a republic based on natural rights, equality, and justice. Consequently, I believe that what we choose to teach our children about race in American history reflects a willingness or unwillingness to face our past squarely by examining a central ideology that has attempted to express complex forms of oppression and injustice. That capacity is not signaled by the willingness of professional historians and social scientists to establish critical dialogue about race among themselves while excluding the masses of learners and citizens from this discussion by omitting it from high school textbooks.

Historical Scholarship on Race in America

A very rich and diverse scholarship not only demonstrates the centrality of race in American and Western life from the eighteenth century to the present but also underscores the fact that race as a body of social thought came into existence in modern times. Such scholars as Frank Snowden, Nicholas F. Gier, Cain Hope Felder, and Charles B. Copher demonstrate that race and racism have not been around since the beginning of time and are a product of the modern era.[4] This is an important lesson that is missing from our textbooks, leading students to the erroneous conclusion that as long as there are multiracial societies there will be racism. These scholars show that although ancient civilizations constituted genuine "multiracial" (they really mean multiethnic) societies (e.g., Memphis), concepts of race and ideologies of racism did not exist.

In order to remain focused on their precise contributions to the study of race and racism, let us consider briefly meanings of the interrelated yet distinct concepts of race, racism, prejudice, and ethnocentrism. Race is the classification of human beings into separate and distinct subdivisions of humankind based on various physical characteristics such as hair texture and shape of head, eyes, lips, and nose, and on such genetic markers as blood groups. It is assumed that all races stem from separate and distinct gene pools dating back to the origin of humankind and that their members share a greater degree of physical and genetic similarity with one another than with other humans. Racism, narrowly defined, is a mode of thought that offers a particular explanation for the fact that population groups that are classified by ancestry are likely to differ in culture, status, and power. Racists make the claim that particular human populations ("races") create superior civilizations, conquer vast territories, and dominate other human groups (other "races") because they are intellectually superior—and that differences between "races" are mainly a result of immutable genetic factors and not of environmental or historical circumstances. Defined this way, the word *racism* is useful for describing a trend in Western thought between the 1700s and the present that has provided one kind of rationale for racially oppressive social systems. Hence, racism is distinct from prejudice—hostility against those perceived as culturally, physically, and religiously different that does not necessarily focus on the overt doctrine of "gene pools" or "blood lines." Consequently, prejudice on the part of tall people against short people does not assume racial difference, nor does prejudice among Protestants against Catholics. Racism is also distinct from ethnocentrism, the latter being a conviction that one's own culture, religion, or political forms are superior to all others. In its pure form, ethnocentrism does not stress physical differences or racial differences and allows, in theory at least, for the conversion and assimilation of those who differ in physical characteristics. For instance, one might assert that religion X is superior to all other religions and that members of all other religions should abandon their faiths and convert to religion X. Importantly, conversion would not be restricted according to physical characteristics.

Scholars do not contend that the ancients were free of prejudice or ethnocentrism. On the contrary, ancients made ethnocentric judgments of other societies and cultures and were prejudiced against foreigners and people judged to be barbarian or heathen. They did not, however, conceive of human beings as belonging to superior and inferior races, did not fall into the error of biological racism, and, on balance, did not make skin color the basis of judging human worth. Several arguments have been advanced to account for the absence of race and racism in late antiquity. Slavery, conquest, and subjugation were all independent of race. Slaves were of all colors and physical types, and therefore the identification of color or phenotype with subjugation did not develop. Hence, people of late antiquity did not make choices that required them to justify the subordination of human beings based on skin color, facial features, hair texture, and so forth. Frank Snowden contrasts this social context with that of modern times, when in the eighteenth century Africans were automatically categorized as slaves. Thus the modern question Why the Negro only as slave? gave rise to all kinds of race theories regarding the innate inferiority of "Negroes." The tendency in the ancient world was not to equate color or physical characteristics with subordination. Snowden concludes that the ancient pattern that doomed all conquered people indiscriminately to slavery precluded race and racism, while the modern pattern that enslaved only the "colored races" compelled a theory of race and an ideology of racism.

Snowden focuses on the images of blacks in Greek and Roman art as a means of substantiating his thesis that the ancients were free of race and racism. To be sure, the pictorial image tells us little about social reality in the period from 500 B.C. to the early Christian era. What is most impressive, however, is the ancients' overriding interest and delight in diversity, the dignity with which most people of color were portrayed, and the enduring capacity of artists for empathy and human expression. Regardless of the complexities and ambiguities of the so-called black image, the artistic heritage from late antiquity presents an unanswerable challenge to later racist societies that have relied on dehumanizing caricature as an instrument of social and economic oppression.

Were the ancients color-blind? The answer is an emphatic *no*. Snowden documents their awareness of color, particularly the Greeks and Romans. But instead of seeing human color differences as nature's code for inferior and superior races, the ancients stressed the beauty and diversity of humans and portrayed differences with a grace that bespeaks an absence of racism.

Since the ancients were not color-blind, and in their paintings, sculptures, poems, prose, and narratives took explicit note of human color and physical differences, how did they explain to themselves why human beings were of different colors and had distinctive eyes, hair, noses, lips, and so forth? Snowden maintains that the ancients accounted for human physical differences in terms of environment and historical circumstances. The Greeks, for instance, explained obvious physical differences as the effects of diverse environments upon a uniform human population, not as the result of separate and distinct gene pools. In short, they perceived color as only skin deep and did not see it as reflective of innate intellectual, cultural, and moral differences among human beings. In late antiquity the image of "black people" was one expression of the infinite diversity of a common human nature. Such a view would have been inconceivable among rulers in later slave societies that were rationalized on the premise of racial inferiority.

Race and racism emerged fully in the eighteenth century, and a number of excellent works examine their intellectual origins and development. Reginald Horsman, in *Race and Manifest Destiny*, argues persuasively that the concept of race was central to Europeans' conceptions of themselves and others as they constructed a history, mythology, and ideology regarding their origin and development, their place in the world, and their common destiny.[5] The concept of a superior Caucasian race (of which the Anglo–Saxons were the elite specimens) as a separate, innately superior people who were destined to dominate the world and bring self-government, commercial prosperity, and Christian morality to all human beings was essentially a product of the first half of the nineteenth century. The social and ideological roots of this concept, however, stretch back to earlier centuries. Indeed, the English colonists who invaded the New World (America) at the beginning of the seventeenth century brought as part of their ideology a clearly articulated religious myth of a pure English Anglo–Saxon church, and in the seventeenth and eighteenth centuries they shared with other English men and women an elaborately developed secular myth of the superiority of Anglo–Saxon political institutions.

The English colonists fully absorbed the mythical view of the English past developed in the seventeenth century. The vision of heroic, freedom-loving Anglo–Saxon England permeated the ideology of America's revolutionary generation, and the myth appeared most strongly in the writings and utterances of Thomas Jefferson, Josiah Quincy, Jr., Samuel Adams, Benjamin Franklin, Charles Carroll, Patrick Henry, and George Washington. They embraced the pro–Caucasian history about the superior character and common racial origins of the Saxons, Danes, and Normans who supposedly descended from the Germanic tribes. This view of Europe's northern people in general and Anglo–Saxons in particular was as unreal as the writings that depicted Arthur's England as a Camelot of brave knights, fair ladies, and magic swords.

This mythical explanation of the European past turned into a more virulent racism between 1750 and 1850, as the enormous task of rationalizing and justifying forced labor on the basis of racial differences was begun in earnest. In the earlier period the Anglo–Saxon myth held that the secret to

European and American success and domination lay in the superior social institutions established by Germanic people. In the eighteenth century the English and Americans transformed the myth of superior Anglo-Saxon institutions into the myth that the secret of their domination lay in their superior blood. In America the conquest and genocide against native peoples and the enslavement of African peoples provided the social context for the shift from notions of a superior climate to notions of superior innate racial characteristics. This change was attended by another shift from merely praising Germans or Saxons to attacking other peoples and defining them into separate and distinct subspecies of humankind.

In the context of slavery, race as a concept became even more persistent, pervasive, and central in American life. Larry Tise, in *Proslavery: A History of the Defense of Slavery in America, 1701-1840*, reminds us that as products of European culture, early American settlers were well acquainted with human bondage and with forms of thought that urged its perpetuation.[6] Even though the institution of slavery had disappeared from many parts of Europe during the Middle Ages, the idea of slavery and many of its moral and legal implications had been kept alive by philosophers, theologians, and other writers. In the New World they learned to equate slavery with the "Negro," and this gave tremendous force to concepts of race and theories of racism. America's first public defender of slavery, John Saffin, a Massachusetts judge, had little difficulty borrowing from and perpetuating proslavery notions already ingrained in European thought. He also connected slavery to emerging concepts of race by arguing that God had intentionally "set different Orders and Degrees of Men in the World" and that while some men were ordained to be "Monarchs, Kings, Princes and Governours," others were ordained "to be born Slaves, and so to remain during their lives." Such proslavery ideology was not unique to slaveholding Americans in the South, but was almost without geographical distinction. To put it another way, defenders of slavery reflected conceptions of race and racism that were part of the developing American culture.

Few seemed to have opposed slavery or the tendency to edge perpetual servitude ever closer to an identity with "African Negroes" until the events and ideas associated with the American Revolution began to challenge the future of slavery on a massive scale.

Gary B. Nash, in *Race and Revolution*, shows that throughout most of the country, on the eve of the Revolution, the feeling had spread among many that slavery was incompatible with the principles of the Revolution, that it could not be reconciled with Christian morality, and that it was an unsatisfactory basis for the economy of the new nation.[7] Others fought back, making the issue of race the great "American dilemma" for the revolutionary generation. As the Jeffersonian presidency proceeded after 1800, a belligerent white supremacy manifested itself throughout the North, signaling the failure of the abolitionist movement. Since white southerners mainly had put forward the abolition plans, and conservative white northerners, not southerners, were, according to Larry Tise, the first Americans to revive the defense of slavery in public, during the second decade of the nineteenth century, both race and slavery remained a national problem, not just a southern problem. Although the ideology of the Revolution did cause white Americans to pause and consider the implications of their practice of slavery, the force of rhetoric was not sufficient to defeat slavery or racism.

Mid–nineteenth–century America was characterized by a nearly universal belief in white supremacy as the ideology of race, which provided justification for various complex political and economic interests, spread across the width and breadth of the nation. Eugene H. Berwanger's *The Frontier against Slavery*, Forrest G. Wood's *Black Scare*, V. Jacque Voegeli's *Free but Not Equal*, Leon F. Litwack's *North of Slavery*, Leonard P. Curry's *The Free Black in Urban America, 1800-1850*, and Lorenzo Johnston Greene's *The Negro in Colonial New England* document the centrality of race in American history from the end of the Revolution to the outbreak of the Civil War.[8] By the mid–nineteenth century race was a central component of American social thought, affecting the whole direction of national deliberations about ourselves as a nation and a democracy. In 1811 antislavery and anti–African-American forces (usually the two were joined) in the Indiana territorial legislature passed laws preventing free African-Americans from testifying in court against white persons, excluding them from militia duty, and barring them from voting. Ohio in 1807 excluded free African-Americans from residence in the state unless they posted a five-hundred-dollar bond for good behavior. In 1813 Illinois ordered every incoming free person of color to leave the territory under penalty of thirty-nine lashes, repeated every fifteen days until the African-American left the state. By the early 1830s all three states had adopted almost identical statutory restrictions against free persons of color. Michigan and Iowa followed suit, and Wisconsin joined them in voting down African-American suffrage by large majorities. During the antebellum era the Middle West never had an African-American population exceeding 1 percent of the region's total population. Hence, the centrality of race in the region did not depend on the existence of large numbers of African-Americans. This is an important lesson for students to learn, since they normally associate discussions of race with the problems of black people. The history of the Middle West during the period 1810 to 1870 demonstrates that discussions of race in the region began not with the problems of African-Americans but with flaws in American democratic ideology and contradictions in the social order. In the Middle West, as elsewhere in America, the ideology of race was linked to nearly all civil and political questions and figured heavily in federal and state issues. Race was a main current of

American social thought irrespective of whether African-Americans were present or absent in a given place.

The attitudes and laws of "race" developed in the Middle West became the models for new territories farther west as midwesterners followed the frontier to the Pacific. In 1849 delegates to the Constitutional Convention of California voted without debate to adopt the same constitutional restrictions on free persons of color that were found in the Middle West. The U.S. Congress admitted Oregon to the union in 1857—the only free state with an African-American exclusion clause in its original constitution ever admitted. In Kansas, three out of four antislavery advocates voted to exclude African-Americans from residing in the territory. Whites on the western plains were also limiting suffrage, public office, and military service to white men. This pattern was followed in Utah, New Mexico, and Nebraska. Similarly, segregation, discrimination, and injustice based on assumptions of racial distinctiveness flourished and often proliferated in the New England region. New York had property qualifications that withheld the ballot from African-American men. The Pennsylvania legislature formally refused African-American men the vote in 1837 and at the same time seriously debated, though it did not pass, a racial exclusion bill. African-Americans in New England lived a thoroughly segregated existence, set apart in church, school, public services, and society, generally excluded from politics and handicapped in the courts of "justice."

Even after the Civil War had ended and the U.S. Congress had forced African-American male suffrage on all the Confederate states, all but seven nonsouthern states excluded African-American men from the polls by law. The voters of Kansas, Ohio, and Minnesota in popular referendums held in 1867, and the voters of Michigan in 1868, overwhelmingly rejected African-American male suffrage. All such actions stemmed from an ideology of race, an ideology that had become deeply embedded in the basic conceptions of democracy and definitions of the national character. Many other works demonstrate clearly that one cannot understand American social thought and culture apart from an understanding of the crucial place of the race concept at the core of the dominant American ideology. Forrest Wood's *The Arrogance of Faith*, Ronald Takaki's *Iron Cages*, C. Vann Woodward's *The Strange Career of Jim Crow*, and many other works underscore the persistence and pervasiveness of race in American culture from the colonial beginnings through the better part of the twentieth century.[9]

Social Science Scholarship on Race in America

In the late 1970s we saw the emergence of professional scholarship challenging claims regarding the continued centrality of race in American politics, culture, and dominant social institutions. The classic work of this era was probably William Julius Wilson's *The Declining Significance of Race* (1978). This work started from the view that the civil rights movement of the 1960s had succeeded in eliminating the physical barriers of racial discrimination: no more segregated buses, no legal obstructions to voting or school attendance, no separate lunch counters, and so forth. Thus, it was claimed that post–civil rights America would witness the declining significance of race in national life and the emerging significance of class as the key determinant of educational opportunity and of political, economic, and cultural life. The emerging consensus of the 1970s and 1980s was that the politics of race had run its course. By implication, the race concept per se had lost its political and social relevance and was declining as a main current of American social thought. Studies by Wilson, Thomas Sowell (*The Economics and Politics of Race*), Nathan Glazer (*Affirmative Discrimination*), and Shelby Steele (*The Content of Our Character*) grabbed headlines from the mid-1970s to the beginning of the 1990s.[10]

Meanwhile, there was developing a cadre of powerful studies by American social scientists, most of whom had no professional interest in the study of race, demonstrating that instead of declining in significance, race was holding strong as a central fact of American life and culture. They took up their research without intending to study race per se. They were examining the key determinants of American political behavior and discovered that race was an ever increasing fundamental component in structuring intergroup relations in America. Edward G. Carmines and James Stimson, in *Issue Evolution: Race and the Transformation of American Politics*, examine the emergence of race as a political issue over the past fifty years and conclude that it, more than any other concern, has restructured American politics. Robert Huckfeldt and Carol Weitzel Kohfeld, in *Race and the Decline of Class in American Politics* state simply: "The politics of race has emerged as the most meaningful boundary in American politics during the last third of the twentieth century." In fact, they contend that class self-consciousness among voters has declined as an organizing principle in contemporary American electoral politics and that the decline of class ideology is directly related to the concurrent ascent of race ideology. Thomas Byrne Edsall and Mary D. Edsall in *Chain Reaction: The Impact of Race, Rights and Taxes on American Politics* argue that the driving forces of politics today are three volatile and overlapping issues: race, rights, and taxes. They contend that

> race leads the way. No longer a straightforward, morally unambiguous
> force in American politics, race now helps to define liberal and conservative
> ideologies, shapes the coalitions during presidential elections, provides a
> harsh, new dimension to concern over taxes and crimes, and drives a
> wedge through former alliances of middle income voters and the poor.

Earl Black and Merle Black, in *The Vital South: How Presidents Are Elected*, conclude that the "Great White Switch" (overwhelming white Democratic domination in the New Deal period followed by overwhelming white Republicanism after the Great Society) in southern presidential politics occurred when Republican presidential candidates began to emphasize a conservative agenda with a heavy emphasis on racial issues. These and other scholarly works demonstrate that the ideology of race in American social thought was not fundamentally transformed by the passage of landmark civil rights legislation in the 1960s. In his 1978 book *The Declining Significance of Race*, Wilson greatly underestimated the depth and persistence of racial ideology in American life and culture. *Enemies: The Clash of Races* by Haki Madhubuti, published in the same year, was much closer to the mark: race thinking, Madhubuti wrote, will carry into the twenty-first century as a central dimension of American political, social, and economic life.[11]

The Textbook View of Race in America

From the professional scholarship on race there seems little doubt as to its centrality in the American story. More importantly, we learn that race is very largely ideology, a product of history, of choices made by human beings—not a product of nature, of biology, or of natural evolution. Race thinking is a process that needs to be understood and explained. As Barbara J. Fields has argued, "Race is not an idea but an ideology. It came into existence at a discernible historical moment for rationally understandable historical reasons and is subject to change for similar reasons."[12] Hence race does not explain the enslavement of Africans. Rather, the enslavement of Africans helps to account for the emergence of race as a central concept in American ideology because race was used to justify enslavement. Indeed, such an approach leads us to ask the following questions: What kind of social relations underlie the ideology of race, and why were notions of race as a biological reality needed as a critical vocabulary for rationalizing and making sense of colonial and revolutionary America? Why did American leaders choose the concept of race as an important medium through which to apprehend and make sense of their broader social world? This is how we learn about race through professional historians engaged in the study of it as a specialized field.

This is not how most people learn about race through history. Most students will never read Fields, and her insightful analyses have not been incorporated into the textbooks that most of our students will read. The majority learn about race in a very different way. To appreciate the difference we must turn briefly to what may appear to be antiquated concepts of race.

Not so long ago, ethnologists, physical anthropologists, geneticists, historians, and social scientists seemed certain that human beings were naturally divided into three principal races. The concept of race signaled the biological divisions of human beings, distinguished by skin pigmentation, texture of hair, color of eyes, stature, bodily proportions, and place of origin on planet Earth. The three principal races were the Negroid, the Mongoloid, and the Caucasoid. There was the Negro, supposedly one of the principal divisions of humankind, generally marked by brown to black skin pigmentation, dark eyes, and woolly or crisp hair—especially the indigenous peoples of Africa south of the Sahara. The Caucasian, a second major biological division of humankind, was characterized as having fair to dark skin, straight to tightly curled hair, and light to very dark eyes and originally inhabiting Europe, parts of North Africa, Western Asia, and India. Finally, the alleged third separate and distinct species of humankind was the Mongoloid—supposedly marked by a yellowish complexion, prominent cheekbones, epicanthic folds about the eyes, and straight black hair—including Chinese, Koreans, Japanese, Siamese, Tibetans, Eskimos, and North American Indians. Over time these classifications have acquired so many unscientific connotations that in essence they are no longer in technical use and the concept of race itself is often replaced by the language of ethnicity. Now we speak of five major ethnic divisions of humankind: American Indian or Alaskan Native, black (not Hispanic), Asian and Pacific Islanders, Hispanic (Spanish ancestral origin regardless of race), and white (ancestral origin in Europe, North Africa, or the Middle East).

Although the current vocabulary has changed, reflecting in part discomfort with traditional conceptions of mutually exclusive races or subspecies of the larger human population, the sense remains that race and ethnicity represent observed facts, permanent gene pools, and physical characteristics that demand classification into separate and distinct subspecies. To put it another way, racial and ethnic groups are perceived to be relatively fixed or, at the very least, known and self-evident categories. We expect individuals to look Indian, Asian, Hispanic, black, white, and even Jewish. Hence racial and ethnic groups are typically "imagined" as if they were natural, real, eternal, stable, and static units. They are also imagined as if they have always been in existence since the origin of humankind, and definitions of race and ethnicity invariably trace each group to its ancestral origin in Europe, North Africa, the Middle East, Far East, Southeast Asia, Africa south of the Sahara, and so forth. The concept of race that results from such premises leads us to believe that the process of belonging and being perceived by others as belonging to an ethnic group or race derives from scientifically accurate classifications of carefully observed facts, reflecting the natural order of humankind. It also encourages the belief that as human beings we naturally feel more comfortable within our own subspecies, and are naturally inclined to be suspicious and even fearful of persons with different physical characteristics. It is assumed, therefore, that individuals are immediately recognizable as belonging to one or another subspecies of humankind and that the direct reflex of a physical impression stimulates a psychic response as to whether a particular human being is one of your own kind or belongs to another kind. In this sense, presupposed biological reality is often held as the primary explanation for historical phenomena such as racial attitudes. Racial prejudice is viewed as a natural consequence of the psychic response compelled by striking differences in physical appearance, which naturally stimulate fear, suspicion, distrust, and separation.

These assumptions about racial prejudice have often appeared in American textbooks. For example, in the secondary school history textbook *Rise of the American Nation* (1977 edition by Todd and Curti), the authors give an account of the Lewis and Clark expedition, particularly of the factors that made the expedition successful. We are told that the expedition's relations with the Indians were aided by York, Clark's black slave whom Clark freed at the end of the expedition: "Because of his dark skin color, York did not seem as strange to the Indians as the white men did."[13] The authors fail to explain that skin pigmentation is always mediated or interpreted within a larger social context that assigns it meaning. We are led to believe that because of his skin color York was received spontaneously by Indians as a natural brother while whites were viewed as natural aliens. This reinforces the notion that human beings are naturally suspicious of people whose skin colors deviate sharply from their own and are naturally more accommodating to people who are closer in skin pigmentation. This leads to the false assumption that shared color sets automatic limits to conflict and oppression and that sharp differences in skin pigmentation make it easy for one group to oppress another.

An interesting case of this kind of race thinking occurred in a recent debate over Martin Bernal's claim that the Egyptians were black Africans. Emily Vermeule offered the following argument as a logical refutation of Bernal's claim:

> Bernal also believes that Egypt was essentially African, and therefore black. But he does not say what we are to make of the historical accounts of Egyptian pharaohs campaigning against black neighbors to the south, in the land of Kush, as when Tuthmosis I of Egypt around 1510 B.C., annihilated a black Kushite army at the Third Cataract and came home with the body of a black prince hanging upside down from the prow of his ship.[14]

Vermeule, obviously assuming that shared skin color generates a sense of peoplehood and therefore sets limits to oppression, concludes that since the Egyptians sought to annihilate the Kushites, and it is known that the latter were black, it is safe to assume that the former must have been white. Such flawed logic stems from the conventional wisdom that differences in skin color or "race" create natural enemies of humans and makes oppression easier, while shared skin color is presumed to be a badge of natural kinship.

Thus, in the textbook *An American History* (1981 edition by Rebecca Brooks Gruver) the author informs us that "it was relatively easy for the colonists to make slaves of the Africans, since by the sixteenth century the English had come to believe that black people were inferior."[15] This use of race makes the erroneous point that Africans fell under the dominion of the English by virtue of being perceived as inferior. Hence the historical process of enslavement need not be explained. The long-standing and complex encounters between Europe and Africa, the slave trade, the middle passage, the economic and political relations in the West Indies and America are all set aside for the simple explanation that race (race prejudice) explains why people of African descent were set apart for enslavement. The English, as Fields points out, had also come to believe that some white people were inferior, particularly the Irish. But their being perceived as inferior did not lead to enslavement in the New World. Fields argues that Africans did not fall under the dominion of the English by virtue of being perceived as inferior, but rather came to be perceived as inferior by virtue of having fallen under the English dominion. Race, particularly the invention of race as a category to justify enslavement, is seen to be part of the historical process, not an explanation of historical phenomena. By restoring to race its proper history, Fields requires us to understand slavery, to see the powerful role that economics and politics played in shaping the whole edifice of social life, including the compulsion to classify people into subspecies of the human race as a means to justify why "nature" supposedly guaranteed freedom to most and slavery to a sizable minority. We seldom learn about race through history in this manner. Usually race is invoked as a category to give quick and simple answers to complex historical developments. This approach fosters many distortions and stereotypes, but, above all else, it fosters ignorance that is the lifeblood of stereotypes.

Loose thinking about race leads to careless language, which in turn promotes much misinformation. Our authors of secondary school history textbooks suggest by their deeds that now only certain people need to be identified as belonging to a race. This brings to memory an episode from the old television situation comedy "All in the Family." In one episode Archie Bunker shared a hospital room with a man of African descent from one of the French West Indies colonies, but they were separated by a partition and he was unaware of the color of his fellow patient's skin. Bunker assumed from the man's accent that he was a white Frenchman. Throughout their stay in the hospital they held good conversations, so good that Bunker invited the man to dinner in his home. Finally, they were both released on the same day, and Bunker saw his newfound friend. Archie was shocked and embarrassed to realize that he had mistakenly invited a "black man" to dinner. He immediately shifted the blame to the West Indian. "Why didn't you tell me that you were black?" exclaimed Archie. "Why didn't you tell me that you were white?" replied the West Indian. "White people don't have to say that they are white," said Archie. Archie would lead us to forget that ethnic identities are not only black, Latino, Asian, Native American, and so on; they are also white. To ignore white ethnicity is to redouble its hegemony by naturalizing it, which was precisely Archie's intent.[16]

We should recall that the root meaning of the word *ethnic* is "nation," and the word *nation* was invented to refer to peoples neither Christian nor Jewish—in other words, "heathen" or "pagan." At one point the word *ethnic* was amalgamated with the word *heathen* to produce *hethnic*. "Ethnic" has always meant "outsider" and peoples are labeled "ethnic" by those who stand within the center of the culture and by virtue of their position have the power to name. Hence, Anglo-Americans do not really see themselves as an "ethnic" group. That is a label they use to describe those perceived as outsiders, as different, and not as "American" as the Anglo-American immigrants and their descendants. The implication is that only certain Americans can define what it means to be American and the rest must constantly seek their approval and acceptance. Archie's rule is the textbook rule. For instance, secondary school textbooks such as *The American People: A History from 1877* (1986), *The American People: A History* (1986), *The Challenge of Freedom* (1984), *America's Story* (1990), and *People and Our Country* (1982) have index entries for "Black Americans" but none for white Americans. Even the textbook *American Indians of the Southwest* has no index for whites, settlers, or Anglo-Americans. Such practices foster the impression that the "race thing" refers automatically to people of color, particularly blacks, but is of no relevance to understanding whites. This use of the concept of race is analogous to the "ethnic foods" sections in grocery stores and the "ethnic look" in fashion: some people—like some foods, clothes, music—belong to an ethnic group, while others are full-fledged Americans, the standard by which all others are judged. Full-fledged Americans do not have to declare an ethnic group or color. That is perceived as a duty of black Americans, Asian-Americans, Mexican-Americans, Native Americans. This use of race and ethnicity contributes to a consciousness of standard and nonstandard (or essential and nonessential) people. The standard people never have to be explained, the nonstandard have to be labeled, explained, and accounted for at all times. Hence, we have scholars and black scholars, whiz kids and Asian-American whiz kids, presidential candidates and black presidential candidates. News reporters who would never say "white presidential candidate

George Bush" unconsciously report on "black presidential candidate Jesse Jackson." They commit an error for which the intellectual community must accept part of the blame.

At the very least, we should appreciate a great irony expressed in one of Barbara J. Fields's observations. She reminds us that "it was not Afro-Americans . . . who invented themselves as a race. Euro-Americans resolved the contradiction between slavery and liberty by defining Afro-Americans as a race."[17] It is all the more interesting, therefore, that those who needed the concept of race so desperately as a subjective expression of complex economic and political realities do not have to wear it, while others are compelled to interpret their every action as racial.

New Perspectives on Race in America

Breaking away from our tradition of miseducation about race in American history will be difficult. The history of race that we learn in high schools and colleges and through popular culture teaches about race as a set of relatively fixed, known, and self-evident categories necessitated by logic and science. A break with tradition will require considerable homework and re-education on the part of the whole society. It will not suffice to add on to traditional syntheses of the American story more information about various minority groups. The current notion of multicultural education is not the answer. Discussions of race and ethnicity at the end of traditional history lessons—or special units on particular minority groups or any other add-on functions—are not going to resolve long-standing problems of misinformation and stereotyping. In fact, they may only serve to abstract issues of race even further from the larger historical context in which they arose and developed. The challenge is to weave the evolution of race as an American ideology into a new synthesis, one that depicts issues of race alongside other issues that were central to the origin and development of our country. That is how issues of race originated and evolved in the actual historical process, and that is how they should appear in the writing and teaching of American history.

A good start is developing history lessons that treat various groups within the same historical moment, paying particular attention to issues of race, demonstrating how interactions among various groups shaped the complex and contradictory character of the race concept. Indeed, the systematic treatment of issues of race across groups will facilitate our ability to interweave the experiences of those groups into a single synthesis, as opposed to the traditional method of studying each group in isolation from the others, except to juxtapose each minority group to the dominant European-American majority. This tends to divide American history into "Indian history," "black history," "Mexican-American history," and so forth, as though the groups were self-contained in insulated historical tracks and did not intersect around issues of race and other issues as well. Thus, traditional history depicts white–Indian relations, white–black relations, and white–Hispanic relations as though the various minority groups remained in isolation from each other and never intersected to shape the complex issues in American history. In fact, however, it is only through looking at the issue of race through the intersection of various groups that we can really appreciate its complexity.

This point is illustrated more concretely by looking briefly at the issue of race as it developed in movements to provide legal definitions of "whites," "Indians," and "Negroes" during the early part of this century. During the early twentieth century, according to Bernice F. Guillaume and J. David Smith, New York and Virginia initiated efforts to define legally what it meant to be Indian or white or Negro.[18] In New York, the issue of race once again emerged during a campaign to close the reservation school belonging to the Unkechaugs. Indian schools had been placed under the direct jurisdiction of New York's superintendent of public instruction since 1856. In 1934, the Unkechaugs' school was thrust into the limelight when a local landowner, who really was seeking to confiscate the Unkechaugs' land, petitioned the New York State Department of Education to close the school. The state, accepting the local landowner's petition, declared that no appropriation would be made to the Unkechaug (Poosepatuck) Indian Reservation School because the persons living there were not Indians. Rather, the state of New York claimed, the Unkechaugs were mixed with "Negro blood," which nullified any claims to an Indian heritage. The state clearly imposed its notion that a right to an Indian heritage presupposed the so-called purity of aboriginal blood. That was a popular conception of race applied to Indians during the period.

The Unkechaugs, however, did not define themselves as a biological division of humankind, or simply in terms of a mythical blood count. One is struck by their view that "even if you have blue eyes and red hair . . . or if your skin is as white as Will Rogers' . . . or as black as Paul Cuffee's . . . you are Indians." In short, the Unkechaugs viewed themselves as a product of history, not as a product of biology or "pure aboriginal blood." Hence, New York's notion that Indians had to be a pure-blooded subspecies of the human race clashed sharply with Indian conceptions of themselves as a nation created by the process of history. Fortunately for the Unkechaugs, the Suffolk County Court agreed with them in this instance.

The other significant point in this discussion derives from Virginia. In 1924 Virginia's General Assembly passed the Racial Integrity Act, which essentially recognized two "racial" groups in Virginia, white and colored. The term "white person" applied only to individuals who allegedly had "no trace whatsoever of any blood other than Caucasian." The term "colored" was based on the opposite of the concept of being pure-blooded. That is to say, anyone with any trace of anything other than so-called Caucasian blood was defined as a member of the "Colored Race." But, like the Unkechaugs in New York, Indians in Virginia would be recognized as Indians only if they provided proof of being pure-blooded aborigines. Without such proof they would be denied the right to marry as Indians, to designate the "race" of their own children on birth certificates, and to claim an Indian heritage. Virginia's registrar of vital statistics, Walter A. Plecker, launched a long, aggressive campaign against the state's Indians that effectively defined them out of existence. Plecker concluded that there were probably no native Virginia Indians who had no "Negro" blood. Since being "mixed with Negro" nullified one's status as an Indian, Plecker declared that there were virtually no real Indians in Virginia. For twenty-five years he denied marriage licenses and birth certificates to people claiming Indian heritage and insisted that Virginia's Indians be assigned to "colored" military units. He literally sought to define Indians out of existence on the grounds that none of them were "pure-blooded."

It is important to expose students to this kind of examination of race in order for them to appreciate varying and conflicting cultural constructions of concepts of race. More importantly, one need only expose them to the kind of historical issues that emerged in New York and Virginia to impress upon them that conceptions of race are permeated with illogic, mythology, and politics.

Consider, for instance, the science, logic, and politics of Plecker's concept of race. He held to a conception of race that required Virginia's Indians to be "pure-blooded." While this definition legally extinguished the Indians, it simultaneously added to the so-called "colored race," because the Indians were redefined as "Negroes." Moreover, Plecker's definition of a "colored race" presupposed "mixed blood" as the basis for race, not "pure blood." This shows clearly that definitions of race often justified and rationalized the exact social opposites. The ideology of race invented to characterize Indians rationalized removing and exterminating them. The concept of race applied to persons of African descent (which emerged in the context of slavery) rationalized enslaving them and increasing their number. This explains in part why the same people could hold a definition of race in which one drop of so-called "Negro blood" could make one a member of the "colored race" while virtually no amount of Indian blood could make one Indian. Did Plecker ever realize that one of his definitions of race, which required human beings to be "pure-blooded," contradicted the other, which presupposed them to be "mixed-blooded"? Indeed, if he had pushed his own logic further, there would have been no Indian race, no Negro race, no Caucasian race, no Anglo-Saxon race, no pure-blooded subspecies of the human race whatsoever. But such is the nature of ideology—it permits people to rationalize contradictory beliefs and behavior, and it requires neither logic nor scientific accuracy. The idea is not to impose definitions on our students, but to provide lessons that will free them from historically conditioned views and enable them to see the subtleties behind issues that are normally regarded as scientific fact or common sense.

A scene from the movie *Norma Rae* makes the point more vividly. Those who have seen the movie will recall that Norma Rae is a southern textile mill hand who works with Reuben from New York to organize the mill workers into a union. Early in their work, Norma Rae becomes curious about Reuben's ethnicity and engages him in the following exchange:

"Are you a Jew?" asks Norma Rae.

"I beg your pardon?" replies Reuben.

"Are you a Jew?"

"Born and bred."

"I never met a Jew before," Norma Rae informs him.

"How are you doing?" says Reuben as he moves forward to shake her hand.

"I heard you all had horns."

"Circumcised, yes; horns, no."

"Well, far as I can see you don't look any different from the rest of us."

"But we are," says Reuben, correcting her again.

"You are? Well, what makes you different?"

"History," says Reuben emphatically.

Norma Rae is clearly puzzled, and her failure to comprehend is in no small part a result of the kind of education that the average American student gets. In writing and teaching about issues of race and ethnicity in American history, we would do well to convey to our students what Reuben tried to tell Norma Rae: that race and ethnicity are, above all else, products of history, that they are not created by nature but by men and women, and that men and women can change them.

NOTES

1. Donald Johanson and Maitland Edey, *Lucy: The Beginnings of Humankind* (New York, 1981).

2. F. James Davis, *Who Is Black?: One Nation's Definition* (University Park, Pa., 1991), pp. 9–11; Virginia R. Domínguez, *White by Definition: Social Classification in Creole Louisiana* (New Brunswick, N.J., 1986).

3. James D. Anderson, "Secondary School History Textbooks and the Treatment of Black History," in *The State of Afro-American History: Past, Present, and Future*, ed. Darlene Clark Hine (Baton Rouge, La., 1986), pp. 253–74.

4. Frank Snowden, *Before Color Prejudice: The Ancient View of Blacks* (Cambridge, Mass., 1983); Nicholas F. Gier, "The Color of Sin/The Color of Skin: Ancient Color Blindness and

the Philosophical Origins of Modern Racism," *Journal of Religious Thought* 46 (Summer-Fall 1989): 42-52; Cain Hope Felder, "Race, Racism, and the Biblical Narratives," in *Stony the Road We Trod: African American Biblical Interpretation,* ed. Cain Hope Felder (Minneapolis, 1991); Charles B. Copher, "3000 Years of Biblical Interpretation with Reference to Black Peoples," *Journal of the Interdenominational Theological Center* 30 (Spring 1986): 225-46.

5. Reginald Horsman, *Race and Manifest Destiny: The Origins of American Racial Anglo-Saxonism* (Cambridge, Mass., 1981).

6. Larry Tise, *Proslavery: A History of the Defense of Slavery in America, 1701-1840* (Athens, Ga., 1987).

7. Gary B. Nash, *Race and Revolution* (Madison, Wis., 1990).

8. Eugene H. Berwanger, *The Frontier against Slavery: Western Anti-Negro Prejudice and the Slavery Extension Controversy* (Urbana, Ill., 1967); Forrest G. Wood, *Black Scare: The Racist Response to Emancipation and Reconstruction* (Berkeley, Calif., 1968); Leon F. Litwack, *North of Slavery: The Negro in the Free States, 1790-1860* (Chicago, 1961); V. Jacque Voegeli, *Free but Not Equal: The Midwest and the Negro During the Civil War* (Chicago, 1967); Leonard P. Curry, *The Free Black in Urban America, 1800-1850* (Chicago, 1981); Lorenzo Johnston Greene, *The Negro in Colonial New England* (New York, 1942).

9. Forrest G. Wood, *The Arrogance of Faith: Christianity and Race in America from the Colonial Era to the Twentieth Century* (New York, 1990); Ronald T. Takaki, *Iron Cages: Race and Culture in 19th-Century America* (Seattle, 1979); C. Vann Woodward, *The Strange Career of Jim Crow* (New York, 1966).

10. William Julius Wilson, *The Declining Significance of Race: Blacks and Changing American Institutions* (Chicago, 1978); Thomas Sowell, *The Economics and Politics of Race: An International Perspective* (New York, 1983); Nathan Glazer, *Affirmative Discrimination: Ethnic Inequality and Public Policy* (New York, 1975); Shelby Steele, *The Content of Our Character* (New York, 1990).

11. Edward G. Carmines and James A. Stimson, *Issue Evolution: Race and the Transformation of American Politics* (Princeton, N.J., 1990); Robert Huckfeldt and Carol Weitzel Kohfeld, *Race and the Decline of Class in American Politics* (Urbana, Ill., 1989); Thomas Byrne Edsall and Mary D. Edsall, *Chain Reaction: The Impact of Race, Rights and Taxes on American Politics* (New York, 1991); Earl Black and Merle Black, *The Vital South: How Presidents Are Elected* (Cambridge, Mass., 1992); Haki R. Madhubuti, *Enemies: The Clash of Races* (Chicago, 1978).

12. For what is undoubtedly one of the most insightful discussions of race in American history, see Barbara J. Fields, "Slavery, Race and Ideology in the United States of America," *New Left Review* 181 (May/June 1990): 95-118, and "Ideology and Race in American History," in *Region, Race, and Reconstruction: Essays in Honor of C. Vann Woodward,* ed. J. Morgan Kousser and James McPherson (New York, 1982).

13. Lewis Paul Todd and Merle Curti, eds., *Rise of the American Nation* (New York, 1977), p. 204.

14. Emily Vermeule, "The World Turned Upside Down," *New York Review of Books,* March 26, 1992, p. 41. Vermeule is reviewing Martin Bernal, *Black Athena: The Afroasiatic Roots of Classical Civilization,* vol. 2, *The Archaeological Evidence* (New Brunswick, N.J., 1991).

15. Rebecca Brooks Gruver, *An American History* (Reading, Mass., 1981), p. 59.

16. David R. Roediger, *The Wages of Whiteness* (London, 1991).

17. Fields, "Slavery, Race and Ideology," p. 114.

18. J. David Smith, "Eugenics, Race Integrity and the Twentieth-Century Assault on Virginia's Indians," and Bernice F. Guillaume, "Dual Dilemma: Ethnology, Politics and the Abolition of the New York State Poosepatuck (Unkechaug Nation) Indian Reservation School, 1875-1944," papers presented to the Organization of American Historians in Louisville, Kentucky, April 11, 1991.

Gender and Historical Understanding

Bonnie G. Smith

A decade ago, Carolyn Lougee of Stanford University presented an elegant new syllabus for a Western civilization course. It integrated women into reading, lecture, and discussion material in strikingly new ways. From then on, Stanford's Western civilization program incorporated Lougee's directions and especially a threefold set of themes. Western civilization courses, Lougee proposed, should present "as accurately as possible the 'condition' of European women." In addition, they needed to highlight "contributions made by women individually and as a gender group to the development of European civilization." Finally, the introductory survey would "resurrect" and "heed" women's voices as found in their autobiographies, fictional writing, letters, and elsewhere.[1]

Lougee's proposals were inspiring to teachers of almost any kind of history, especially to those with the energy to search out material for presenting women's voices. It took time for teachers to find women contributors to history and to learn enough about those contributions to make changes in curricular materials. As for determining the "experience" of women, that was and remains a tall order, for women's experience runs the gamut from women influential in courts and queens responsible for reproducing dynasties to market women, members of disorderly crowds, women marrying and maintaining agricultural life. The abundant experience of all of them has filled up entire courses, to say nothing of enriching survey courses. The only excuse for not integrating has been time—the material is so vast that one can no longer keep up.

A decade has passed, and in those few years yet another revolution has occurred in thinking about women and survey courses. This revolution developed in part from the sheer mass of information and the premonition that despite the abundance there was still more to be discovered about women.

107

The anticipation of more to come, more crucial books and articles still to read, ever more material to integrate into courses already teeming with kings, wars, great philosophers, and literary men, awakened an urgent need to figure out what the "knowledge explosion," when it came to women, meant for history. Was history a democratic phenomenon in which everyone should have a "voice"? Many people felt it was not. How did one justify substituting women's voices and narratives for wars and kings? Many could not. Indeed, commentators began to think that teaching about women had gone far enough; in the past few years, many people have felt it was time to stop for fear of corrupting the field's high standards.

The unease many feel about a history that includes women stems from the field's development in the nineteenth century, which still sets the terms for the discipline today. As it professionalized, its practitioners usually came from at least the respectable and more often the well-to-do classes. It was practiced in universities, libraries, and archives—places associated (falsely, as we know) with gentility. Moreover, professionalizing historians had a way of removing all sense of the personal or subjective from their work. As the great French historian Fustel de Coulanges put it, "Gentlemen, it is not I who speak, but History which speaks through me."[2] In this way, the historian created a historical narrative articulated by an invisible "I," one without an ego or a persona, universally valid and certainly ungendered. Professional history claimed to stand beyond those issues of class, race, and sex that were so heatedly discussed in Europe and the United States in the nineteenth century.

The nineteenth-century professionalization of history, with its attendant focus on scientific models, also worked a momentous change in the field as a literary genre. Emphases on objectivity, on special skills like paleography and epigraphy, on the development and uses of archives and other repositories, on the creation of seminars and courses of advanced study, on the conferral of advanced degrees, on the phenomena of professional meetings and the founding of scholarly journals—all these transformed the production of historical texts. History rested on an apparent shift in focus from historical writing itself to pretextual efforts. An endorsement of archives and uncovering the facts they contained—popularly attributed to a "founding father," Leopold von Ranke—constructed the modern discipline, with its quickly developed repositories, its credentialing of researchers, its secret research methods passed down only after twenty years of schooling. Avoiding romantic excess, the historical text itself was not to revolve around an exciting narrative (although Ranke initially was drawn to history in part because of its narrative possibilities) but rather to unfold the results of investigations with documents, in archives, employing a range of professional methods for ascertaining facts. It resulted, in the words of Lord Acton, from the "heroic study of records."[3] Professionals denounced their predecessors' emphasis on rhetorical and literary skills and in so doing tried to shift attention to their efforts not as writers but as researchers.

This revolutionary move worked to undermine the truth claims of history's rivals, not only the closely related antiquarianism, but also the more important and ever growing genres, the novel and the newspaper. The truth of so-called scientific history (unlike that of the novel) resided in its absolute factuality and in its evolution from secret, privileged sites like archives and libraries, manuscripts hidden away and unearthed, documents from the past examined for the first time in centuries. The new historical knowledge was so recondite that the French historian Ernest Lavisse protectively locked the door of his classroom while his seminar was in session. The newspaper, by contrast, counted on public, accessible, and current knowledge. Its greatest sin was its literary nature, which it shared with the novel and with the heroic history of Carlyle, Macaulay, and that archenemy Sir Walter Scott. Trapped in fact within a whole circuit of sins, these unscientific challengers incited textual excitement, deployed larger-than-life heroes, and cast their net to entrap a wide audience.

Amidst the claims to "neutrality" and "objectivity," to being immune to class, race, and sex interests, the reconstruction of history within the new institutional setting of the university and historical association left behind it traces of gender. Alongside the concern for basing historical writing on data, facts, and objective standards, a lightly sketched path reveals an involvement with masculinity, femininity, and sexual difference. Leopold von Ranke, for instance, professed to have a "desire for the data." Hidden away in archives, the facts contained in ancient documents were "so many princesses, possibly beautiful, all under a curse and needing to be saved." Hardly neuter, the metaphors of professionalization exuded heterosexuality in which an adventurous (male) historian rescued the beautiful princess. In another instance, Ranke referred to a Venetian collection of documents, hitherto unseen, as "the object of my love . . . a beautiful Italian, and I hope that together we shall produce a Romano-German prodigy."[4] And, finally, an unseen archive was "an absolute virgin. I long for the moment I shall have access to her . . . whether she is pretty or not."[5]

Ranke invested his fight against the idealist or romantic version of history with libidinal energy. In this he hardly differed not only from many contemporaries but also from those who continued to seek the heroic past offered in romantic history where the knight in shining armor had his way with one and all. Professional history in the nineteenth and twentieth centuries formed a chivalric haven for the development and play of masculine desires and libidinal activities. As a site invested with aspects of masculine identity—a heroism, for instance, in discovering records or acquiring knowledge (embodied today in the "archive jock" who has visited every municipal archive in France, for instance)—historical study was and remains a properly important but hardly unproblematic place. So a first point is to see the masculine investment in the "heroic" act of research, in the creation of archive "jockery," and in the erotic relationship developed in the pursuit of facts.

Operating from this metaphoric space, scientific history, around which the profession constituted itself, proceded to engage its literary enemy on a gendered terrain. The *English Historical Review* began with the promise not to offer "allurements of style" to its readers.[6] It praised works for their "utter want of tinsel embroidery" and their refusal to "adorn a tale."[7] Other periodicals pointed to the "tawdry trappings" of literary works.[8] Allurements, adornments, tawdry trappings, and tinsel embroidery in the nineteenth century were the wherewithal of prostitution, of public women and their sexuality. Romantic history, like the whore, was all decked out. Historic imagery and heroic narratives paraded about like so many strumpets, leading the public to sin and infecting it. "Clio is going to be just a gal-about-town," wrote one American university historian to a colleague, "on whom anybody with two bits worth of inclination in his pocket can lay claims."[9] The course of professionalization unwittingly followed the lure of sexualized language and the metaphors of whoredom.

At the same time, amateurs began castigating professionals in a similarly sexual way. The *Atheneum* found Gardiner a "Dryasdust," someone whose "pulse was slow," and in another review said, "Of Cecil's scandalous private life, of his sumptuous lodgings, of his secret orgies, of his intrigues with Lady Suffolk and other frail women, the writer has no conception."[10] In fact, whether amateur or professional, scientific or romantic, the voice of history betrayed a dependence on heterosexual articulations and conventions. These conventions remain powerful today, for instance, in the charge that whole fields like African-American and women's history are "sexy," "hot," or "fashionable." In fact, historiographical works, like the recent and popular work of Peter Novick, revel in repeating gendered or sexual metaphors, slurs, and bons mots of previous historians to make their claims. The language of bad history was and remains the language of women.

History's second characteristic in the nineteenth century, a characteristic on which its entire legitimacy rested, involved fashioning scientific history as a discourse of politics and creating linkages to governmental power and the workings of the state. The English historian J. R. Seeley put it most succinctly when he said, "History is past politics." Although Ranke had a feeling that literature and the arts were appropriate to history, his best energy was spent in political and institutional history. The project of the Enlightenment and romanticism to widen the historical field—as seen in the work of Voltaire, Herder, and de Staël—ended, leaving the historical narrative to spin out a thick description, daily more intricate, of the state, its great and even minor personalities, its rituals, obsessions, and struggles. When concerns for other aspects of history — such as social movements or intellectual life — revived, they did so guided by political chronology, the research methods for political history, the language of facts and objectivity, and so on.

Meanwhile, historical methodology reveled in this connection to the state. Ranke touted the importance of reading secret ambassadorial reports as a way of knowing about the workings of power. Later in the century, Lord Acton marked the next stage in the development of scientific and professionalized history "when the war of 1859 laid open the spoils [that is, the archives] of Italy."[11] From then on, he continued, every country was forced to open its records. Or, as Acton's teacher Ignaz von Doellinger put it in the 1860s, "Every library corner [in Europe] has been searched."[12] This forcing open of governmental sources, this unveiling and probing of secrets, these articulations of historical method were intertwined with the course of politics. According to Ranke, Acton, and later historians, the ways of the historian, particularly the skills for discovering and assessing the workings of politics, were precisely those needed by the successful leader. Had the leaders of the French Revolution studied history from a scientific perspective, Fustel de Coulanges maintained, they would not have made the "inept imitation of antiquity" that led to the Terror.[13] History no longer involved narrative virtuosity but rather feats of archival discovery and investigation. So too politics at the turn of the century eschewed the plumed man on horseback (as Max Weber first suggested) for the bureaucratic administrator and parliamentary politician. Historical work, like political rule, involved the language of bureaucratic power and distinterested methods of factual appraisal.

The subject of history was politics, the methodology of governing was historical, and the historian and the politician were often one and the same — Guizot, Thiers, and Jaurès are a few French examples. In England, Gladstone did scholarly writing and spent his happiest moments in the company of Lord Acton and often went to Germany to visit the historian Doellinger. As for Doellinger, much of his work was motivated by a struggle with the papacy. Ranke and Treitschke were also on the list of historians who mingled and even merged with their subject matter. Male politicians from Napoleon to John F. Kennedy have professed to love history, and many historians from Ernest Lavisse to Arthur Schlesinger, Jr., have written about, fantasized about, and wielded political power. If political power was for men, then so was professional history, its subject matter and methodology, and even its fantasies. Historians revived the call of the second-century historian Lucian for scholars whose professional qualities duplicated the masculinity of their political, military, and diplomatic subject matter:

[Give us the historian] with the mind of a soldier combined with that of a good citizen, and a knowledge of generalship; yes, and one who has at some time been in a camp and has seen soldiers exercising or drilling and knows of arms and engines; again, let him know what "in column," what "in line" mean, how the companies of infantry, how the cavalry are maneuvered, the origins and meaning of "lead out" and "lead around," in short not a stay-at-home or one who must rely on what people tell him.[14]

Participating in political debate, sharing military knowledge, and interrogating politicians, historians could construct genealogies of greats, of "masters," and in the process continue history as a discourse of patriarchy and power, one that had little space for women.[15]

Women for as long as professional history has existed have attempted not only to enter the field as researchers and university teachers but also to integrate women into the master narrative. Their efforts have often appeared to be bizarre, unnecessary, or cruelly subversive of the great aims of history. It was difficult to find the right persona in a world so redolent of masculine images such as "masters," "monks," "soldiers," and others that the great professionalizers used to describe their enterprise.[16] It was no less difficult to introduce evidence about the lives of women. Let me give but one example from the work of Lucy Maynard Salmon, who taught history at Vassar College from late in the 1890s until the 1920s. Salmon started her career with a prize-winning study of the appointing powers of the presidency, but then turned to a history of household service, a work the *Nation* found "unworthy of her."[17] That study shaped her endeavor to teach a history of everyday life, and one that was gendered. In her seminars at Vassar, she would fling down all sorts of ordinary artifacts for her students to scrutinize—cookbooks, railroad schedules, laundry lists, newspapers—instead of political documents.[18] Salmon in her pathbreaking "History in a Backyard" challenged the archive as a source by opening with the conceit of not being able to go to Europe for research one summer. This piece was summarily rejected by the *Yale Review* and other journals, as were pieces with such improbable titles as "The Family Cookbook," "On Beds and Bedding," and "Ode to a Kitchen Sink." Trying to insert women into history, she left the realm of historical prose in, for example, a history of the cookbook. Here Salmon displays images of cooking that recalled the family:

Aunt Hannah's loaf cake, Cousin Lizzie's waffles, Grandmother's cookies, Grandma Lyman's marble cake, Sister Sally's quince jelly, Mother's raspberry vinegar, Warren's cake, Jennie's gingerbread, Jack's oyster stew, Mercy's nasturtium pickles, johnny cake, brown betty, and carolines.

Or she found place names of cooking:

Lady Baltimore cake, Philadelphia ice cream, Irving Park cake, Bangor
pudding, Nuremberg cakes, Banbury tarts, Bavarian cream, Irish stew,
Scotch broth, English muffins, and Hamburg steak.[19]

Recounting the domestic—not the political—past, Salmon often ended up
in the realm of sheer poetics. The poetic, Gaston Bachelard reminds us,
leaves concern for cause and effect behind in favor of evocations, reverber-
ations, and echoes.[20] Salmon, like the housewife who was "emancipated
from time and space" into poetry, could become absorbed in reverie and invention but not, perhaps, history:

> Birds on canapes, bird's-nest pudding, floating islands, apples in bloom,
> shadow potatoes, cheese aigrettes, apple snow, snowballs, gossamer
> gingerbread, fairy gingerbread, aurora sauce, moonlight cake, lily cake,
> lady fingers, and amber pudding.[21]

Salmon took up the Rankean challenge by constituting and exploring new
kinds of sources. Her poetic history rejected the heroic and heart-thumping
sagas of Scott, but she and others were never able to overcome the standards
of significance set by political history.

The work of pioneers like Salmon, viewed from today's vantage point,
indicate some of the boundaries of history, and their careers remind us of the
ways in which history was never a neutral profession, but rather one con-
figured as male and disguised by the language of science and universalism.
Women historians and women's history have confronted a tradition in
which their very presence was a sign of the amateur and of bad history. But
recent attention to the issue of gender in history has begun to denaturalize
those claims to science, universality, and truth. It has shown that the marking out of masculinity and femininity has constituted the fundamental work
of society, economics, and politics—and, yes, of history. Rather than maintaining the singular importance of such a thing as "women's voice," the interpretation that power has devolved from an ongoing process of "gendering" suggested that history itself was a highly gendered process that did an
immense amount of masculinist work by the ways in which it was constructed. By foregrounding "difference," the idea of gender has allowed us
to see the ways in which history has been based on identity, sameness, and
the universalizing of all that is male.[22] Political, economic, and cultural
power has been sustained by their coincidence with this definition of history
as sameness, identity, and masculinity. A history emphasizing difference
would have entirely other shapes and consequences from that based on
knowing which king followed which.

How can we feature discussions of difference in our courses? One way to redraw the map of history and to integrate material on gender and women is to reconsider our teaching of areas and events where we already have evidence that would allow us to integrate and revise. For instance, one major locus of the workings of gender power or patriarchy has been at the basic level of replenishment of the population, although these workings have been interpreted as private, not political, and thus not historical. Just as the production of goods for human sustenance occurs in a matrix of social and political arrangements, so too reproduction constitutes a major endeavor from which political, social, and cultural power evolve. It was convenient to think of reproduction as "natural" and thus beyond the realms of power and social arrangements; such a supposition placed it outside historical narrative and analysis. Yet reproductive experience, changes in population, and demographic behavior in general have a history and have influenced history. So basic a category has yielded power and produced politics.

During the last three decades historians realized that the family was not "natural" but rather historical. Old and young, men and women had different kinds of power, different duties, and so on. Familial rules at any particular time involved assigning tasks so that productive work would sustain the family unit, while reproductive rules (such as age at marriage, courtship customs, breast-feeding patterns, and the like) worked to arrange just the right number of children to permit familial and community survival. The development of women's history has forced us to consider how the organization of reproduction and its effect on determinations of sexuality and sexual orientation may work differentially in the lives of men and women, both in so small a unit as the family and in so large a one as the state. Connecting the history of reproduction with insights about gender, students can discuss how the differentials in reproductive arrangements yield differentials in power, whether it is the power of a father, of a tribal chief, or of a national leader.

Specific areas where material about gender and reproductive organization can fit history are abundant. For example, over the past decade historians have come to consider the condition and experience of women in the ancient world. They note that the transition from the so-called dark age in Greece to that period when classical institutions arose involved a transition from a perilous population situation after wars and an accompanying agricultural decline. Simultaneously, women were disadvantaged when it came to participating in that new construct of the "polis" and specifically in what is called Athenian democracy. Discussion of women usually follows descriptions of how Athenian democracy operated and assessments of its conceptual importance to the development of political systems. Democracy was not yet complete, new accounts proceed, because for the moment it excluded slaves and women. In this way Western civilization serves as a Whiggish celebration of an expanding democracy, made complete when slavery ultimately disappeared and women could vote.

Rewriting such a scenario is crucial. The exclusion of women from the polis was not incidental to democracy; rather, it was intrinsic to democracy. The idea of including women and slaves or of "liberating" them was outside the Athenian conceptional framework. Rather, a fundamental social and political process was at work in defining rights and access to politics in terms of male and female. Acting as warrior, as free landholder, as citizen, as theater-goer, and as lover were the attributes of masculinity. In that particular society, "adding" women or "liberating" them would have destroyed the social and political edifice because gender definitions would have collapsed. Moreover, the sexual segregation involved in the gendering of classical Greek society helped restore population and political order. Political regulations marked off spaces for masculine and feminine functioning and defined reproductive duties so that population growth would reoccur tranquilly.

The period of the French and Industrial Revolutions is another instance: demographic change and the reorganization of reproductive habits seem crucial to understanding the cataclysms of those years. In the eighteenth century population surged as never before. As people wandered the countryside homeless and begging in ever greater numbers, concern for population restraint appeared not just among political economists like Malthus. Segments of the European population began to reorganize the reproductive system and reduce fertility. Should we not ask our students (and ourselves) whether this affected the shape of the Age of Revolution, especially in France and England? One friend, hearing this suggestion, emphatically maintained that, despite all the new information about women during the French and Industrial Revolutions, those events were about less faddish, more transcendent matters like liberty, class, power, and so on. (And, of course, writing about the French Revolution has made more than one career.)

Yet one can hardly ignore that the revolutionary epoch redefined masculinity and femininity and changed conditions for the replenishment of the species. The conscientious teacher will make some attempt to see the relationship between the revolutions in politics and production on the one hand and the demographic and gender revolutions on the other. Only such considerations allow us to make sense of the French revolutionary legislation proscribing women from attending political clubs, from meeting to talk politics, from gathering in groups of more than three. Only such considerations help us make sense of the regulation of women and reproduction in the provisions of the French Civil Code. Husbands were given all the economic power; married women had no right to property, had to follow their husbands wherever they might move, and legally had to reside with them.

Instead of seeing these provisions as mere expressions of transcendent ideals, as whimsical acts, or as predictable expressions of Napoleonic misogyny, we need to consider revolutionary legislation as part of an effort to regulate population and to redefine the terrain of men and women. What was the early onset of the birth control revolution in France but the result of the legislation of equal inheritance? A modern political ethos arose through the impulse to regulate and reshape society along the lines of privatized (rather than community-based) control of fertility and the expansion of male political prerogatives.

Another modern historic situation — imperialism — adds to our sense of how the relationship between masculine and feminine constructs are crucial to historical understanding and pertinent to the Western civilization survey. We are now able to teach our students how a phenomenon such as imperialism intersected with ideas of masculinity and femininity. Europeans by the late nineteenth century had created an identity that depended on controlling other races. But gender also structured the idea of what "European" meant. White men forged identities as colonial soldiers and administrators, as hunters, and as journalists and scholars expert in the ways of native peoples. In a complementary way, politicians maintained that imperialist domination, and thus the survival of entire nations like Britain, depended on the efforts of wives and mothers. To preserve the nation, they had to create an imperial race by nourishing, clothing, and otherwise tending their families more vigorously and more successfully than they had in the past. This was no incidental task, for those imperialist nations would collapse as they were then organized without the gendered roles of masculine and feminine to carry out the imperial mission. Finally, imperialism reached its crescendo precisely when one of the most central developments in Western history was taking place: the precipitous 50 percent decline in the birthrate between the late nineteenth century and 1930 and the concomitant creation of a dramatic new approach to reproduction. Politicians in France questioned the potency of French men; other European leaders felt that women in general had rejected their maternal identity for the sake of being "new women." Without doubt the ethos of imperial society and the history of its politics were intertwined with gendered and reproductive concerns.

Analyzing the rise of Adolf Hitler and nazism for Western civilization classes also calls for an understanding of gender, race, and ethnicity as pivotal to politics. Even the most conservative historians will note that Nazis and fascists displayed misogynist tendencies. Misogyny was hardly incidental to nazism, but rather permitted the deployment of the rest of its program. The Nazi ideologue's power rested on his being distinct from the women around him, on redefining himself as warrior and male after the shattering experiences of World War I. Hitler's first year in power saw major legislation working toward reestablishing gender clarity and the power of masculinity within the bounds of race and ethnicity. That legislation mandated the removal of women from civil service and university jobs (male professors in particular responded with gusto) and provided subsidies for women who would stop working in order to have families. Not just legislation but the demeanor and speeches pointed to the ways in which nazism built on the power derived from rebuilding the differences between men and women.

Nazism also depended on anti-Semitism in word and deed to heighten its power and drive its policy. Throughout history, misogyny and anti-Semitism have been conjoined. The student of Western civilization will see Chaucer, for instance, putting the vicious anti-Semitism of his society in the prim mouth of the distasteful prioress. In the modern period we often see nineteenth- and twentieth-century Jewish men described in feminine terms and thus defined as a threat to traditional definitions of masculinity. The Jew had the metaphorical power to destroy gender definition and thus society. By the twentieth century anti-Semitism increased in potency as the gender order and the reproductive order (given the birth control revolution and the blows to traditional definitions inflicted by war, feminism, and economic catastrophe) weakened. Genocide was so primal a matter because it worked to reorder all that. It signaled renewed control over the entire reproductive order as whole groups could be racially defined and then encouraged to reproduce or, alternatively, be destroyed. Nazism, and ultimately the Final Solution, were about determining how biology would work. Aryans would be encouraged to reproduce; Slavs, Jews, gypsies, and other peoples marked out by those with political power would be destroyed as racial groups.

Will we continue to learn history as a universal truth, a story of reality that tells us everything it is important to know when in fact its truths have been so partial? Even as teachers continue the important task of finding women's voices and describing their experiences, even as we try to make our history courses more democratic in terms of gender, race, and ethnicity, we must consider that the results are still unsatisfactory. Our efforts seem feeble because of the claims history makes to being about objective Reality and universal truth when in fact it is so partial and so filled with fantasies of masculinity—not only those of researchers, but of readers as well. We can only suppose that women historians and women students bring their own prejudices, desires, and psychic needs to the field. But as long as either set of fantasies is unacknowledged, as long as we try to fit a few women into a narrative that assigns primacy to the details of political struggle and great men, learning history will remain a far from benign enterprise. Rather than touting only our objective standards, we must see what fantasies and partial truths accompany them, what contests and struggles for power have occurred in every realm of society, what different story lines have made up history and been repressed by the profession for being "insignificant" or "natural." If historical understanding has been deeply gendered, then history teaching has the urgent task of gendering history as well.

NOTES

1. Carolyn Lougee, "Toward a Two-Sex History: A Model for the European Survey Course from the Renaissance to the French Revolution," in *The Introductory History Course. Six Models*, ed. Kevin Reilly (Washington, D.C., 1984), pp. 1-17. The account summarizes a fifty-page proposal Lougee presented at an American Historical Association conference on the introductory history course in 1980.

2. This oft-quoted remark from a lecture was cited in the *English Historical Review* (vol. 5) but appears in different versions in many printed sources and in the lore of the profession.

3. John Dalberg-Acton, *Lectures on Modern History* (1906; reprint New York, 1961), p. 22.

4. Letter to Ferdinand Ranke, November 11, 1836, Leopold von Ranke, *Neue Briefe*, ed. Bernhard Hoeft and Hans Herzfeld (Hamburg, 1949), p. 230.

5. Ibid.

6. "Prefatory Note," *English Historical Review* 1 (1886): 5.

7. *English Historical Review*, reviews of S. Gardiner, *History of the Commonwealth and Protectorate 1649-1660*, and Georg Busolt, *Handbuch der griechischen Geschichte*, vol. 13 (1898), pp. 167, 125. See also Lord Acton's praise for Ranke's writing "without adornment" (*Lectures*, p. 39).

8. "Gardiner's Personal Government of Charles I," *Saturday Review*, December 22, 1877, p. 774.

9. Quoted in Peter Novick, *That Noble Dream: The "Objectivity Question" and the American Historical Profession* (Cambridge, 1988), p. 193.

10. *Atheneum*, 1863, pp. 392-93; 1869, p. 629.

11. Acton, *Lectures*, p. 29. This statement also shows the dependence of what was called scientific methodology on nation building.

12. John J. Ign. von Doellinger, *Fables Respecting the Popes of the Middle Ages*, trans. Alfred Plummer (London, 1871), p. 9.

13. N. D. Fustel de Coulanges, "Inaugural Lecture," in *The Varieties of History: From Voltaire to the Present*, ed. Fritz Stern (New York, 1956), p. 187.

14. Lucian, *How to Write History*, trans. K. Kilburn (Cambridge, 1959), vol. 6, p. 49.

15. Historians also used real cases to eliminate women from this discourse of masculine identity, for instance, the noted, much-written-about Pope Joan, notorious in nineteenth-century scholarship. Dozens of prominent historians, Doellinger among them, spent enormous energy proving that Joan did not exist. They also discussed issues like the "droit du seigneur," the right of a lord to intercourse with a new bride. All of this continued to give historical research libidinal interest, but cases like Pope Joan were used to demonstrate that women and gender were beyond the limits of political history.

16. See my "Historiography, Objectivity, and the Case of the Abusive Widow," *History and Theory*, Beiheft 31 (December 1992): 15-32.

17. Quoted in Louise Fargo Brown, *Apostle of Democracy: The Life of Lucy Maynard Salmon* (New York, 1943), p. 83.

18. Caroline Ware, a student of Salmon's, speaking informally at the first Evalyn A. Clark Conference, October 12, 1985, Vassar College. Another former student, the historian J. B. Ross, provided a similar picture of Salmon's classes in interviews in May 1985 in Washington, D.C.

19. Lucy Maynard Salmon, "The Family Cookbook," *Vassar College Quarterly* 11 (March 1926): 101-11 passim.

20. Gaston Bachelard, *The Poetics of Space* (Boston, 1969).

21. Salmon, "The Family Cookbook," p. 105. Mary Beard sometimes ended up in a similar place—for instance, in *On Understanding Women*, where for pages she employed free verse. On early professional women's responses to scientific history, see my "Gender, Objectivity, and the Professionalization of History," in *Objectivity and Its Other*, ed. Wolfgang Nader (Lexington, Ky., forthcoming).

22. See especially the work of Joan Scott and in particular her *Gender and the Politics of History* (New York, 1988).

Canons, Texts, and Contexts

Dominick LaCapra

Advocacy of a canon of "great books" in education and in the study of culture in general has recently become the object of renewed affirmation as well as attack. Unfortunately, the most heated affirmation has been part of a neoconservative revival that has placed the blame for contemporary problems on education and educators, especially in the humanities, and has seen the return to "great books" as the true path to salvation. The recent plaints of Allan Bloom, William Bennett, and Lynne Cheney chime with a long-standing tendency in American culture to divert attention from the socioeconomic and political sources of problems by scapegoating intellectuals; they also reaffirm a displaced religious sense of the sacred text as the beacon of common culture for an educated elite.

The neoconservative defense of an authoritative and culture-building canon has exacerbated the desire to decenter or even demolish canons. This desire has been pronounced among various groups, including neo–Marxists, feminists, students of popular culture, and proponents of ethnic and Third World studies.[1] To the extent that the exclusionary bias of canons is aggravated rather than mitigated by the neoconservative initiative, the critique of canons acquires increased plausibility and appeal. Moreover, the broad issue of cultural and sociopolitical practice can in no sense be reduced to a debate over canonicity. At the very least, there is the prior question of access to literacy and, even more basically, the issue of equality of opportunity in general. Indeed, debates about the canon, especially when they are conducted without an awareness of their limitations and assumptions, may serve as a displacement of, or even a diversion from, a broader analysis of social and political structures.[2] The question, however, is whether the limited significance of the issue of canonization and the valid objections to certain social, political, and cultural functions of canons — or of overcharged debates about canonicity—entail the simple abandonment of careful study of texts and artifacts that have traditionally been included in canons. I would answer that question in the negative but insist that recent discussions raise the question of precisely how one should undertake both a critique of canonicity and a qualified defense of the careful reading of certain canonical texts.

I would like to begin with a few general considerations that serve as a framework for my other comments. One should distinguish between the texts or artifacts that have been included in canons and the process of canonization that entails acts of inclusion and (explicit or implicit) exclusion. The latter has, I think, been the primary object of both attacks upon and defenses of the canon. Through canonization texts are presumed to serve certain hegemonic functions with reference to dominant values and structures, and the extent to which they do depends upon the way in which they are interpreted and the uses to which they are put. The process of canonization raises the question of the reception of texts with reference both to the constitution of disciplines or professions and to processes, such as socialization, operative in the larger society and polity. The open question is the extent to which texts that are canonized may be argued to invite or resist canonical functions.

A critique of a canon may proceed in two fashions. First, it may insist upon the noncanonical reading of canonized texts in order to bring out the ways in which those texts resist or contest the canonical functions they are presumed to serve. For what may be quite forceful in canonization is the tendency to bracket the critical and even transformative potential of texts. Ideally, noncanonical reading examines the manner in which canonized texts must be interpretively bowdlerized to make them adjust to canonical functions. It also brings out their critical sides and investigates their relations to whatever ideologically reinforcing functions a text may be argued to have.

A second and equally important mode of criticizing canons is to insist upon the importance of sets of texts and artifacts that have been not simply bowdlerized but marginalized or altogether excluded with the effect that certain counterhegemonic traditions are effaced from the historical record. Until recently, texts of women and minorities have undergone this process of suppression and repression. The effort to include formerly excluded or marginalized texts is altogether crucial, as is the historical and critical study of how and why processes of exclusion take place. I would, however, like to argue that the two modes of criticizing canons I have mentioned should be seen as mutually reinforcing rather than as mutually exclusive options. Choices have to be made between these procedures not on a theoretical level but on pragmatic and problematic grounds when one confronts the issue of assigning material in a course or treating it in a study. But the unavoidable difficulties these choices pose should not be made to obscure the point that both procedures raise comparable problems and hold out similar promises.

One problem is that critiques of the canon may share a propensity with defenses of a canon—the tendency to fetishize the canon and fixate attention on it. The result is a monolithic idea of the historical role of canons as well as an inclination to consign to the shadows issues that cannot be centered on the question of canonicity. To the extent that a canon is dominant or at least prominent in a field of study, concern about its composition and functions is warranted. Still, one should not lose sight of the point that the goal—indeed, the promise—of a critique of canons should be the displacement of the very problem of canonicity and the realization that the crucial factor in the selection and interpretation of texts is their relationship to a set of crucial issues. The emphasis should be on certain issues and what texts may be argued to disclose or conceal with reference to them. Among the most intensely pressing issues we confront today are those relating to gender, race, class, and species—issues that involve the legitimate rights of women, oppressed minorities and classes, and animals other than the human being. These and comparable issues, such as the relation of work and play in society and culture or, in another register, between texts and contexts in interpretation, should be the focus of our concern and the guides in our debates, and the issue of the selection and interpretation of texts and other artifacts should be decentered in the sense that it becomes one limited but not unimportant subject of discussion and controversy in the light of significant problems. One would still have to select certain texts or artifacts for special attention, but one would be constrained to make arguments and provide reasons for one's choices. Although co-optation is always a clear and present danger in a commodity system, the resultant choices would not simply amount to a canon in the conventional sense insofar as they are self-critical and do not serve—or even actively resist—canonical functions and reappropriations. Indeed, until we start asking certain questions about significant issues, we do not know how the texts of the past will respond. Moreover, we ought to be open to the possibility—in certain cases the likelihood—that in reading a text our very conception of significant issues will be challenged or changed—shown to be too restricted or simplistic. This outcome of reading is itself a hallmark of texts from which we may have most to learn and to which we should be inclined to return.

In view of these observations and contentions, one should recognize the need to criticize the very concept of "great book," which is encrusted with neoconservative and Arnoldian connotations. This concept should be displaced in the direction of text and artifact in general. (Often I shall use "text" in its expanded sense as a metonym for artifact or signifying practice in general.) This process of substituting "text" for "great book" is already well under way, especially in literary criticism and certain forms of intellectual history. Texts in the literal sense are not the only and not the most important objects of study or of life. I would, however, contend that without careful, critical attention to at least certain literal texts, one's own intellectual and political culture (at least in the context of modern Western societies) may prove to be rather thin, if not superficial, and one may well be in no position to reconstruct past — or to analyze contemporary — social, political, and cultural practices with any degree of subtlety and acumen. In fact, one may find oneself implicitly relying on the perspective of an overly restricted subset of more or less canonical figures (or "modern masters") whose limitations are not offset by the arguments and perspectives that could conceivably be elaborated on the basis of the work of other, unread figures. This is not, however, to say that the sole guide to critique is the written text or, for that matter, the artifact of traditional elite culture in general. On the contrary, the very opposition between elite and popular culture should be both investigated historically and questioned politically. And one should be open to the critical potential of noncanonical artifacts or traditions (including oral traditions) that may deserve broader dissemination if not centrality. Indeed, attention should be directed to an important but problematic distinction that may help in salvaging the valid component in the notion of especially significant texts (in the expanded or general sense).

I would propose that all texts are worth thinking *about*, but some texts are especially valuable to think *with*, and in certain cases they have proven this value in renewed ways over time. The texts that are worth thinking with enable a more pointed discussion of texts and aspects of texts — including aspects of texts worth thinking with — that are less deserving of emulation. They may also assist in the recognition of those critical aspects or utopian possibilities that may at times be found in even the most debased or commercialized cultural artifacts. Despite its problematic nature and the difficulty in applying it to specific artifacts, this distinction between that which is worth thinking with and that which is worth thinking about is required as a general guide in coming to terms with texts in ways that actively invite continual self-questioning. It would, however, be a mistake to take this distinction as a binary opposition, and its variable application to specific texts is always open to reconsideration. But critical thought is in a worse position without this distinction than with it. The danger in certain reading technologies, including deconstruction and the new historicism, is that this distinction may be obliterated insofar as all texts and artifacts are read in the same terms either as self-deconstructive or as culturally and politically symptomatic.[3]

How does one identify the texts that are particularly worth thinking with — texts that help to develop critical abilities in cultural studies? No text entirely transcends an uncritical implication in contemporary ideologies and prejudices. No text in this sense is without its blind spots. But certain texts are submerged in blindness and regenerate or even reinforce ideologies in relatively unmodulated fashion. Propaganda on the political level and advertising on the commercial level tend to be ideologically reinforcing or to employ potentially critical modes, such as irony and parody, only within safe and self-serving limits.

In significant but not total contrast, some texts help one to foreground ideological problems and to work through them critically. And they may assist one in elaborating a critically self-reflective approach to a field of study as well as procedures for investigating contexts in an other than narrowly historicist manner. For these texts may be argued to frame their ideologies and prejudices in a specific fashion and to help put the reader in a better position to confront them critically. No text or cultural artifact can in and of itself critically rework or transform society. But some are particularly effective in engaging critical processes that interfere with the regeneration or reinforcement of ideologies and established contexts in general; they provide bases for the critique of their own blindnesses by helping to initiate a process of reflection that may educate us as readers and have practical implications. These are the texts and artifacts that have a special claim to be included in self-contestatory "canons" that are themselves always open to questioning and renewal, particularly as we discover blindnesses and limitations in what we earlier thought were exemplary texts or dimensions of texts. A challenge in the reading of any text or artifact is to ascertain the specific configuration of symptomatic (or ideologically reinforcing), critical, and potentially transformative forces it puts into play—a challenge that involves us as readers in both reconstruction of and dialogic exchange with the past. This objective should never be divorced from close, formal inquiry into the manner in which a text does what it does, for this mode of inquiry is crucial in delineating precisely how a text relates to its contexts or reworks its contents. Formal inquiry is not simply formalistic to the extent that it does not confide in a simple separation of form from context or content. Such inquiry is necessary not only for the critic but also for the historian who recognizes what should be obvious: texts or artifacts are events that cannot be reduced to contextual forces or employed as mere documentary sources insofar as they make a historical difference by refiguring their contexts or reworking their material. To make this point is not to subscribe to a quasi-transcendental notion of textuality or "literariness" that relegates contexts to an ancillary status and affirms a purely performative or abysmally self-canceling conception of language. It is rather to insist upon a careful, historically specific, and self-questioning inquiry into the manner in which texts interact with their contexts of writing and reception.

There is clearly a need in historiography to address the question of the contexts of reading and interpretation over time. Indeed, there is no simple choice among contextualization, textual interpretation, and self-critical dialogue with the texts of the past. To oppose the reconstruction of contexts to textual analysis or dialogic exchange is to create an artificial and debilitating dichotomy. But historical understanding should not for that reason be conflated with contextualism in its narrowly historicist and documentary sense.

While no text transcends an implication in contexts, one cannot read all texts indiscriminately as straightforward signs of the times. "Context" easily becomes a Procrustean bed on which we cut all artifacts to the measure of our familiarizing, preestablished modes of understanding and satisfy our hunger for hefty "factoids" and thick descriptions. What is thereby eliminated is the manner in which certain texts make claims on us and may even disrupt the explanatory or interpretive molds in which we try to contain them. For the contextualizing historicist, history—understood in a very conventional manner—is the answer. For the historian, history should be a problem, that is to say, something that calls for critical reflection and for continual reinvestigation as to its very nature.

It is, moreover, important to note that one cannot essentialize the nature of the work performed on ideologies and contexts by texts that are worth thinking with. Or, to put the point another way, one cannot essentialize or fetishize the notion of critique itself. In this sense, it would at best be of limited value to try to arrive at a uniform, purely formal, or universally determining set of criteria with which to identify texts worth thinking with, for what might serve critical thought in certain circumstances might not in others. For example, at a certain point in history, it might be both aesthetically and politically challenging for a member of an oppressed group to make use of a traditional literary form, such as the *Bildungsroman* or the autobiography—a form that might serve a critical function for a member of a privileged class only if it were subjected to certain telling variations. And, within a given reference group, a technique (such as free indirect style or montage) that was experimental and thought-provoking at one time may become banal and accommodating at another. In this sense, a concern for context is directly related to the appreciation of the critical or at least provocative potential of given texts or procedures at a given time and over time. Moreover, on the level of reception, one must try to understand as fully as possible why it is that even the most heinous and disastrous ideologies or the most stereotypical texts have been able to exercise a hold over people, including some of the seemingly most critical intellectuals. When critique becomes autonomous and emerges as one's own form of naïveté, the very appeal of ideologies may escape one's grasp. One may also become blind not only to the limits of one's own thought but also to the way in which certain aspects of an existing set of contexts may in fact be worth preserving, reinforcing, or reworking. (This point applies, for example, to civil liberties in our own context.) Other aspects of a status quo may by contrast be ready for radical criticism and major reconstruction. In addition, one's perspective on which contextual aspects fall into one or another category may change over time, thereby indicating that understanding has a delayed or belated — what Freud termed a *nachträglich* — dimension. This unsettling dimension, whereby one is able to see things or ask questions that were not available to oneself or others in the past, is bound up both with traumatic effects and with the very ability to learn from an exchange with the past. *Nachträglichkeit* ("belatedness") would be utterly misconstrued if it became a pretext for simplistic teleological narratives in which earlier phenomena are portrayed as causing or leading unilaterally to later ones. But the attempt to reduce its role to the vanishing point (for example, by an indiscriminate dismissal of "anachronisms") may itself be criticized as an extreme manifestation of a certain kind of historicism that attempts to evade present contexts in favor of total empathy with, or autonomized reconstruction and pure interpretation of, an excessively restricted and idealized idea of past contexts.

With respect to existing disciplines, the departure from canons has had some dubious consequences that underscore the need to be attentive to the nature and implications of one's critique. Canons have been more evident in literary criticism, philosophy, and art history than they have been in history or social science. In addition, the former fields have had canons both on the level of so-called primary texts and on the level of theoretical texts or commentaries taking "primary" texts as objects of analysis or emulation. The critique of canons has for obvious reasons also been more vociferous and forceful in these fields than in history or social science. The near-fixation on canons in the traditional humanistic disciplines tended to obscure an entire range of important problems, including the very problem of the emergence, institutionalization, and often dubious functions of a canon.

Still, there is one function of a canon that is difficult to gainsay. A canon does provide a shared set of reference points for discussion, even when one insists that these reference points should not only be approached critically but also selected in part because of their very ability to stimulate critical thought that may be applied elsewhere. The role of such a set of reference points would seem to be directly related to the importance of theory and of traditions of theorizing in a field not modeled on the natural sciences. In other words, it is difficult to see how one could relegate texts to an instrumental status and elaborate an autonomous body of theory in fields in which meaning, interpretation, and critical self-reflection are at issue. In these fields, specific texts would seem to be inextricably bound up with problems and have a special status as media of dialogic exchange.

There is an obvious but nontrivial sense in which any common program of studies with requirements institutes a canon that may well exclude or underemphasize certain topics. And the effects of such a program, on however local or evanescent a level, can be very constraining. But disciplines or fields taken as a whole do reveal some noteworthy divergences, at least with reference to a canon in the weightier sense of a pantheon of authors and a long-standing list of consecrated texts believed to be privileged objects of reading for generations. Certain fields have for some time not had a canon in this delimited sense, and in them the movement toward a more critically defined set of textual reference points would not involve dismantling such a traditional edifice. In fact, it might well involve arguing for the necessity of non-traditional, self-contestatory "canons."

One sign of a science is that it no longer reads its canonical authors. To put it another way, it does not have a textual canon or even competing canons. It has relatively autonomous theories, textbooks, and problems; a disciplinary matrix; and occasional papers in which the valuable findings — in contrast to the texts — of earlier figures are assumed to be integrated. To the extent that science has exemplary texts, they lead a very short life and would seem to have a largely instrumental value. Hence, a contemporary physicist qua physicist need not read Newton or Einstein. I would be inclined to object that reading Newton and Einstein, as part of a broader definition of a historically informed, self-reflective physicist, should be prevalent and valued within the profession, but the dominant criteria for good physics do not require it.

The social sciences have in large part attempted to follow the natural sciences in this dimension of self-understanding. In this minimal sense, they seem to have become more "scientific." Yet the consequences are questionable. It is problematic in the extreme to believe that whatever is valuable in Marx, Weber, Freud, and Durkheim has been integrated into the state of the art in a manner that releases social scientists from the need to read carefully the texts of these figures and to offer courses on them. Other crucial figures such as C. L. R. James and W. E. B. Du Bois are often excluded and therefore ignored as parts of the history of the discipline. The belief that the social sciences may emulate the natural sciences in this "noncanonical" respect helps to void them of a critical, self-reflective dimension and fosters a narrowly scientistic self-conception. It also tends to make them adaptive to the status quo in an extremely confining manner.

One may argue that an attempt to come to terms with the past of a discipline is part and parcel of a broader cultural, philosophical, and self-critical understanding of that discipline; it requires some sense of a "canon" of relevant texts as a shared but critically appropriated and essentially contested set of reference points. Yet one may question the extent to which professional historiography itself has had a theoretically informed relation to its own past, in which certain texts provide a basis for argument and self-reflection. The "research imperative" often appears to be dominant — an imperative in accordance with which past texts are documents having an instrumental value as sources of information that are used to test a hypothesis or to flesh out a narrative. When it exists at all as part of an undergraduate or graduate program, the "theory" seminar may stress works that are of restricted methodological interest in furthering research rather than those that stimulate more basic critical and self-critical reflection, and it may be even more narrowly geared to immediate, practical payoffs in the assignment of very recent historiography that may be directly emulated (or "trashed") by aspiring professionals. Of course, a seminar cannot do everything; difficult choices have to be made, and a great deal depends upon how assignments are discussed. But the conflation of methodology with theory and the neat separation between recent historians and those who wrote more than a generation ago may induce both diminished self-understanding and the relegation of past historians to the history of historiography, thereby inhibiting a tense interaction between contemporary work and a dialogue with the past. In addition, one often slights the possibility that attention to the nature and role of the historian's own discourse does not entail an "aestheticization" of history or a simple-minded reduction of history to fiction but rather a cognitively responsible effort to achieve critical understanding of theoretical problems with implications for historical practice—problems such as subject position, voice, and the negotiation of the transferential relation between the historian and the past.[4]

In philosophy, the analytic turn, while not eliminating entirely the rereading of past philosophers, tended to reduce their work to quarries for insights into present problems. In this sense, Plato not only would be treated very selectively but might just as well have published—after the requisite editorial work—in *Mind* or the *Philosophical Review*. The study of the past could not in this sense aid in providing perspective on the present or even in generating a reorientation of significant questions. Thus, when Richard Rorty argued for a conception of philosophy as a conversation with the past, his initiative came as something of a shock, even though it was still very much indebted to a now familiar analytic idiom and often kept conversation within rather gentlemanly parameters and bourgeois-liberal assumptions that tended to downplay more intense modes of controversy and conflict.

Recently, history and philosophy have become somewhat more open to debates about their orientation. Philosophers have become more attentive to the possibility that the manner in which one comes to terms with the past is crucial to one's activity in the present and future.[5] In historiography, debates about theory and method are no longer confined to a small group of intellectual historians. A significant number of historians believe they must be up on current controversies about theory and method, if only at times to resist the allures of newer orientations and reaffirm an established convention or the tried-and-true proclivities of a mentor. And historians in general are increasingly apprehensive not only about the threat of invading troops but also about the deceptive maneuvers of invading tropes. The fact that the *American Historical Review*—until recently not notable as a forum for self-reflection—could devote almost an entire issue (94:3 [June 1989]) to methodological and theoretical debates is a surprising and welcome turn of events.[6]

With respect to a critical and self-critical historiography, I would maintain that there is and ought to be a tension between two related approaches to which I have already alluded. While both are in certain ways necessary, they cannot be simply integrated or subsumed in a classical synthesis. Rather, the two exist in a tense and open dialectical relationship that may be negotiated with greater or lesser success. Indeed, they may—and perhaps should—take different inflections in the work of different scholars (or even in different dimensions of the work of the same scholar). Each approach involves a claim about how to construe texts and implies how implausible it is to maintain that texts simply read themselves. These two approaches are contextualization in terms of the conditions of production and reception in the past, and dialogic exchange with texts in terms of an interaction between past and present with possible implications for the future.

The contextualizing approach stresses the detailed embeddedness of texts in their own time and over time. It frequently relies on the provision of extensive background information that cannot be derived from the text itself, and it typically insists upon a very broad sampling of texts from the same or related genres. In the form given to it by such recent figures as Quentin Skinner, J. G. A. Pocock, and David Hollinger, it aims to reconstitute an idiom or discursive framework that formed the broad yet particularized context for the text or corpus of texts under consideration. This approach has resulted in notable achievements, and the reconstruction of a shared field of discourse is both important in itself and necessary in the appreciation of how certain texts rework or transform common assumptions. But at times there is a tendency in the profession to identify contextualization with historical understanding itself. For many historians, to historicize is to contextualize. Careful and well-informed contextualization is, as I have intimated, an altogether necessary dimension of historical understanding, but it should not be equated with historical understanding *tout court*. The limitations of contextualism emerge most sharply when it becomes historicist in the sense criticized by Walter Benjamin in his "Theses on the Philosophy of History."[7]

The second approach is prevalent among literary critics and philosophers. It stresses our dialogic exchange with the past, and it may emphasize if not focus exclusively upon the performative and creative way in which we rewrite the past in terms of present interests, needs, and values. In this view, we awaken the dead in order to interrogate them about problems of interest to us, and the answers we derive justifiably tell us more about ourselves than about a context we could not fully recreate in the best of circumstances even if we wanted to. Here priority is given to the novel and stimulating interpretation that tests our methods and theories and enables the texts of the past to be read as addressing us, whether in an intemporal sense or in a more disorienting and uncanny manner in which conventional notions of time may be unsettled. What is often lost sight of, however, is the caveat that the ability of a powerful reading method to reprocess in its own terms any object of inquiry should not be seen as a solution to problems but as itself a deeply problematic and disturbing phenomenon.

In philosophy, this second approach has at times led to "rational reconstructions" in which the work of past philosophers is rethought to make it relevant to present concerns, at times by working out more coherently lines of inquiry that were either cut short or poorly elaborated in the texts under scrutiny. In literary criticism, new criticism and more recent approaches such as deconstruction differ in how they interpret texts, but they converge in showing little interest in past contexts for their own sake. For example, Rousseau's status in the Enlightenment and his relation to the French Revolution — problems that have traditionally preoccupied historians — may not even be mentioned, or in any case are not given a privileged status. In Jacques Derrida's *Of Grammatology*, for example, the history of primary concern is the long and tangled heritage of metaphysics, and Rousseau is an exemplary figure in a problematic in which we are still very much implicated.[8]

A somewhat different formulation of the different stresses of recent interpretive approaches would distinguish those who read for the plot and those who plot for the read.[9] Those who read for the plot are concerned with eliciting patterns that actually or potentially characterize a set of texts, and their emphasis could be seen as a mode of contextualization in the form of intertextuality — one that may be adjusted in a variety of ways to contextualization in terms of social, political, and cultural matters. Those who plot for the read may refer to contextual forces, including intertextual ones, but their objective is to provide as fine-grained a reading of specific artifacts as possible, and this emphasis may well induce a creative exchange that at times seems to depart from what might plausibly be argued to be happening in a text. Instead, it prompts imaginative or intricately theoretical initiatives on the part of the reader. Structuralists often seem to read for the plot, while deconstructors plot for the read — typically the read that brings out the paradoxes or aporias of plotting itself and indicates how we are read by what we attempt to read.

I have oversimplified somewhat, and a closer investigation of the figures and movements I have mentioned might lead to a fuller appreciation of how they may be of use in elaborating the perspective I am about to enunciate. I would contend that contextualization and dialogic exchange, reading for the plot and plotting for the read, supplement one another in a number of important and, at crucial moments, tense and even conflict-ridden ways in our attempts to read and interpret texts. For one thing, they are different inflections of the transferential relation that binds us to the past and through which the problems we investigate are repeated in displaced and sometimes disguised form in our very discussions of them. Extreme contextualization of the past in its own terms and for its own sake may lead to the denial of transference through total objectification of the other and the constitution of the self either as a cipher for empathetic self-effacement or as a transcendental spectator of a scene fixed in amber. By contrast, unmitigated "presentist" immersion in contemporary discourses, reading strategies, and performative free play may at the limit induce narcissistic obliteration of the other as other and the tendency to act out one's own obsessions or narrow preoccupations. An analogue of working through problems in interpretation would at the very least require a critical and self-critical way of putting into language the tense and shifting relation between contextualization and dialogic exchange. In other words, we must attempt to listen attentively to the voices of the other as we respond in voices that necessarily bear the imprint of our own formative and at times conflict-ridden contexts. But to formulate the point this way is not to make apostrophe a pretext for mythologization or to reify the text as the autonomous bearer of its own readings. It is rather to insist on our implication in a complex interactive process whereby readings and interpretations must be defended by arguments that direct attention to features of the object and engage contrasting understandings of it.

In addition, the very manner in which texts of the past responded to their own multiple contexts makes radical or historicist contextualization a relatively adequate mode of interpretation only with respect to the most banal and reproductive artifacts. Even in these artifacts, reproduction is not simple replication of contexts but does something to them (typically in terms of reproducing and further legitimating an ideology or stereotype) that must be examined carefully. If a text could be totally contextualized, it would paradoxically be ahistorical, for it would exist in a stasis in which it made no difference whatsoever. It would be immobilized in its own era. If contextualization were fully explanatory, texts would be derivative items in which nothing new or different happened. But especially with texts that are good to think with, the work or play on contexts is far-ranging, and it necessarily engages us in dialogic exchange. By giving of themselves, certain texts are especially effective in inducing us to give of ourselves. Thus, certain texts may be exemplary in demonstrating that historical interpretation requires not only contextualization but also the insistent investigation of the variable and never-to-be-fixated limits of contextualization.

Another way to put the point concerning transference, dialogic exchange, and working-through is to say that if we probe far enough, no significant problem is purely anachronistic. Anachronism takes two inversely related forms: projection of the present onto the past and projection of the past onto the present. Objectivity requires that we check projection, but the process of projection cannot be entirely eliminated. It is related to commitment and to intense interest and investment in what we do. In a basic sense, it is entailed by the fact that we are always implicated in the things we analyze and try to understand. The ideal of objectivity should not be made to neutralize the problem of the historian's voice in narration or analysis. Checking projection requires that we listen to the other, not that we efface or transfix the self. It may also require that we examine carefully the complex manner in which the other is in the self and the self in the other. Here an example may be helpful. David Hollinger writes the following in defense of contextualization as the more "authentic" way to understand William James historically:

> Advocates of this or that currently popular epistemology or metaphysical doctrine will claim James as their own, or set him up as a representative defender of some opposing doctrine. The anachronistic readings of James that sometimes result are not difficult to live with, but a more accurate comprehension of what James himself was doing can make a more authentic James available for use in these contemporary debates. This authentic, historical James is also the one we must have if we wish to get right the intellectual history of the United States.
>
> A truism about James is that he worried over the relation of science to religion. Yet this concern has been distant from the minds of most of the philosophers and scholars of the last fifty years who have drawn inspiration from, and sought to interpret, James's work. . . . An accurate reading of James requires that we not screen out as an irrelevant curiosity the anxiety about the fate of religion in an age of science that James frankly shared with most of the people who heard him lecture and bought his books during his lifetime. By taking this anxiety seriously, we can more easily discern in James's texts what I argue here was James's center of intellectual gravity: A radically secular, naturalistic vision of the process by which knowledge is produced, and a hope that religiously satisfying knowledge might still be forthcoming if only enough people would bring to inquiry—and place at risk in it—their religious commitments.[10]

Hollinger is to the point in stressing the limitations of even anodyne "presentist" rational reconstructions that filter out concerns deemed to be irrelevant and reconfigure the past to serve an excessively truncated idea of contemporary interests. And he may well be correct in asserting that "anxiety about the fate of religion in an age of science" was not a concern in the James scholarship to which he refers. But one can criticize these tendencies without identifying contextualization as authentic and confining historical understanding only to the reconstruction of past contexts. One may instead conclude from Hollinger's remarks that philosophers who eliminated religion from the picture were misled and that the historian need not covertly corroborate or at best invert their form of anachronism by identifying authentic historical understanding with an interpretation that itself situates religion and the concern about the relation between science and religion squarely in the past. And one may ask whether a "radically secular, naturalistic vision" may conceal displaced religious elements in the thought of its proponents and itself induce an underestimation of the role of religion in contemporary social life. Hollinger wrote at a time when the revival of religion, at times in its most fundamentalist forms, was already becoming obvious as a feature of contemporary American culture and politics. And he says enough about the historical role of religion in America to indicate that the very belief that religion is a thing of the past is a short-sighted historical judgment. In fact, the relevance of Emerson to the pragmatic tradition may be in placing in the foreground the union of pragmatism and evangelism in American culture—a topic that is both studied and reenacted in Cornel West's 1989 book *The American Evasion of Philosophy: A Genealogy of Pragmatism*.[11] I would even be tempted to say that if you scratch a pragmatist, you may well find an evangelist (or at least an edifying "discourser").

There is, however, another observation to be made in this respect. The fixation on anachronisms tends to obliterate the ways in which the past is repeated in the present with more or less significant variations. This process is crucial to our transferential relation to the past, and only by investigating it closely can we hazard a judgment about just how different a past context or period indeed was. With respect to religion, the obvious question is whether the so-called secularization thesis should be reformulated not in the simplistic form of an identity between religion and secular ideologies or in the tendentious form that leads one to reject as nefarious heresies ideologies one opposes. Rather, secularization should itself be understood as a typically conflictual process of repetition with change—at times disruptive or traumatic change. In opposing a simplistic version of the secularization thesis, Hans Blumenberg may well have offered a better and more psychoanalytically acute interpretation of secularization in terms of reoccupation: an older, typically religious or theological cultural territory or set of concerns is reoccupied or reinvested ("recathected" in Freud's sense) by contemporary modes of thought and practice, which may in the process be deformed or disfigured in unconscious ways.[12] In this sense, the very notion of anachronism, while having certain obvious but significant uses, may be superficial insofar as it diverts attention from the intricate process in which older forms are regenerated or reaffirmed with more or less significant differences over time. One might even venture to say that old problems never die, or even fade away. They tend to return as the repressed. Coming to terms with them requires a process of "working through" that is cognizant of their role and the possibilities or difficulties it creates for interpretation and for life.

The line of thought I have tried to sketch leads to a conception of differential economies of loss and gain that should become objects of debate and options to be actively engaged in different departments and disciplines. Even if one recognizes the claims of both contextual particularization and dialogic exchange, one may strike different balances or imbalances under different circumstances. To the extent one emphasizes the insertion of a text or problem in past contexts, one may well be interested in elaborately detailed features of the inferentially reconstructed past. And one may insist that only through contextualization will one be able to provide the perspective on problems or artifacts that is altogether necessary (although not sufficient) in critically understanding them. At times scholarly erudition may take precedence over criticism and dialogic exchange. And the focus on context—especially on the grand panoramic picture of the immediate time and place—may lead to excessively reductive readings of texts or at least to a directed and very selective use of them.[13] By contrast, an interest in criticism will typically be linked to a desire for pointed, provocative, even micrological readings that renew or at least upset prior ways of understanding a text or problem. One may emphasize the need to generalize within cases, that is, to draw out the implications of local knowledge for larger themes and grander theories. Yet one may also be drawn into the text and its complexities in ways that limit or downplay the role of extensive research into more immediate contexts—perhaps the role of historical understanding in general. Even in the best of cases, the concern for dialogic exchange will probably induce one to stress basic, long-term contexts as they are reworked in texts or to raise the very issue of contextualization in a manner that underscores our implication in the problems we treat.[14]

I have already intimated that the partial contrast between a dialogic exchange with texts and an insertion of them in past contexts should not be promoted to the status of a sheer dichotomy.[15] In fact, it may be mitigated and displaced in a manner I have signaled at certain points—a manner that is becoming a concern among historians and theorists.[16] Aside from stressing the need to work through the tensions among contextualization, textual interpretation, and dialogic exchange, I would note the importance of providing a close, critical reading of contexts themselves that might enable a self-critical exchange with them. In this respect, documents, while not losing their evidentiary function, would be objects of interrogation and analysis, and inquiry into their specific situation and workings would complement and complicate the necessary use of them as sources of information about the past. Instead of restricting one's use of documentary sources to quarries for facts, it might even be desirable to thematize the problem of the nature of documents (notably, such documents as inquisition registers and police reports) in relation both to their historical role in networks of power and authority and to the more or less warranted inferential reconstructions one bases on them. Instead of simply assuming that one's goal is to find order in chaos, to structure and fully explain one's material, or to find meaning in the past, one would rather try to set up an exchange between sources and inferential reconstructions such that the elaboration of a context — including the crucial issue of the appropriate use of language in rendering it — would be constituted as a genuine problem in historical inquiry. This effort — for example, in the study of the Holocaust — might enable one to combat more effectively revisionist abuses that only accentuate the deficiencies of both positivistic method and theories about the "fictive" nature of all interpretive structures and inferential reconstructions.

It would also be desirable to include in one's account selections from unpublished sources and archival material that are sufficient to allow the reader to evaluate one's analysis or narrative. At least equally desirable would be an attempt to give a context to one's approach in terms of one's own subject position and relation to the contemporary conflict of interpretations and reading strategies. Especially with respect to controversial topics, nothing is more misleading for a reader than the impression that an account simply relates the facts or explains a problem without having a formative and ideologically weighted relation to other accounts. This effort to read documents as texts, to pose as a problem the question of the relation between various sources (including memory) and the inferential reconstruction of contexts, and to offer the interlocutor or reader some perspective on oneself in terms of a present context of debate would not transcend all tensions; on the contrary, it would place them in the foreground. It might, however, further the chances of working out a more comprehensive account of problems that would at least counteract the one-sidedness of both historicist contextualism and presentist reprocessing of the past in and through contemporary forms of reading. It would also indicate how various options may engage one another most provocatively and constructively when they incorporate an active awareness of the claims of other interpretive modes and the differential stresses and strains attendant upon any choice in interpretation. Indeed, such a field of forces may give rise to hybrid modes of thought of delicate hue and complex configuration that attest to the way critical thinking is positioned on thresholds, open to its own historicity, and prone to unforeseen transitions.

NOTES

1. See, for example, Terry Eagleton, *Literary Theory: An Introduction* (Minneapolis, 1983);

Peter Stallybrass and Allon White, *The Politics & Poetics of Transgression* (Ithaca, N.Y., 1986); Jane Tompkins, *Sensational Designs: The Cultural Work of American Fiction* (New York, 1985); Henry Louis Gates, Jr., *Figures in Black: Words, Signs, and the "Racial" Self* (New York, 1987); and Houston Baker, *Blues, Ideology, and Afro-American Literature: A Vernacular Theory* (Chicago, 1984). On canonization in general, see Robert von Hallberg, ed., *Canons* (Chicago, 1983). See also Joseph Gibaldi, ed., *Introduction to Scholarship in Modern Languages and Literatures* (New York, 1992), especially Robert Scholes, "Canonicity and Textuality," pp. 138-58, and David Bathrick, "Cultural Studies," pp. 320-40.

2. For an elaboration of this argument, see John Guillory, "Canonical and Non-Canonical: A Critique of the Current Debate," *ELH* 54 (1987): 483-527. In *Professing Literature: An Institutional History* (Chicago, 1987), Gerald Graff questions the extent to which processes such as canonization have in fact been effective in successfully inculcating dominant values, at least in the United States. He writes: "Literary studies have been no beacon of political enlightenment, but they have not been an instrument of dominant ideology and social control either—or, if so, they have been a singularly inefficient one" (p. 14). Scholars with political concerns are prone to overestimate the actual impact of their own areas of study even if only to criticize the results. But one obviously has here a problem that requires extensive empirical research on the level of dissemination and reception.

3. On these problems, see my *Soundings in Critical Theory* (Ithaca, N.Y., 1989). In the recent controversy over the early World War II journalistic articles of Paul de Man, some commentators sympathetic to deconstruction have tended to read markedly symptomatic, propagandizing texts as if they were self-questioning—indeed, to read de Man as if his very early texts were as intricate and self-contestatory as his later ones often are. To some extent, this tendency was unfortunately authorized by Derrida in "Like the Sound of the Deep within a Shell: Paul de Man's War" (*Critical Inquiry* 14 [1988]: 590-652; reprinted in Werner Hamacher, Neil Hertz, and Thomas Keenan, eds., *Responses: On Paul de Man's Wartime Journalism* [Lincoln, Neb., and London, 1989], pp. 127-64).

4. See, for example, Perez Zagorin, "Historiography and Postmodernism: Reconsiderations" (*History and Theory* 24 [1990]: 263-74), in which rhetorical analysis of historical texts tends by and large to be reduced to—and dismissed as—an "aestheticization" of history, and any attempt to foreground the problem of the historian's use of language is seen as diversionary with respect to the central concerns of historiography. For a contrasting view, see Philippe Carrard, *Poetics of the New History: French Historical Discourse from Braudel to Chartier* (Baltimore and London, 1992). See also my forthcoming review of this book in the *Journal of Modern History*. On the problem of transference, see my "Psychoanalysis and History" in *Soundings in Critical Theory*, pp. 30-66. See also Saul Friedlander, "Trauma, Transference, and 'Working Through' in Writing the History of the *Shoah*" in *History & Memory* 4 (1992): 39-59, and Peter Loewenberg, *Decoding the Past* (New York, 1983). In transference, as I adapt the term from psychoanalysis, the historian or analyst tends to repeat with more or less significant variations the problems active in the object of study. The point is not to deny transference or simply to act it out but to attempt to work through it in a critical manner.

5. Especially significant in this respect is the Ideas in Context series edited by Richard Rorty, J. B. Schneewind, Quentin Skinner, and Wolf Lepenies for Cambridge University Press. For the more interpretive approach to social science, which has probably been strongest in professional anthropology, see, for example, Paul Rabinow and William M. Sullivan, eds., *Interpretive Social Science: A Reader* (Berkeley, Calif., 1979), and James Clifford and George E. Marcus, eds., *Writing Culture: The Poetics and Politics of Ethnography* (Berkeley, Calif., 1986).

6. Discussion of theoretical and methodological problems has continued to be combined with monographic research in subsequent issues of the journal under the excellent editorship of David L. Ransel. With particular reference to certain arguments in the present essay, see Russell

Jacoby, "A New Intellectual History?" (*American Historical Review* 97 [1992]: 405-24), and Dominick LaCapra, "Intellectual History and Its Ways" (ibid., pp. 425-39).

7. *Illuminations*, edited and with an introduction by Hannah Arendt (1955; New York,
1969), pp. 253-64. Benjamin writes in Thesis VII (p. 256): "To historians who wish to relive an
era, Fustel de Coulanges recommends that they blot out everything they know about the later
course of history. There is no better way of characterizing the method with which historical
materialism has broken." It is often easier to know what Benjamin is criticizing in the Theses
than what he is advocating. But I take his critique of full empathy in the attempt to reconstruct
the past purely in its own terms and for its own sake to imply that it is only through a diacritical
comparison with later times that one can even attempt to reconstruct and understand what
something meant at its own time. I would also take it to imply that contextualization is most
thought provoking when it brings out obscured features or submerged possibilities of the past
that still (if only by contrast) raise questions for us. And contextualization must be supple-
mented by critical dialogic exchange if we are to elicit and probe the past's unexamined assumptions and belated effects, thereby enabling us to put them in self-critical contact with our
own assumptions (whose very disclosure may be facilitated by our attempt to articulate past
assumptions).

8. Jacques Derrida, *On Grammatology*, trans. Gayatri Chakravorty Spivak (1967; Baltimore
and London, 1974).

9. *Reading for the Plot* is of course the title of Peter Brooks's important book (New York,
1984). The book is dedicated to Paul de Man, one of the exemplars of plotting for the read.

10. David Hollinger, *In the American Province: Studies in the History and Historiography of Ideas*
(1985; Baltimore and London, 1989), pp. 3-4.

11. Cornel West, *The American Evasion of Philosophy: A Genealogy of Pragmatism* (Madison,
Wis., 1989).

12. See *The Legitimacy of the Modern Age*, trans. Robert M. Wallace (1966; Cambridge,
Mass., and London, 1985). The notion of reoccupation offers an obvious way of reading the
first of Walter Benjamin's "Theses on the Philosophy of History": "The story is told of an
automaton constructed in such a way that it could play a winning game of chess, answering
each move of an opponent with a countermove. A puppet in Turkish attire and with a hookah
in its mouth sat before a chessboard placed on a large table. A system of mirrors created the
illusion that this table was transparent from all sides. Actually, a little hunchback who was an
expert chess player sat inside and guided the puppet's hand by means of strings. One can imagine a philosophical counterpart to this device. The puppet called 'historical materialism' is to
win all the time. It can easily be a match for anyone if it enlists the services of theology, which
today, as we know, is wizened and has to keep out of sight" (*Illuminations*, p. 253).

13. Excessively reductive reading has, I think, been prevalent in the historical profession. A
recent and especially impressive example is Richard Wolin's important book *The Politics of Being: The Political Thought of Martin Heidegger* (New York, 1990). Wolin succinctly and cogently
puts forth contextual considerations that must be taken into account in a reading of Heidegger,
and he convincingly argues that recent disclosures concerning the significance of Heidegger's
affiliation with the Nazis should foster a hermeneutics of suspicion in reading Heidegger's
texts. But he also pursues the more dubious goal of employing Heidegger's Nazi affiliation to
thoroughly discredit all of his thought from *Being and Time* (1927) to his latest writings, thereby
denying the role of all tensions and counterforces in his work, including those that might be
argued to question the bases of his affiliation with the Nazis. Wolin in effect reverses the tendency to read markedly symptomatic, ideologically saturated texts as if they were self-critical
by emphatically reading even texts with certain critical currents as if they were predominantly
if not totally symptomatic.

14. The concern with dialogic exchange has in different ways characterized the work of
Mikhail Bakhtin, Martin Heidegger, Hans-Georg Gadamer, and Jacques Derrida. I have tried

in my own work to explore selectively and critically the relevance of their approaches for historiography and to relate them to the problem of contextualization.

15. I offer the following incomplete list of texts in which the tension between dialogic exchange and contextualization is addressed or negotiated in a thought-provoking manner: Roger Chartier, "Intellectual History or Sociocultural History? The French Trajectories," in *Modern European Intellectual History: Reappraisals and New Perspectives*, ed. Dominick LaCapra and Steven L. Kaplan (Ithaca, N.Y., and London, 1982), pp. 13–46; Saul Friedlander, *Reflections of Nazism: An Essay on Kitsch and Death*, trans. Thomas Weyr (New York, 1984); François Furet, *Interpreting the French Revolution*, trans. Elborg Forster (Cambridge, 1981); Martin Jay, *Fin-de-Siècle Socialism and Other Essays* (New York and London, 1988); Joan Scott, *Gender and the Politics of History* (New York, 1988); Eric L. Santner, *Stranded Objects: Mourning, Memory, and Film in Postwar Germany* (Ithaca, N.Y., and London, 1990); and Richard Terdiman, *Discourse/Counter-Discourse: The Theory and Practice of Symbolic Resistance in Nineteenth-Century France* (Ithaca, N.Y., and London, 1985). I would also make special mention of Karl Marx's *Eighteenth Brumaire* and (despite its very reductive and tendentious reading of Enlightenment figures) Alexis de Tocqueville's *Old Regime and the French Revolution*.

16. See, for example, Carrard, *Poetics of the New History*, especially pp. 121-33.

Part III
Popular Films and Historical Memory

The Historical Film:
Looking at the Past in a Postliterate Age
Robert A. Rosenstone

Historians and Film

Let's be blunt and admit it: historical films trouble and disturb professional historians. Have troubled and disturbed historians for a long time. Listen to Louis Gottschalk of the University of Chicago, writing in 1935 to the president of Metro–Goldwyn–Mayer: "If the cinema art is going to draw its subjects so generously from history, it owes it to its patrons and its own higher ideals to achieve greater accuracy. No picture of a historical nature ought to be offered to the public until a reputable historian has had a chance to criticize and revise it."[1]

How can we think of this letter today? As touching? Naive? A window onto a simpler age that could actually conceive of Hollywood as having "higher ideals"? All of these? But if the attitude seems dated, the sentiments surely are not. Most historians today would be capable of saying, or thinking, the same thing. Give reputable scholars the chance to criticize and revise scripts, and we will surely have better history on the screen.

Question: Why do historians distrust the historical film?

The overt answers: Films are inaccurate. They distort the past. They fictionalize, trivialize, and romanticize people, events, and movements. They falsify history.

The covert answers: Film is out of the control of historians. Film shows we do not own the past. Film creates a historical world with which books cannot compete, at least for popularity. Film is a disturbing symbol of an increasingly postliterate world (in which people can read but won't).

Impolite question: How many professional historians, when it comes to

141

fields outside their areas of expertise, learn about the past from film? How many Americanists know the great Indian leader primarily from *Gandhi*? Or Europeanists the American Civil War from *Glory*, or—horrors!—*Gone with the Wind*? Or Asianists early modern France from *The Return of Martin Guerre*?

Dislike (or fear) of the visual media has not prevented historians from becoming increasingly involved with film in recent years: film has invaded the classroom, though it is difficult to specify if this is due to the "laziness" of teachers, the postliteracy of students, or the realization that film can do something written words cannot. Scores, perhaps hundreds, of historians have become peripherally involved in the process of making films: some as advisers on film projects, dramatic and documentary, sponsored by the National Endowment for the Humanities (which requires that filmmakers create panels of advisers but—to disappoint Gottschalk—makes no provision that the advice actually be taken); others as talking heads in historical documentaries. Sessions on history and film have become a routine part of academic conferences (such as the one that gave birth to this book), as well as annual conventions of major professional groups like the Organization of American Historians and the American Historical Association. Reviews of historical films have become features of academic journals: *American Historical Review, Journal of American History, Radical History Review, Middle Eastern Studies Association Bulletin, Latin American Research Review*.[2]

All this activity has hardly led to a consensus on how to evaluate the contribution of the "historical" film to "historical understanding." Nobody has yet begun to think systematically about what Hayden White has dubbed *historiophoty*—"the representation of history and our thought about it in visual images and filmic discourse."[3] In essays, books, and reviews, the historical film is dealt with piecemeal. Yet it is fair to say that two major approaches predominate.

The explicit approach takes motion pictures to be reflections of the social and political concerns of the era in which they were made. Typical is the anthology *American History/American Film*, which finds "history" in such works as *Rocky* (problems of blue-collar workers), *Invasion of the Body Snatchers* (conspiracy and conformity in the fifties), *Viva Zapata* (the cold war), and *Drums along the Mohawk* (persistence of American ideals).[4] This strategy insists that any film can be situated "historically." As indeed it can. But it also provides no specific role for the film that wants to talk about historical issues. Nor does it distinguish such a film from any other kind of film. Which leads to this question: why not treat written works of history in the same way? They, too, reflect the concerns of the era in which they were made, yet we historians take their contents at face value and not simply as a reflection of something else. Why consider history books in terms of contents and historical films in terms of reflections? Is it that the screen itself only reflects images? That the analogy to Plato's cave is too close to allow us to trust what messages the shadows deliver?

The implicit approach essentially sees the motion picture as a book transferred to the screen, subject to the same sorts of judgments about data, verifiability, argument, evidence, and logic that we use for written history. Involved here are two problematic assumptions: first, that the current practice of written history is the only possible way of understanding the relationship of past to present; and, second, that written history mirrors "reality." If the first of these assumptions is arguable, the second is not. Certainly by now we all know that history is never a mirror but a construction, congeries of data pulled together or "constituted" by some larger project or vision or theory that may not be articulated but is nonetheless embedded in the particular way history is practiced.

Let me put it another way: historians tend to use written works of history to critique visual history as if that written history were itself something solid and unproblematic. They have not treated written history as a mode of thought, a process, a particular way of using the traces of the past to make that past meaningful in the present.

The notion of history as constituted and problematic is hardly news to anyone familiar with current debates in criticism, but it needs to be stressed. For to talk about the failures and triumphs, strengths and weaknesses and possibilities of history on film, it is necessary to pull back the camera from a two-shot in which we see history on film and history on the page square off against each other, and to include in our new frame the larger realm of past and present in which both sorts of history are located and to which both refer. Seen this way, the question cannot be, Does the historical film convey facts or make arguments as well as written history? Rather, the appropriate questions are: What sort of historical world does each film construct and how does it construct that world? How can we make judgments about that construction? How and what does that historical construction mean to us? After these three questions are answered, we may wish to ask a fourth: How does the historical world on the screen relate to written history?

Varieties of Historical Film

We cannot talk about the historical "film" in the singular because the term covers a variety of ways of rendering the past on the screen. (Written history, too, comes in different subcategories—narrative, analytic, quantitative—but we have the notion that they all are part of some larger story about the past. Film seems more fragmented, perhaps because there exist no broad film histories of nations, eras, or civilizations that provide a historical framework for specific films.) It is possible to put history on film into a number of categories—history as drama, history as antidrama, history without heroes, history as spectacle, history as essay, personal history, oral history, postmodern history—but for heuristic purposes this essay will collapse all of these into three broad categories: history as drama, history as document, and history as experiment. Most of what follows will focus on history as drama, the oldest and most common form of historical film.

If you say "historical film," history as drama is probably what comes to mind. A staple of the screen ever since motion pictures began to tell stories, this form of film has been regularly produced all over the world—in the United States, France, Italy, Japan, China, Russia, India—wherever films are made. Some of the most beloved motion pictures have been dramatized history, or at least dramas set in the past. Among them are the kind of works that have given the historical film such a bad reputation—*Gone with the Wind, Cleopatra, The Private Life of Henry VIII*.

It has been suggested by Natalie Davis that history as drama can be divided into two broad categories: films based on documentable persons or events or movements (*The Last Emperor, Gandhi, JFK*) and those whose central plot and characters are fictional, but whose historical setting is intrinsic to the story and meaning of the work (*Dangerous Liaisons, The Molly Maguires, Black Robe*).[5] But this distinction does not in fact have much explanatory power, for the categories quickly break down. A recent film, *Glory*, which I will analyze later in this essay, follows the common strategy of placing fictional characters next to historical characters in settings alternately documentable and wholly invented.

History as document is a more recent form than history as drama. Growing—at least in the United States—out of the social problem documentary of the thirties (*The Plow That Broke the Plains*), it was given a boost by the post–World War II patriotic retrospective (*Victory at Sea*), and an even bigger boost by public money, which has been funneled by the National Endowment for the Humanities into historical films in the past two decades. In the most common form, a narrator (and/or historical witnesses or experts) speaks while we see recent footage of historical sites intercut with older footage, often from newsreels, along with photos, artifacts, paintings, graphics, newspaper and magazine clippings.

Professional historians trust history as document rather more than history as drama because it seems closer in spirit and practice to written history—seems both to deliver "facts" and to make some sort of traditional historical argument, whether as a feature (*The Wobblies, Huey Long, Statue of Liberty*) or as a series (*The Civil War, Eyes on the Prize*). But a major problem for documentary lies precisely in the promise of its most obviously "historical" materials. All those old photographs and all that newsreel footage are saturated with a prepackaged emotion: nostalgia. The claim is that we can see (and, presumably, feel) what people in the past saw and felt. But that is hardly the case. For we can always see and feel much that the people in the photos and newsreels could not see: that their clothing and automobiles were old-fashioned, that their landscape lacked skyscrapers and other contemporary buildings, that their world was black and white (and haunting) and gone.

History as experiment is an awkward term for a variety of filmic forms, both dramatic and documentary and sometimes a combination of the two. Included here are works made by avant-garde and independent filmmakers in the United States and Europe as well as in former communist countries and the Third World. Some of these films have become well known, even beloved (Sergei Eisenstein's *Oktober* and *Battleship Potemkin*, Roberto Rossellini's *The Rise of Louis XIV*). Some have achieved local or regional fame (*Ceddo* by Senegal's Ousmane Sembene, *Quilombo* by Brazil's Carlos Diegues). Others remain intellectual and cinematic cult films, more written about by theorists than seen by audiences (Alexander Kluge's *Die Patriotin*, Trinh T. Minh-ha's *Surname Viet Given Name Nam*, Alex Cox's *Walker*, Jill Godmilow's *Far from Poland*).

What these films have in common (apart from lack of exposure) is that all are made in opposition to the mainstream Hollywood film. Not just to the subject matter of Hollywood but to its way of constructing a world on the screen. All struggle in one or more ways against the codes of representation of the standard film. All refuse to see the screen as a transparent "window" onto a "realistic" world.

Why, you may ask, discuss such films? Why take time for works few people want to or can see? Because, as I have argued elsewhere, such works provide the possibility of what might be called a "serious" historical film, a historical film that parallels—but is very different from—the "serious" or scholarly written history, just as the standard Hollywood film parallels more popular, uncritical forms of written history, the kind history "buffs" like. At its best, history as experiment promises a revisioning of what we mean by the word *history*![6]

How Mainstream Films Construct
a Historical World

The world that the standard or mainstream film constructs is, like the world we live in and the air we breathe, so familiar that we rarely think about how it is put together. That, of course, is the point. Films want to make us think they are reality. Yet the reality we see on the screen is neither inevitable nor somehow natural to the camera, but a vision creatively constructed out of bits and pieces of images taken from the surface of a world. Even if we know this already, we conveniently forget it in order to participate in the experience that cinema provides.

Less obvious is the fact that these bits and pieces are stuck together according to certain codes of representation, conventions of film that have been developed to create what may be called "cinematic realism"—a realism made up of certain kinds of shots in certain kinds of sequences seamlessly edited together and underscored by a sound track to give the viewer a sense that nothing (rather than everything) is being manipulated to create a world on screen in which we can all feel at home.

The reason to point to the codes of cinema (which have a vast literature of their own) is to emphasize the fundamental fiction that underlies the standard historical film—the notion that we can somehow look through the window of the screen directly at a "real" world, present or past. This "fiction" parallels a major convention of written history: its documentary or empirical element, which insists on the "reality" of the world it creates and analyzes. The written work of history, particularly the grand narrative, also attempts to put us into the world of the past, but our presence in a past created by words never seems as immediate as our presence in a past created on the screen.

History as drama and history as document are, in their standard forms, linked by this notion of the screen as a window onto a realistic world. It is true that the documentary—with its mixture of materials in different time zones, with its images of the past and its talking heads speaking in the present—often provides a window into two (or more) worlds. But those worlds share, both with each other and with history as drama, an identical structure and identical notions of document, chronology, cause, effect, and consequence. Which means that in talking about how the mainstream film creates its world, it is possible to make six points that apply equally to the dramatic film and the documentary.

1. The mainstream film tells history as a story, a tale with a beginning, middle, and an end. A tale that leaves you with a moral message and (usually) a

feeling of uplift. A tale embedded in a larger view of history that is always progressive, if sometimes Marxist (another form of progress).

To put it bluntly, no matter what the historical film, be the subject matter slavery, the Holocaust, or the Khmer Rouge, the message delivered on the screen is almost always that things are getting better or have gotten better or both. This is true of dramatic films (*Glory, Reds, The Last Emperor*) and true of documentaries (*The Civil War*). It is also true (perhaps especially true) of radical documentaries like *The Wobblies, Seeing Red, The Good Fight,* and other hymns of praise to lost causes.

Often the message is not direct. A film about the horrors of the Holocaust or the failure of certain idealistic or radical movements may in fact seem to be a counterexample. But such works are always structured to leave us feeling Aren't we lucky we did not live in those benighted times? Isn't it nice that certain people kept the flag of hope alive? Aren't we much better off today? Among those few films that leave a message of doubt about meaningful change or human progress, one might point to *Radio Bikini*, with its lingering questions about the possibility of controlling atomic energy or regaining an innocent faith in government, the military, or the scientific establishment. Or to *JFK*, with its worries about the future of American democracy, though the very fact that a big star like Kevin Costner, playing New Orleans attorney Jim Garrison, expresses these doubts tends to reassure us that the problems of the security state will be exposed and solved.

2. Film insists on history as the story of individuals. Either men or women (but usually men) who are already renowned, or men and women who are made to seem important because they have been singled out by the camera and appear before us in such a large image on the screen. Those not already famous are common people who have done heroic or admirable things, or who have suffered unusually bad circumstances of exploitation and oppression. The point: both dramatic features and documentaries put individuals in the forefront of the historical process. Which means that the solution of their personal problems tends to substitute itself for the solution of historical problems. More accurately, the personal becomes a way of avoiding the often difficult or insoluble social problems pointed out by the film. In *The Last Emperor* the happiness of a single "reeducated" man stands for the entire Chinese people. In *Reds*, the final resolution of a stormy love affair between two Americans becomes a way of avoiding the contradictions of the Bolshevik Revolution. In *Radio Bikini*, the fate of a single sailor stands for all of those who were tainted with radiation from the atomic-bomb tests of Operation Crossroads.

3. Film offers us history as the story of a closed, completed, and simple past.

It provides no alternative possibilities to what we see happening on the screen, admits of no doubts, and promotes each historical assertion with the same degree of confidence. A subtle film like *The Return of Martin Guerre* may hint at hidden historical alternatives, at data not mentioned and stories untold, but such possibilities are never openly explored on the screen.

This confidence of the screen in its own assertions can trouble even historians who are sympathetic to the visual media. Natalie Davis, the historical consultant on the film, worries about the cost of the "powerful simplicity" of *Martin Guerre*: "Where was there room in this beautiful and compelling cinematographic recreation of a [sixteenth-century] village for the uncertainties, the 'perhapses,' the 'may-have-beens' to which the historian has recourse when the evidence is inadequate or perplexing?"[7] Davis followed her work on the film by writing a book (with the same title) in order to restore this important dimension to the story of Martin Guerre. But anyone other than an expert viewing a historical film is confronted with a linear story that is unproblematic and uncontested in its view of what happened and why.

This is equally true of the documentary, despite the fact that it may call on various witnesses and experts who express alternative or opposing points of view. Through editing, these differences are never allowed to get out of hand or call into question the main theme of the work. The effect is much like that of dissenting minor characters in a drama, people whose opposing positions heighten the meaning of whatever tasks the heroes undertake. Ultimately, these alternative viewpoints make no real impact. They only serve to underline the truth and solidity of the main world or argument.

4. Film emotionalizes, personalizes, and dramatizes history. Through actors and historical witnesses, it gives us history as triumph, anguish, joy, despair, adventure, suffering, and heroism. Both dramatized works and documentaries use the special capabilities of the medium—the close-up of the human face, the quick juxtaposition of disparate images, the power of music and sound effect—to heighten and intensify the feelings of the audience about the events depicted on the screen. (Written history is, of course, not devoid of emotion, but usually it points to emotion rather than inviting us to experience it. A historian has to be a very good writer to make us feel emotion while the poorest of filmmakers can easily touch our feelings.) Film thus raises the following issues: To what extent do we wish emotion to become a historical category? Part of historical understanding? Does history gain something by becoming empathic? Does film, in short, add to our understanding of the past by making us feel immediately and deeply about particular historical people, events, and situations?

5. Film so obviously gives us the "look" of the past—of buildings, land-

scapes, and artifacts—that we may not see what this does to our sense of history. So it is important to stress that more than simply the "look" of things, film provides a sense of how common objects appeared when they were in use. In film, period clothing does not hang limply on a dummy in a glass case, as it does in a museum; rather, it confines, emphasizes, and expresses the moving body. In film, tools, utensils, weapons, and furniture are not items on display or images reproduced on the pages of books, but objects that people use and misuse, objects they depend upon and cherish, objects that can help to define their livelihoods, identities, lives, and destinies.

This capability of film slides into what might be called false historicity. Or the myth of facticity, a mode on which Hollywood has long depended. This is the mistaken notion that mimesis is all, that history is in fact no more than a "period look," that things themselves *are* history, rather than *become* history because of what they mean to people of a particular time and place. The baleful Hollywood corollary: as long as you get the look right, you may freely invent characters and incidents and do whatever you want to the past to make it more interesting.

6. Film shows history as process. The world on the screen brings together things that, for analytic or structural purposes, written history often has to split apart. Economics, politics, race, class, and gender all come together in the lives and moments of individuals, groups, and nations. This characteristic of film throws into relief a certain convention—one might call it a "fiction"—of written history. The analytic strategy that fractures the past into distinct chapters, topics, and categories. That treats, say, gender in one chapter, race in another, economy in a third. Daniel Walkowitz points out that written history often compartmentalizes "the study of politics, family life, or social mobility." Film, by contrast, "provides an integrative image. History in film becomes what it most centrally is: a process of changing social relationships where political and social questions—indeed, all aspects of the past, including the language used—are interwoven."[8] A character like Bertrande de Rols in *Martin Guerre* is at once a peasant, a woman, a wife, a property owner, a mother, a Catholic (but possibly a Protestant), a lover, a resident of Languedoc, a subject of Francis I of France.

How Experimental Films Construct a Historical World

The only collective way to characterize history as experiment is as films of opposition: opposition to mainstream practice, to Hollywood codes of "realism" and storytelling, to the kind of film described above. Certainly most experimental films will include some of the six characteristics of the standard film, but each will also attack or violate more than one of the mainstream conventions. Among films defined as history as experiment, it is possible to find the following: works that are analytic, unemotional, distanced, multicausal; historical worlds that are expressionist, surrealist, disjunctive, postmodern; histories that do not just show the past but also talk about how and what it means to the filmmaker (or to us) today.

How does history as experiment contest the characteristics of mainstream film? Here are some examples:

1. History as a story set in the framework of (moral) progress: Director Claude Lanzmann suggests in *Shoah* that the Holocaust was a product not of madness but of modernization, rationality, efficiency—that evil comes from progress. Alex Cox, in *Walker*, highlights the interpenetration of past and present and points to Manifest Destiny (with its assumptions of political and moral superiority and uplift) not as an impulse confined to pre-Civil War America but as a continuing part of our relationships with Central America.[9]

2. History as a story of individuals: Soviet directors in the twenties, particularly Eisenstein in *Potemkin* and *Oktober*, created "collectivist" histories in which the mass is center stage and individuals emerge only briefly as momentary exemplars of larger trends (much as they do in written history). The same strategy has been pursued more recently by Latin American filmmakers (Jorge Sanjines in *Power of the People*, Carlos Diegues in *Quilombo*).

3. History as a closed, uncontested story: Jill Godmilow in *Far from Poland* presents a "history" of the Solidarity movement through competing voices and images that refuse to resolve into a single story with a single meaning. Chris Marker in *Sans Soleil* and Trinh T. Minh-ha in *Surname Viet Given Name Nam* both dispense with story in favor of historical incident, pastiche, rumination, essay.

4. History as emotional, personal, dramatic: Roberto Rossellini made a series of sumptuously mounted but wholly de-dramatized films—including *The Rise of Louis XIV* and *The Age of the Medici*—in which amateur actors mouth lines rather than act them. The Brazilian Glauber Rocha achieves a similar Brechtian, distanced, unemotional past in such works as *Antonio Das Mortes* and *Black God, White Devil*.

5. History with a "period look": Claude Lanzmann in *Shoah* tells a history of the Holocaust without a single historical image from the thirties or forties; everything was shot in the eighties, when the film was made. The same is largely true of Hans-Jürgen Syberberg's *Hitler—A Film from Germany*, which re-creates the world of the Third Reich on a soundstage with puppets, parts of sets, props, actors, random historical objects, all illuminated by back-projected images.

6. History as process: Director Alexander Kluge in *Die Patriotin* creates history as a series of disjunctive images and data, a kind of collage or post-modern pastiche. Juan Downey in *Hard Times and Culture* uses a similar approach in a study of fin-de-siècle Vienna. Chris Marker in *Sans Soleil* envisions the past as made up of disconnected, synchronous, and erasable events.

History as experiment does not make the same claim on us as does the realist film. Rather than opening a window directly onto the past, it opens a window onto a different way of thinking about the past. The aim is not to tell everything, but to point to past events, or to converse about history, or to show why history should be meaningful to people in the present. Experimental films rarely sanitize, nationalize, or reify the past, though they often ideologize it. They tend to make bits and pieces of our historical experience accessible, sometimes in all its confusion. Such films rarely claim to be the only or the last word on their subject; many hope to make us think about the importance of a subject ignored by written history.

Experimental films may help to revision what we mean by history. Not tied to "realism," they bypass the demands for veracity, evidence, and argument that are a normal component of written history and go on to explore new and original ways of thinking the past. Although such films are not popular, and although "reading" them can at first seem difficult for those who expect "realism," their breakthroughs often are incorporated into the vocabulary of the mainstream film. The revolutionary montage effects of Eisenstein were long ago swallowed up by Hollywood. More recently, a German film, *The Nasty Girl*, uses a variety of avant-garde techniques (back projection rather than sets, composite shots, overtly aburdist elements) to portray the continuing desire of middle-class Germans to deny local complicity with the horrors of the Third Reich.

Reading and Judging the Historical Film

Our sense of the past is shaped and limited by the possibilities and practices of the medium in which that past is conveyed, be it the printed page, the spoken word, the painting, the photograph, the moving image. Which means that whatever historical understanding the mainstream film can provide will be shaped and limited by the conventions of the closed story, the notion of progress, the emphasis on individuals, the single interpretation, the heightening of emotional states, the focus on surfaces.

These conventions mean that history on film will create a past different from the one provided by written history; indeed, they mean that history on film will always violate the norms of written history. To obtain the full benefits of the motion picture — dramatic story, character, look, emotional intensity, process — that is, to use film's power to the fullest, is to ensure alterations in the way we think of the past. The question then becomes Do we learn anything worth learning by approaching the past through the conventions of the mainstream film (conventions that are, through global Hollywoodization, understood virtually everywhere in the world)?

A slight detour: it must always be remembered that history on film is not a discipline in which historians participate (to any great extent). It is a "field" whose standards historians may police but, with rare exceptions, only as onlookers. When we historians explore the historical film, it is "history" as practiced by others. Which raises the ominous question By what right do filmmakers speak of the past, by what right do they do "history"? The answer is liberating or frightening, depending on your point of view. Filmmakers speak of the past because, for whatever reasons — personal, artistic, political, monetary — they choose to speak. They speak the way historians did before the era of professional training in history, before history was a "discipline." Today the historian speaks by virtue of this discipline, by virtue of special training and the standards of a profession. Filmmakers have no such standard training, and no common approach to history. Few, if any, devote more than a minor part of their careers to history; it is more likely that they are moved over the years to make one or two historical statements on film. (Though some major directors have devoted major parts of their careers to history, including Roberto Rossellini, Akira Kurosawa, Masahiro Shinoda, Carlos Diegues, Ousmane Sembene, John Sayles, and Oliver Stone.) One result: history on film will always be a more personal and quirky reflection on the meaning of the past than is the work of written history.

The haphazard nature of history on film, and the lack of professional control, makes it all the more necessary that historians who care about public history learn how to "read" and "judge" film. Learn how to mediate between the historical world of the filmmaker and that of the historian. This means that historians will have to reconsider the standards for history. Or learn to negotiate between our standards and those of filmmakers. We will have to adapt to film practice in order to criticize, to judge what is good and bad, to specify what can be learned from film about our relationship to the past. The film world will not do this, for it has no ongoing stake in history (though some individual filmmakers do). The best we historians can hope for is that individual filmmakers will continue to create meaningful historical films that contribute to our understanding of the past. For only from studying how these films work can we begin to learn how to judge the historical film.

Among the many issues to face in learning how to judge the historical film, none is more important than the issue of invention. Central to understanding history as drama, this is the key issue. The most controversial. The one that sets history on film most apart from written history, which in principle eschews fiction (beyond the basic fiction that people, movements, and nations occurred in stories that are linear and moral). If we can find a way to accept and judge the inventions involved in any dramatic film, then we can accept lesser alterations—the omissions, the conflations—that make history on film so different from written history.

History as drama is shot through with fiction and invention from the smallest details to largest events. Take something simple, like the furnishings in a room where a historical personage sits—say Robert Gould Shaw, the chief character in *Glory*, a colonel and leader of the Fifty-fourth Regiment of African-American troops in the American Civil War. Or take some process, such as the training of the black volunteers who served under Shaw, or the reconstruction of the battles they fought. The room and the sequences are approximate rather than literal representations. They say this is more or less the way a room looked in 1862; these are the sorts of artifacts that might have been in such a room. This is more or less the way such soldiers trained, and the battles they fought must have looked something like this. The point: the camera's need to fill out the specifics of a particular historical scene, or to create a coherent (and moving) visual sequence, will always ensure large doses of invention in the historical film.

The same is true of character: all films will include fictional people or invented elements of character. The very use of an actor to "be" someone will always be a kind of fiction. If the person is "historical," the realistic film says what cannot truly be said: that this is how this person looked, moved, and sounded. If the individual has been created to exemplify a group of historical people (a worker during a strike, a shopkeeper during a revolution, a common soldier on a battlefield) a double fiction is involved: this is how this sort of person (whom we have created) looked, moved, and sounded. Both can obviously be no more than approximations of particular historical individuals, approximations that carry out some sense that we already have about how such people acted, moved, sounded, and behaved.

The same is true of incident: here invention is inevitable for a variety of reasons—to keep the story moving, to maintain intensity of feeling, to simplify complexity of events into plausible dramatic structure that will fit within filmic time constraints. Different kinds of fictional moves are involved here, moves we can label Compression, Condensation, Alteration, and Metaphor.

Consider this example: when Robert Gould Shaw was offered command of the Fifty-fourth, he was in the field in Maryland, and he turned down the offer by letter. A couple of days later, urged by his abolitionist father, he changed his mind and accepted the position. To show the internal conflict expressed in this change within a dramatic context, *Glory* compresses Gould's hesitation into a single scene at a party in Boston. The actor, Matthew Broderick, uses facial expression and body language to show Gould's inner conflict. When he is offered the command by the governor of Massachusetts, he says something noncommital and asks to be excused. There follows a scene with another officer, a kind of alter ego, an officer who voices Shaw's own unspoken doubts about the costs of taking such a command. These doubts register on Broderick's face, and we literally watch Shaw make this difficult decision, see that accepting the commission is a matter of conviction triumphing over fear. All of this scene, including the fellow officer, is invented, yet it is an invention that does no more than alter and compress the spirit of the documentable events into a particular dramatic form. In such a scene, film clearly does not reflect a truth—it creates one.

The difference between fiction and history is this: both tell stories, but the latter is a true story. Question: Need this be a "literal" truth, an exact copy of what took place in the past? Answer: In film, it can never be. And how about the printed page, is literal truth possible there? No. A description of a battle or a strike or a revolution is hardly a literal rendering of that series of events. Some sort of "fiction" or convention is involved here, one that allows a selection of evidence to stand for a larger historical experience, one that allows a small sampling of reports to represent the collective experience of thousands, tens of thousands, even millions who took part in or were affected by documentable events. One may call this convention Condensation too.

But isn't there a difference between Condensation and invention? Isn't creating character and incident different from condensing events? Is it not destructive of "history?" Not history on film. On the screen, history must be fictional in order to be true!

Why? Because filmic "literalism" is impossible. Yes, film may show us the world, or the surface of part of the world, but it can never provide a literal rendition of events that took place in the past. Can never be an exact replica of what happened (as if we knew exactly what happened). Of course, historical recounting has to be based on what literally happened, but the recounting itself can never be literal. Not on the screen and not, in fact, in the written word.

The word works differently from the image. The word can provide vast amounts of data in a small space. The word can generalize, talk of great abstractions like revolution, evolution, and progress, and make us believe that these things exist. (They do not, at least not as things, except upon the page.) To talk of such things is not to talk literally, but to talk in a symbolic or general way about the past. Film, with its need for a specific image, cannot make general statements about revolution or progress. Instead, film must summarize, synthesize, generalize, symbolize—in images. The best we can hope for is that historical data on film will be summarized with inventions and images that are apposite. Filmic generalizations will have to come through various techniques of condensation, synthesis, and symbolization. It is the historian's task to learn how to "read" this filmic historical vocabulary.

Clearly, we must read by new standards. What should they be? At the outset, we must accept that film cannot be seen as a window onto the past. What happens on screen can never be more than an approximation of what was said and done in the past; what happens on screen does not depict, but rather points to, the events of the past. This means that it is necessary for us to learn to judge the ways in which, through invention, film summarizes vast amounts of data or symbolizes complexities that otherwise could not be shown. We must recognize that film will always include images that are at once invented and true; true in that they symbolize, condense, or summarize larger amounts of data; true in that they impart an overall meaning of the past that can be verified, documented, or reasonably argued.

And how do we know what can be verified, documented, or reasonably argued? From the ongoing discourse of history; from the existing body of historical texts; from their data and arguments. Which is only to say that any "historical" film, like any work of written, graphic, or oral history, enters a body of preexisting knowledge and debate. To be considered "historical," rather than simply a costume drama that uses the past as an exotic setting for romance and adventure, a film must engage, directly or obliquely, the issues, ideas, data, and arguments of the ongoing discourse of history. Like the book, the historical film cannot exist in a state of historical innocence, cannot indulge in capricious invention, cannot ignore the findings and assertions and arguments of what we already know from other sources. Like any work of history, a film must be judged in terms of the knowledge of the past that we already possess. Like any work of history, it must situate itself within a body of other works, the ongoing (multimedia) debate over the importance of events and the meaning of the past.

False Invention/True Invention

Let me compare two films that invent freely as they depict historical events—*Mississippi Burning*, which uses "false" invention (ignores the discourse of history), and *Glory*, which uses "true" invention (engages the discourse of history).

Mississipi Burning (directed by Alan Parker, 1988) purports to depict Freedom Summer, 1964, in the aftermath of the killing of three civil rights workers, two white and one African–American. Taking for its heroes two FBI men, the film marginalizes blacks and insists that though they are victims of racism, they in fact had little to do with their own voting rights drive. The resulting message is that the government protected African–Americans and played a major role in the creation of Freedom Summer. Yet this is palpably untrue. This story simply excludes too much we already know about Mississippi Freedom Summer and the rather belated actions of the FBI to solve the murder of the three civil rights workers.[10] The central message of that summer, as responsible historians have shown, was not simply that blacks were oppressed, but that they worked as a community to alleviate their own oppression. This is the theme that the film chooses to ignore. By focusing on the actions of fictional FBI agents, the film engages in "false" invention and must be judged as bad history. Indeed, by marginalizing African–Americans in the story of their own struggle, the film seems to reinforce the racism it ostensibly combats.

Glory (directed by Edward Zwick, 1989) is as inventive as *Mississippi Burning*, but its inventions engage the historical discourse surrounding the film's subject: the Fifty-fourth Massachusetts Regiment commanded by Robert Gould Shaw, and, by implication, the larger story of African–American volunteers in the American Civil War.

Here are examples of how specific strategies of invention work in *Glory*:

Alteration. Most of the soldiers in the Fifty-fourth were not, as the film implies, ex-slaves, but in fact had been freemen before the war. One can justify this alteration by suggesting that it serves to bring the particular experience of this unit into line with the larger experience of African–Americans in the Civil War, to generalize from the Fifty-fourth to what happened elsewhere in the Union to slaves who were freed.

Compression. Rather than creating characters from regimental histories, the film focuses on four main African–American characters, each of whom is a stereotype—the country boy, the wise older man, the angry black nationalist, the Northern intellectual. The filmic reason is obviously dramatic: such diverse individuals create a range of possibilities for tension and conflict that will reveal character and change. The historical reason is that these four men stand for the various possible positions that blacks could take toward the Civil War and the larger issues of racism and black-white relations, topics that are not solely "historical"—or that, like all historical topics, involve an interpenetration of past and present.

Invention. Although there is no record of this happening, in the film the quartermaster of the division to which the Fifty-fourth belongs refuses to give boots to the black troops. His ostensible reason is that they will not be used in battle, but the real reason is that he personally does not like African-Americans nor think them capable of fighting. Clearly, this incident is one of many ways the film has of pointing to the kinds of Northern racism that black soldiers faced. Another way of showing the racism might have been by cutting to the antiblack draft riots in New York, but such a strategy could vitiate the intensity of the film and the experience of our main characters. This incident is an invention of something that could well have happened; it is the invention of a truth.

Metaphor. Robert Gould Shaw is shown practicing cavalry charges by slicing the tops off watermelons affixed to poles. Did the historical Shaw practice this way? Does it matter? The meaning of the metaphor is obvious and apropos.

Question: does using a white officer as a main character violate the historical experience of these African-American volunteers? Answer: No, it provides a different experience, a broader experience. Even if the decision to have a white main character was in part made for box office reasons (as it surely must have been), the film provides another explanation. Throughout *Glory* we see and hear Robert Gould Shaw saying (in voice-over extracts from original letters) that though he admires them, he cannot comprehend the culture of these men he leads. The clear implication is that we too will never fully understand their life. We viewers, in other words, stand outside the experience we are viewing just as Shaw does. Which suggests that film itself can only approximate that lost historical life. We do not understand the life of the soldiers because we are always distant spectators of the experience of the past, which we may glimpse but never fully understand.

For all its inventions, *Glory* does not violate the discourse of history, what we know about the overall experience of the men of the Fifty-fourth Regiment—their military activities, their attitudes and those of others toward them.[11] At the same time, the film clearly adds to our understanding of the Fifty-fourth Regiment through a sense of immediacy and intimacy, through the empathic feelings of emotion and that special quality of shared livingness and experience that the film conveys so well. To share the up-close danger of Civil War battles as rendered on the screen, for example, is to appreciate and understand the possibilities of bravery in a new way. (All this was recognized by James McPherson, author of a recent highly acclaimed work, *Battle Cry of Freedom: The Civil War Era*, in his review of the film in *New Republic*.)[12]

There is no doubt that the film simplifies, generalizes, even stereotypes. But it proposes nothing that clashes with the "truth" of the Fifty-fourth Regiment or the other black military units that fought for the Union—that men volunteered, trained under difficult conditions, and gave their lives in part to achieve a certain sense of manhood for themselves and pride for their people. Only the moral may be suspect: when the bodies of the white officer and one of his black men (the angriest, the one most suspicious of whites, the one who refuses to carry the flag, the one who has been whipped by this same officer) are pitched into a ditch and fall almost into an embrace, the implication seems to be that the Fifty-fourth and the Civil War solved the problem of race in America. How much more interesting, how much truer, might have been an image that suggested that the problems of race were to continue to be central to the national experience.

A New Kind of History

Of all the elements that make up a historical film, fiction, or invention, has to be the most problematic (for historians). To accept invention is, of course, to change significantly the way we think about history. It is to alter one of written history's basic elements: its documentary or empirical aspect. To take history on film seriously is to accept the notion that the empirical is but one way of thinking about the meaning of the past.

Accepting the changes in history that mainstream film proposes is not to collapse all standards of historical truth, but to accept another way of understanding our relationship to the past, another way of pursuing that conversation about where we came from, where we are going, and who we are. Film neither replaces written history nor supplements it. Film stands adjacent to written history, as it does to other forms of dealing with the past such as memory and the oral tradition.

What, after all, are the alternatives? To try to enforce Gottschalk's dicta? To insist that historians begin to make films that are absolutely accurate, absolutely true (as if this were possible) to the reality of the past? Not only is this impossible for financial reasons, but when historians do make "accurate" films (witness *The Adams Chronicles*), they tend to be dull as both film and history, for they do not make use of the full visual and dramatic power of the medium. A second alternative: history as experiment. But whatever new insights into the past experimental films provide, they tend to give up large audiences. A final alternative: to wish film away, to ignore film as history. But this would be to surrender the larger sense of history to others, many of whom may only wish to profit from the past. Worse yet, it would be to deny ourselves the potential of this powerful medium to express the meaning of the past.

It is time for the historian to accept the mainstream historical film as a new kind of history that, like all history, operates within certain limited boundaries. As a different endeavor from written history, film certainly cannot be judged by the same standards. Film creates a world of history that stands adjacent to written and oral history; the exact location of the understanding and meaning it provides cannot yet be specified.

We must begin to think of history on film as closer to past forms of history, as a way of dealing with the past that is more like oral history, or history told by bards, or griots in Africa, or history contained in classic epics. Perhaps film is a postliterate equivalent of the preliterate way of dealing with the past, of those forms of history in which scientific, documentary accuracy was not yet a consideration, forms in which any notion of fact was of less importance than the sound of a voice, the rhythm of a line, the magic of words. One can have similar aesthetic moments in film, when objects or scenes are included simply for their look, the sheer visual pleasure they impart. Such elements may well detract from the documentary aspect, yet they add something as well, even if we do not yet know how to evaluate that "something."

The major difference between the present and the preliterate world, however obvious, must be underscored: literacy has intervened. This means that however poetic or expressive it may be, history on film enters into a world where "scientific" and documentary history have long been pursued and are still undertaken, where accuracy of event and detail has its own lengthy tradition. This tradition, in a sense, raises history on film to a new level, for it provides a check on what can be invented and expressed. To be taken seriously, the historical film must not violate the overall data and meanings of what we already know of the past. All changes and inventions must be apposite to the truths of that discourse, and judgment must emerge from the accumulated knowledge of the world of historical texts into which the film enters.

NOTES

1. Quoted in Peter Novick, *That Noble Dream: The "Objectivity Question" and the American Historical Profession* (New York, 1988), p. 194.

2. There is no single book that satisfactorily covers the topic of history and film. The broadest discussion takes place in a forum in *American Historical Review* 93 (December 1988): 1173-1227, which includes the following articles: Robert A. Rosenstone, "History in Images/History in Words: Reflections on the Possibility of Really Putting History onto Film"; David Herlihy, "Am I a Camera? Other Reflections on Film and History"; Hayden White, "Histori-

ography and Historiophoty"; John J. O'Connor, "History in Images/Images in History: Reflections on the Importance of Film and Television Study for an Understanding of the Past";
Robert Brent Toplin, "The Filmmaker as Historian."

3. White, "Historiography and Historiophoty," p. 1193.

4. John J. O'Connor and Martin A. Jackson, eds., *American History/American Film: Interpreting the Hollywood Image* (New York, 1979).

5. Natalie Zemon Davis, " 'Any Resemblance to Persons Living or Dead': Film and the
Challenge of Authenticity," *Yale Review* 76 (September 1987): 457-82.

6. Not much has been written on experimental historical films. For a brief window onto
the issue see my articles "What You Think About When You Think About Writing a Book on
History and Film," *Public Culture* 3 (Fall 1990): 31-66; "Contemporary Filmmakers and the
Construction of the Past," *Comparative Studies in Society and History* 32 (1990): 822-37; and
"Walker: The Dramatic Film as Historical Truth," *FilmHistoria* 2, no. 1 (1992): 3-12.

7. Natalie Zemon Davis, *The Return of Martin Guerre* (Cambridge, Mass., 1983), p. viii.

8. Daniel J. Walkowitz, "Visual History: The Craft of the Historian-Filmmaker," *Public
Historian* 7 (Winter 1985): 57.

9. For a full discussion of *Walker* see my article "Walker: The Dramatic Film as Historical
Truth."

10. Books on Mississippi Freedom Summer include Doug McAdams, *Freedom Summer*
(New York, 1988), and Mary A. Rothschild, *A Case of Black and White: Northern Volunteers and
the Southern Freedom Summers, 1964-1965* (Westport, Conn., 1982). For an older account that
remains useful, see Leon Holt, *The Summer That Didn't End* (London, 1965).

11. For a history of the Fifty-fourth Regiment, see Peter Burchard, *One Gallant Rush: Robert
Gould Shaw and His Brave Black Regiment* (New York, 1965).

12. "The 'Glory' Story," *New Republic* 202 (January 8, 1990): 22-27.

Introduction to "Interventions in the *Field of Dreams* with Ariel Dorfman"

Ariel Dorfman

It is particularly appropriate that I should be speaking to you here today, because my presence comes to you thanks to history, or should I say thanks to President Nixon's sponsorship of this event. I would not be in the United States if in 1973 the elected government of your country had not succeeded in destabilizing and overthrowing the legal, constitutional, and freely elected government of my country, Chile. I am here, quite simply, because I had to leave my country as a result of the state terrorism perpetrated against the followers of Salvador Allende.

After seven years of exile in Europe, I wound up in the United States in 1980, in the very country that was in great measure responsible for unleashing violence upon my land and my people. And what I found when I came here was that the story of how the leader of the free world and the paragon of democracy (I am talking about your country, in case you don't recognize the description) devastated both freedom and democracy in another country had basically been forgotten. The part played by the United States in the overthrow of the Allende government had been amply documented by journalists and even by an official investigative committee headed by Senator Frank Church. For a brief while this occupied the front-page headlines, and then it slipped into the oblivion of the last pages and finally faded totally. It was not that Pinochet, the general who overthrew Allende and succeeded him, or the general's atrocities were not mentioned, but that their mention gradually diminished. Phrases like "U.S.-sponsored coup" and "sufferings created by the United States" began to evaporate into insignificance, as if, somehow, to mention the event was in bad taste.

Mention of the past, of the U.S. sponsorship of the military takeover, began to appear ever more infrequently as part of a limbolike parenthesis, and then all of a sudden there was no parenthesis; there wasn't even the quotation mark, there wasn't even the parenthesis between the parenthesis, there wasn't even the blank space; even the omission, even the disregard weren't there anymore. Basically, a piece of history had disappeared, an event that had been a major part of history. I was berated by a letter writer for not mentioning the U.S. sponsorship of the coup in an article I wrote for *Harper's*. My answer was, "I'm not the one who's got to bring it up. You did it to us." My job as a Chilean is to look at what we did to ourselves and not what you did to us. If I'm bringing the matter up here, it is because what was done to Chile—the same overthrow, the same oblivion—was also done to the elected governments of Guatemala, the Congo, Iran, and Indonesia. These recurring events indicate that the absence cannot be understood as a mere oversight, an accident.

If the story of what was done to Chile were burning in the core of American consciousness; if it were told to Americans over and over in newspapers and television programs and billboards and radio programs; if it were repeated so often that people knew it like the alphabet, like their own myths, like George Washington's cherry tree or something like that; if what was done to my nation and to other nations in your nation's name was so much a part of the flesh of American consciousness, if that were so, then events like these would become in the future absolutely unthinkable, impossible, and ridiculous.

One recent example will do. How could one fund a contra war against the Nicaraguan government in the name of democracy if everybody knew—and I mean everybody knew it, knew it like you know Babe Ruth—that the United States had during this whole century done everything in its power to destroy Nicaraguan democracy. It would be difficult to publicly justify the war, given this knowledge.

This introduction may seem elusive, but it leads into the theme of popular culture. I bring up this process of collective amnesia because we cannot possibly think about how we learn history unless we examine how certain uncomfortable, inconvenient parts of it have been selectively and systematically unlearned. For this procedure of unlearning to be successful, it cannot be carried out only at the obviously political and discursive levels of public speeches, reports, government briefings, editorials, and policy books. What is being suppressed, after all, is the story of how things happen, a messy, violent, bothersome version of what happened—the story that, if it were remembered, would cause pain, inconsistency, discomfort, aches, doubts, screams, would violate and make violent the smooth surface of everyday life.

A certain variety of the past keeps coming up, resurfacing, sticking its tongue out, refusing to behave, stepping out of the parentheses, dancing back into consciousness. Even in those margins of consciousness, we are there, those who cannot be totally suppressed. So the only way to be really

rid of the pest of the past, the pest of the past of that old story, is with another story.

And this is where popular culture comes in, because American popular
culture is the most powerful storyteller of our times. In fact, it is the most
powerful storyteller of all times. There has never been one quite like it. And
this culture, this industry as it is called, derives a great deal of its strength,
profitability, and entertainment value from the obvious skills and talents it
sucks into its maelstrom: some of the best minds, most creative brains, best
image makers, and best scriptwriters and wits. Elsewhere I have written
that if Shakespeare were alive today, he wouldn't be denouncing the Ninja
Turtles, he would be writing their scripts. No Old Globe for him, the
whole globe for him. But that strength also derives from the ability of many
cultural images to tame and domesticate what I would call the perturbation,
the furious perturbation, the other subversive stories. Subversive means
subversion of, another version of, a version underneath, the submarine version, the version that comes with its periscope in the middle of the ocean.
Because these stories constantly pose problems and then relieve us, the audience, of the burdens of having to confront the pain of history, the pain of
memory. They try to make things seamless again.

But I have decided not to confront this entertainment industry with a
speech about it. Last year, Jon Beller, a graduate student in literature at
Duke, and I—with the help of a group of Duke undergraduates—filmed the
way in which I dealt with that most popular of movies of a few years back,
Kevin Costner's *Field of Dreams*. Ours is a modest effort, from a resource
standpoint. With the budget of that Hollywood movie we could probably
finance one hundred thousand videos like ours.

Allow me this. If your country could intervene in the field of the dreams
of my country, and by doing so end up bringing me here to the United
States, it is fitting that I use my presence here to intervene in your field, your
dreams, and your field of dreams and your conference. So here is my gentle
intervention. It is called "Interventions in the Field of Dreams."

Print Edition of
"Interventions in the *Field of Dreams*
with Ariel Dorfman"
Jonathan L. Beller

(On the still image of a tiger the following letters are typed) "It's 8:30 do you know where your brains are?" ("Brains" is then crossed out and replaced by "Dreams." Then) "Paper Tiger Television Presents:"

(Cut to DORFMAN sitting in an empty movie theater.)

DORFMAN: I don't know what the media would do with this sort of intervention but . . .

(Universal Studio's logo, "UNIVERSAL," comes up, cutting DORFMAN off abruptly. The music from Field of Dreams *rolls, along with an abbreviated version of the credits from* Field of Dreams: *"Kevin Costner," "Field of Dreams," etc. More music and visual cut to an imposing image of DORFMAN's face on a television screen. The title of the piece types itself out:) "Interventions in the* Field of Dreams *with Ariel Dorfman."*

(Cut to first image of Field of Dreams, *a turn-of-the-century photograph of a boy sitting in a wheat field. Kevin Costner's voice tells the history of his character, RAY KINSELLA, while the screen shows us photographs and films from RAY's history. This sequence is taken directly from* Field of Dreams. *The photographs and films, which we subtitle with the names of the technologies used to produce them and the supposed dates of their production, recapitulate the evolution of media from early large-format black and white cameras to Polaroids and thirty-five-millimeter color*

"Interventions in the *Field of Dreams* with Ariel Dorfman," Jonathan Beller, director, Jim Halff, editor, was made for Paper Tiger Television in cooperation with Duke University in 1990. It has been shown on cable television in New York, San Francisco, Los Angeles, and Baltimore. For rental information, contact Paper Tiger Television, 339 Lafayette Street, New York, New York, 10012; phone 212-420-9045.

print film to super-8 movie film to sixteen-millimeter movie film, and finally, when we are in the film's present, to the "reality" of thirty-five-millimeter cinema. The subtitles underscore the power and range of contemporary cinema's ability to construct and "authenticate" history by simulating antecedent forms of representation and appropriating them for its own purposes. The images described above and Costner's voice-over are allowed to run. We interrupt it where indicated.)

RAY: My father's name was John Kinsella. It's an Irish name. He was born in North Dakota in 1896 and never saw a big city until he came back from France in 1918. He settled in Chicago where he quickly learned to live and die with the White Sox. Died a little when they lost the 1919 World Series; died a lot the following summer when eight members of the team were accused of throwing that series. He played in the minors for a year or two but nothing ever came of it. Moved to Brooklyn in '35, married mom in '38 and was already an old man working at the naval yards when I was born in 1952. My name is Ray Kinsella. Mom died when I was three and I . . . suppose dad did the best he could. I was put to bed at night to stories of Babe Ruth, Lou Gehrig, and the great Shoeless Joe Jackson. Dad was a Yankees fan then so of course I rooted for Brooklyn. But in '58 the Dodgers moved away so we had to find other things to fight about. We did. And when it came time to go to college I picked the farthest one from home I could find.

(Cut to ARIEL DORFMAN sitting in a wood-paneled studio.)

DORFMAN: The problem with the imagination, as it is posited in this film, is that the magic is there in order to stop history and not impulse us towards history. What they're imagining in the film, and what the filmmakers are asking you to imagine, is a perfect ideal form of history where you will not have to change it. Where you'll be satisfied with the way in which history has been constructed, in which you will take care, on the imaginary playing field, of the dreams . . . of all the problems of history, by being absolutely passive. You don't have to go out from the dreams into the real world to change anything, because it's being changed for you. Now that's bogus magic; that's not real magic. The real magic occurs when a lot of people come together and they feel activated to really change their circumstances, the real problems that have come to them from the past. When in fact the way in which they dialogue with the past, with the dead, is to change the present. Not to fall in love with what is gone and cannot be brought back ever.

(Cut back to series of images and Costner's narration.)

RAY: Officially my major was English, but really it was the sixties. I marched; I smoked some grass; I tried to like sitar music; and I met Annie *(sixteen-millimeter images of hippies)*.

(Cut to close-up of DORFMAN, outside.)

DORFMAN: Well, that was supposedly the sixties. But this is the nineties and this is a film, *Field of Dreams*, for the nineties. Of course, it does look back, and Kevin Costner or Ray Kinsella has got a problem, really two problems: One is that he rebelled against society as a child of the sixties and now he's got to figure out how to reintegrate, how to reincorporate himself into the society. And also, he broke with his father, he had a rupture with the tradition of America, with the working tradition of America . . . with his dad who's dead and its difficult to bring him back to life . . .

(Abrupt cut back to series of images and Costner's narration.)

RAY: After graduation we went to the Midwest and stayed with her family as long as we could . . . almost a full afternoon. Annie and I got married in June of '74. Dad died that fall. A few years later Karen was born. She smelled weird, but we loved her anyway. Then Annie got the crazy idea of buying a farm. I'm thirty-six years old, I love my family, I love baseball, and I'm about to become a farmer . . .

(At this point RAY and ANNIE are standing on a field next to a SOLD sign. There is a white house in the background. This scene is shot in sixteen millimeter. The motion is arrested and half of the now still scene is wiped away, leaving just RAY, ANNIE, and the SOLD sign. Onto the other half of the screen walks DORFMAN.)

DORFMAN *(speaking to us about the frozen half-image on screen right)*: "Sold!" but what are they buying? The land. Seems to be a foolhardy thing to do in this time when there is such a crisis in land and agriculture, but they are fulfilling the dreams of the sixties of going back to the land, of producing things and growing crops so people can eat. But maybe they're buying into something else. Let's see what happens.

(DORFMAN now gets wiped off the screen by the film and Kevin Costner picks up where he left off.)

RAY: . . . but until I heard the voice I had never done a crazy thing in my whole life.

(Cut to thirty-five-millimeter film footage of RAY working in his cornfield. The VOICE OF AMERICA beckons him.)

VOICE: If you build it he will come.

RAY: All right, that's it. Who are you, huh? What do you want from me?

VOICE: If you build it he will come.

(RAY looks up and sees the baseball field he is to build, glistening on the horizon. Cut to excerpts from scenes of RAY building a baseball diamond.)

LOCAL VOICE 1: What the hell is he doin'?

LOCAL VOICE 2: He's plowin' under his corn.

RAY: Third highest in history . . . and the name stuck . . .

LOCAL VOICE 3: He's gonna lose his farm . . .

LOCAL VOICE 4: Damn fool.

(Cut to DORFMAN sitting outside with a group of students. He pulls up a piece of grass. The bottom quarter of the television screen is a window in which Field of Dreams *continues to run from where we left off, but now on fast forward. In the field of dreams, RAY continues his frantic work.)*

DORFMAN: Well, that's a crazy thing to do, right? Plow up the grass, plow up the field. But he's keeping some sort of a dream alive. You know, this has become a society where people don't dream, don't do crazy things any more, so we can connect with that. And who knows, there may be some money in it.

(The window at the bottom of the screen opens up the screen covering DORF-MAN's scene and revealing Field of Dreams *full size. The frantically moving film slows down to speed. RAY and ANNIE are talking at their kitchen table. Their daughter, KAREN, is off screen.)*

ANNIE *(with a worried look)*: We used up all our savings on the field, Ray.

KAREN: Daddy?

RAY: Just a minute, Karen. So what are you saying? We can't keep the field?

ANNIE: Not if we want to keep the farm.

KAREN: There's a man out there in the lawn.

(Stunned, RAY gets up and walks across the room to look out the front door. There in the field he sees his father's hero, SHOELESS JOE JACKSON. As he looks, SHOELESS JOE dissolves to DORFMAN swinging a bat out in the middle of another baseball field. Close-up of RAY's face. He's excited. Film runs normally.)

ANNIE: I'll put up some coffee. Why don't you go on outside.

(This scene repeats itself, but the second time the film image is rendered broken up and in black and white.)

ANNIE: I'll put up some coffee. Why don't you go on outside.

(Cut to ANNIE walking out the front door some days later.)

ANNIE: Ray, dinner!

(The 1919 WHITE SOX now tease RAY, mocking his domesticity.)

THE TEAM: Ray, dinner. Dinner, Ray.

(While the image plays, DORFMAN comes in on a voice-over. A ball is tossed from one player to another.)

DORFMAN: Well, this is where the sexual revolution of the sixties ended up, right? *(Cut to DORFMAN swinging a bat that would connect with the tossed ball.)* With this bat. I mean that's where it ended up. You've got the men on the baseball field, Shoeless Joe come back from the dead—he's gonna play games with Kevin Costner and Annie is making the coffee. "Dinner." If she weren't here none of these dreams could be marketed, none of this field could be possible.

(Cut back to the film. While RAY and ANNIE watch, SHOELESS JOE walks off into the corn in order to disappear in his usual fashion. During the next two lines images from elsewhere in the film that depict ANNIE doing different forms of housework are inserted in squares over the basic film image.)

SHOELESS JOE: Hey, is this heaven?
RAY: No. It's Iowa.

(ANNIE continues to work in the inserts as JOE disappears into the corn.)

RAY *(turning to ANNIE; the inserts are gone)*: We're keeping this field.

(Cut to DORFMAN in the studio skeptically watching this section of the film on television.)

ANNIE: You bet your ass we are.

DORFMAN *(in the studio with the monitor. He hits PAUSE.)*: You bet your ass they are; but there's a problem. *(DORFMAN pushes PLAY on the VCR.)*

THE BANKER: You're gonna lose your farm, pal.

DORFMAN *(pushing PAUSE; the film image remains frozen on the monitor screen)*: "You're gonna lose your farm, pal." This is just a typical ploy and strategy of all American cinema. You've got the good guys and the bad guys. In this case you've got the bad owners, the guys who control the banks, and you've got the good owners, the people who control the fields. The idea here is that there are people who are going to corrupt and exploit America, and there are people who are going to take care of America. They're both owners. What is not said is that Kevin Costner and his people are going to end up exploiting . . . you. Let's see how that happens.

(Out of the monitor screen the still image begins to move and emerge. As it expands to cover DORFMAN's face, we see that RAY is tending the field.)

THE VOICE (back in the field): Ease his pain.

RAY: What? Sorry, what? I didn't understand.

THE VOICE: Ease his pain.

RAY: Ease his pain? What the hell does that mean?

(Cut to DORFMAN standing on the pitcher's mound of a baseball diamond.)

DORFMAN: Well, there's a lot of pain in America. There's the pain of racial segregation. There's the pain of a nation divided by the sixties and Vietnam. There's the pain of fathers and sons [who] can't agree. There's the pain of women left out. There's a lot of pain in America. A lot of exploitation in America. And how is Kevin Costner going to ease that pain? Well, it's really not that difficult, at least the film thinks not. It's going to be done right here, with the baseball field. Baseball is going to ease that pain. All the political pain in America is going to be resolved in this imaginary field.

(Cut to RAY washing his hands at the kitchen sink.)

ANNIE: Come on, honey, wash up, we got the PTA meeting after dinner. They're talking about banning books again. Really subversive books like *The Wizard of Oz, The Diary of Anne Frank.*

(Cut to PTA meeting.)

A PARENT: The so-called novels of Terence Man . . .

(Cut to ANNIE, irate.)

ANNIE *(gesturing toward the PARENT and addressing the assembly)*: Who's for Eva Braun here? Who wants to burn books? Who wants to spit on the Constitution of the United States of America? Anybody? *(She surveys the crowd; no one moves.)* All right. Now. Who's for the Bill of Rights? Who thinks freedom is a pretty darn good thing? C'mon, let's see those hands! *(A few hands go up.)* Who thinks we have to stand up to the kind of censorship that they had under Stalin? *(A few more hands. After a time she has a tentative majority.)* All right! There you go, America! I love you! I'm proud of you! I mean it!

RAY *(interrupting)*: Annie?

ANNIE: What?

RAY: We gotta go.

ANNIE *(to the PTA)*: We gotta go. This is great!

(Cut to DORFMAN leaning impassively on a television monitor that is running the scene that we have been watching.)

RAY *(leaving with ANNIE)*: I figured it out, I figured it out.

ANNIE: Was that great or what?

RAY: I figured it out.

ANNIE: God, it's just like the sixties again!

DORFMAN *(hitting PAUSE on the VCR, he takes a breath)*: So the sixties can live again. They're back again. But of course they're back in a very non-controversial way where everybody in the audience can identify with the two sixties activists. I mean, what Annie is defending is the Constitution of the United States, she's defending the freedom of speech, she's against censorship, against Stalinism, basically. That's what she's defending, and of course all Americans would agree with that. So that's what the sixties has come down to. Notice that she doesn't ask for a vote on things that deeply divide Americans today, such as abortion or nuclear energy or what happens to the farm land or what policy you have in foreign countries. No, all those things are left outside, just like all the issues that deeply divided this country in the sixties are left outside. *(Pause.)* In other words, the sixties was an incredible rupture in the consciousness of this country, in which a great part of this nation, especially the younger people, but those who had been excluded, demanded their place in history, demanded a radical change in the way in which America thought itself, attacked the basic myths of the United States. That has all been reduced now to a series of lonely gestures, gestures that don't have any real activism, any real substance behind them. And that's why Annie can be so happy about them. And that's why the protagonist can go off to find Terence Man, who is the voice of the sixties.

(RAY's Volkswagen bus travels across country in fast forward to music from the Grateful Dead. He is going to find TERENCE MAN.)

RAY *(practicing)*: Hi. Hi, I'm Ray Kinsella. Hi. *(As TERENCE MAN opens the door the film slows down somewhat, but the entire conversation takes place in 125 percent fast forward. The effect is that their chipmunk voices estrange and ironize the content of their conversation.)* Mr. Man, if I could just have one minute, please.

TERENCE: Look, I can't tell you the secret of life and I don't have any answers for you. I'm no longer a public figure. I just want to be left alone. So piss off! *(He tries to slam the door.)*

RAY *(sticking his neck out)*: Wait! I've come fifteen hundred miles to see you at the risk of losing my home and alienating my wife. All I'm askin' is one minute.

TERENCE: I don't do causes anymore.

RAY: This isn't a cause. I don't need money or endorsement.

TERENCE *(a look of revelation coming over his face)*: You're from the sixties?

RAY: Well, yes.

TERENCE: Out! *(He picks up a cylinder of bug spray and begins spraying RAY vehemently.)* Get back to the sixties while you still can! There's no place for you here in the future! Out!

RAY *(with his foot in the door again)*: You've changed, you know that?

TERENCE: I suppose I have. How's about this? *(making a peace sign with his hand)* Peace, love, dope! Now get the hell out of here! *(He slams the door.)*

(Cut to the studio; the door opens and DORFMAN enters.)

DORFMAN: In the sixties, this sign *(he makes a peace sign)* meant something more than just a caricature of peace, love, and dope. *(As DORFMAN speaks, a fast-forwarded section of* Field of Dreams *appears inserted into the window on the studio door as if the field of dreams is trying to get in.)* Terence Man is a double caricature. First, he is a caricature of what the sixties was, and then he is a caricature of what happened to the people of the sixties: that they grew disappointed, that there was nothing more that could be done. But of course a lot of those agendas are still absolutely valid, a lot of the problems that the sixties were trying to address are still around in this country: peace, love, dope, etc. Always look for what's being omitted, look for what's being withheld, look for the things that perturb the audience. Because if those things were in the film, it wouldn't be that easy to integrate—*integration*—this black radical into the contemporary American field of dreams establishment. *(During the next few lines magical music from* Field of Dreams *interrupts DORFMAN and makes some of his message inaudible. His image is taken over by Kevin Costner and James Earl Jones at a baseball game.)* And of course the man is disappointed. *(Music and the VOICE of the field: "Go the distance.")* The man is embittered. But because he has been constructed in such a way, he can then go off with his friend, Huck and Jim once again, searching for the solutions to all his problems.

(Cut to RAY's Volkswagen van running backwards to music from Field of Dreams *["China Grove" by the Doobie Brothers].)*

TERENCE MAN *(voice-over)*: We're going to Minnesota to find Moonlight Graham.

HELPFUL WOMAN *(speaking to RAY and TERENCE in an office along the route of their search for America)*: Doc Graham is dead. He died in 1972.

(Video compression [fast forward] of the section of the film where RAY magically walks out into a night in 1972 and encounters the still living DR. GRAHAM.)

RAY *(seeing DR. GRAHAM)*: Dr. Graham? My name's Ray Kinsella, I'm from Iowa. Are you Moonlight Graham?

MOONLIGHT: No one's called me Moonlight Graham in fifty years.

(Cut to DORFMAN in the studio standing by the monitor.)

DORFMAN: Why? Because that's Burt Lancaster right? Wrong. That's you. And if you don't believe that Burt Lancaster is standing in for you, for the audience, just listen to James Earl Jones. *(DORFMAN pushes PLAY on the VCR. James Earl Jones begins to speak.)*

TERENCE: . . . he did for these people. If he had gotten a hit, he might have stayed in baseball.

(DORFMAN pushes PAUSE, but the image on the monitor begins to run in fast forward and the sounds from Field of Dreams *emerge in a high-pitched fast-forward that interferes temporarily with DORFMAN's analysis.)*

DORFMAN: If he'd gotten a hit, Doc Graham would have stayed in baseball. But that would have been pretty difficult and pretty dangerous. I mean, if everybody who dreams of being a star ends up being a star, if everybody who has a dream plows up their cornfield, if everybody leaves their profession of doctor to become a baseball player, if everybody's Kevin Costner, well, society's not going to work. So there must be some people up on the screen, and some people who participate, you people, us, just by watching.

(Visual cut to fast-forward footage from Field of Dreams. *A young MOONLIGHT GRAHAM gets into the red Volkswagen with TERENCE and RAY.)*

DORFMAN *(continuing)*: When James Earl Jones and Kevin Costner go off to the farm . . . back to the farm, they pick up a young boy named Moonlight Graham, *(DORFMAN's face appears on the back of the rearview mirror of RAY's van)* another way in which a young form of old America is coming back to life, one more father figure made young, resurrected, to play on the field of dreams.

*(*Field of Dreams *comes down to speed and runs normally.)*

MOONLIGHT GRAHAM *(as a young boy)*: Hi. I'm Archie Graham *(TERENCE and RAY exchange looks of intimate disbelief).*

(Cut to a time a few hours later in their road trip. RAY and TERENCE are having a heart-to-heart road conversation.)

RAY: Anyway, when I was seventeen, I packed my things, said something awful and left. Son of a bitch died before I could take it back. Before I could tell him . . . you know . . .

(Cut to DORFMAN sitting in a red Volkswagen van. He leans out the window.)

DORFMAN: I can really identify with this man. He has, like we all have, something to repent, something that he did to somebody in the past and in this case to somebody who is dead. You can't take back what you've said and done to the dead. Or can you? Well, Kevin Costner is going to find the typical American way of rewriting the past, of bringing his father back from the past, bringing back his father's hero from the past. He's going to do it the American way, by cleaning the past, Sanforizing the past, making sure that the past does not continue to make trouble for you now. [He's going to re-write the past in a way that] allows you to settle into the present and the future. Get rid of it, really: amnesia, instant, total amnesia, the American way.

(Cut to a gardener with his shirt off mowing a baseball field.)

DORFMAN: Meanwhile, back at the farm . . .

(Cut to shot of BANKER talking to ANNIE.)

BANKER: Annie, you got no choice in the matter.

(Outside now, RAY, KAREN, ANNIE, TERENCE, and BANKER talking on the field.)

RAY: Look, I'm not selling the farm.

BANKER: Ray, you have no money! You have a stack of bills to choke a pig and come fall you've got no crop to sell. But I do have a deal to offer you that's gonna allow you to stay on the land.

KAREN: Daddy, you don't have to sell the farm.

BANKER: Why would anybody pay money to come here?

KAREN: To watch the game. It'll be just like when they were little kids a long time ago, and they'll watch the game and remember what it was like.

BANKER: What the hell is she talking about?

KAREN: People will come.

TERENCE *(with revelation in his face)*: People will come, Ray. *(A speck of light about the size of a gadfly begins to dog TERENCE MAN's face as he speaks.)* They'll come to Iowa for reasons they can't even fathom. *(The speck of light hovers and begins to expand. Now we see that it is a television monitor with DORFMAN's face on it. DORFMAN, whose televised face now hovers in midair, coldly observes TERENCE's "poetic" speech concerning the marketability of American history correctly presented.)* They'll turn up your driveway not knowing for sure why they're doing it. They'll arrive at your door as innocent as children longing for the past. "Of course we won't mind if you look around," you'll say. "It's only twenty dollars per person." And they'll pass over the money without even thinking about it. For it is money they have and peace they lack.

BANKER: You're broke, Ray. You sell now or you lose everything.

TERENCE: The one constant *(the monitor closes up again and begins to swoop at TERENCE like a troubled insect or a fighter plane)* through all the years, Ray, has been baseball. America has rolled by like an army of steamrollers; it's been erased like a blackboard, rebuilt, and erased again. But *(TERENCE raises a finger)* baseball has marked the time. This field, this game is a part of our past, Ray. It reminds us of all that once was good and it could be again. Oooooh, people will come, Ray, people will most definitely come.

(The flying television bearing DORFMAN's watching visage makes two more swoops at James Earl Jones and comes up full on the screen. From inside of the television set DORFMAN begins to speak. During the lines that follow, the camera pulls out, revealing that DORFMAN is sitting in the studio next to the monitor that bears his image. We see him speaking on the monitor and in the flesh. This image represents an entirely different relation to the production of images than that embodied by Field of Dreams.*)*

DORFMAN: James Earl Jones says that people will come without even thinking about it, to fork over twenty dollars, but I'm urging you, you people who have forked over a lot of money to watch a lot of films like this one, to think about it, think about what he's really saying. He's saying that you can take a dream and you can market it precisely because you can line up millions of people willing to pay twenty dollars or five dollars or two dollars fifty just so they can participate, so they can identify again with the deepest sense of what they really are, of what America is. And he's saying that America is really about baseball. He says, "America has been like a blackboard, erased over and over again." — He's sort of the blackboard [that] is being erased over and over again — and what remains is a spectacle. What remains is something that speaks about how America once was — the deepest past — and what America once again can be. Therefore, what the whole film has been talking about is getting rid of all the things that need to be erased out of America, and that can then be put back into a film and marketed to comfort all you people out there. The mythical America has been recreated *(cut to shot of DORFMAN and monitor on the edit monitor in postproduction studio; zoom out reveals the editor at the controls, making the cut that we are seeing)* and the reason why it can be a success is [that] people are willing to pay twenty dollars apiece without even thinking about it. Think about it.

(Cut to Field of Dreams *footage. BANKER, ANNIE, TERENCE, RAY, and KAREN continue to talk.)*

RAY: Can't do it, pal.

BANKER: You turn your daughter into a damn space case!

RAY: Get your hands off her!

(They struggle over KAREN and she falls backwards off the bleachers, landing on the ground with a dull thud.)

ANNIE: Karen? Is she all right?

RAY: I don't know.

ANNIE: Is she breathing?

TERENCE: Should I get the car?

(ARCHIE GRAHAM looks out from the baseball field and steps up to the edge of the field.)

ANNIE: I'm gonna call emergency.

RAY *(seeing ARCHIE GRAHAM)*: Just wait.

(ARCHIE GRAHAM drops his glove, hesitates, and takes a step off the field. As his foot goes down in this moment of high tension, it dissolves into DORFMAN's foot stepping across the baseline. For a moment we see DORFMAN standing in the studio and then we are back to ARCHIE dropping his glove again. This time, as he steps off the field, he becomes, as he ought to according to the logic of Field of Dreams, *Burt Lancaster as the older MOONLIGHT—or, rather, DOCTOR GRAHAM.)*

MOONLIGHT GRAHAM *(having a look at Karen)*: What have we got here?

RAY: She fell.

(Cut to DORFMAN standing in the studio.)

MOONLIGHT GRAHAM'S VOICE: This child's choking to death.

*(Field of Dreams *sound fades out.)*

DORFMAN: So Doc Graham's been brought back. Back from the past, back from the dead, back from middle America, outside history, in order to save all of our children, in order to keep on doing the things that ordinary people do all the time. He's had his hit (*while DORFMAN talks, his screen peels back to reveal the film footage of DOC GRAHAM walking off the field and resignedly disappearing into the corn, then peels forward, restoring DORF-MAN still speaking in the studio*), he's in the history books, now he must sit back and enjoy the spectacle—be part of the spectacle only by watching it. That's the fate of most of us, unless we're on the field of dreams, unless we're in the movies themselves, and that's the way it is.

But Doc Graham has been preparing us for another sort of ordinary man, the dockworker, somebody from middle America, ordinary America, the traditional values of America, which now Kevin Costner must relate to. And of course that is the father. This was really all the time about bringing back the father from the past (*DORFMAN screen peels back to reveal RAY and his youthful father walking on the baseball field; it then peels forward, restoring DORFMAN*), this ordinary guy, finding out that his values and the values of this rebellious son really were not that much in collision, they weren't clashing, but that they could find themselves on the field of dreams, in the spectacle. And the idea is that as long as you've omitted everything from this dream, in other words, as long as you've taken all the nightmare elements out—as long as you can, for instance, get rid of James Earl Jones, he's a black guy, get rid of him very quickly (*DORFMAN's screen peels back again and James Earl Jones is disappearing into the corn, then it peels forward, restoring DORFMAN*), send him to the other side of heaven to report—as long as you can keep on omitting these things, as long as you can put the women up on the porch with the daughters, then finally you can have the culminating scene that we've all been waiting for, that began at the very beginning, which is, of course, the nineties. How do you bring back the dead father and the future son, how do you have them playing catch together on the field of dreams—which is, of course, the movie we're watching?

(*DORFMAN's image spins, revealing behind it RAY and his father walking on the baseball diamond. As DORFMAN's spinning image fades out entirely, the sensitively climactic violin music from the end of* Field of Dreams *comes full on.*)

RAY: Dad, you wanna have a catch?

DAD: I'd like that.

(*The music builds to a crescendo. We see ANNIE on the porch watching RAY and his father toss the ball on the diamond. DORFMAN's face fades in for a full-screen close-up while the end of* Field of Dreams *continues to run. We see in this double exposure the film through DORFMAN and DORFMAN through the film.*)

DORFMAN: So this is how it all ends. You have dad and junior playing catch on the field, you have the past and the future, you have two versions of America: traditional America and rebellious America coming together on this white patch in the middle of the blackness. But the blackness is not really the cornfield, because, as you can see *(DORFMAN points toward the line of hundreds of cars pulling up to the field at night)*, winding like a serpent towards it is the whole of the United States, all of the spectators of America, coming to watch the TV screen, coming to watch this patch of white screen. In other words, the field of dreams is simultaneously the movie screen. And on that screen what they are watching is the reconciliation of everything that has divided the United States. It is the resolution of all the conflicts that have made this country such a troublesome place in the last thirty to forty to fifty, in fact, to sixty years. The whole of the United States' history has been reconciled. First of course it has been omitted, caricatured, and then it's been reconciled in this film of dreams. If you look you can see. You have . . .

(DORFMAN's image freezes in mid-word and from his arrested mouth comes an electronic buzzing like a scream. He is a frozen image, revealed as another technological production. His frozen face melts off the screen, revealing him behind himself, seated back in the studio.)

DORFMAN: The problem with the imagination as it is posited in this film is that the magic is there in order to stop history and not in order to impulse us towards history. *(Fade to black. Cut to artwork from the boxes for various videotapes flipping on the screen one by one. We see* The Last Emperor, The Longest Day, Kinjite, Iron Eagle 2, *etc.)* What the filmmakers are asking us to imagine is a perfect, ideal form of history where you will not have to change it, where you'll be satisfied with the way in which history has been constructed—which means basically that you can be absolutely passive. You don't have to go out from the field of dreams into the real world to change anything, because it is being changed for you. Now that's bogus magic. *(Cut to shot of a room made by three walls of shelves full of black videotape boxes.)* The real magic is when a lot of people come together and they feel activated to really change their circumstances. When, in fact, the way in which they dialogue with the past, with the dead, is to change the present.

(Credits flash over still of a room completely full of videotapes)

Direction: Jon Beller

Edition: Jim Halff

Production: Liz Asch, Jon Beller, Hope Creal, Lea Davis, Melinda Frank, Mel-issa Goldberg, Kurt Jeannine, Adam Joyce, David Messinger, Laura Tawney, Tom Whiteside.

(and the title repeats)

Interventions in the Field of Dreams *with Ariel Dorfman.*

Commentary on
"Interventions in the *Field of Dreams*
with Ariel Dorfman"

Ariel Dorfman

Before opening the debate to everyone, I'd like to make a few additional comments. First, I don't believe in conspiracies. I want to put this as forcefully as possible because, strangely enough, whenever I bring this up newspapers and critics tend to suggest that I am in favor of a conspiracy. Over and over again, even if in my books I keep saying no, that this is not five people getting together and snickering, "How are we going to screw America?" It is, rather, the way in which many people work out their problems just like you work out your problems. I am against that conspiracy theory because it means that we can solve this problem by exterminating, by getting rid of a couple of dangerous enemies out there, and that leads to Stalinism. This process comes out of deep crises, and unless people have built a real possibility of finding spaces where they can exercise and practice a real critique in their everyday lives, they are defenseless against these stories. So there is nothing condemnatory about liking popular films. I cry each time I see *Field of Dreams*, because I also have problems with history and I also would like to be able to bring back the dead, and I worship the power of the imagination. These films speak about very legitimate concerns that you have, that I have. And I don't want to feel superior, though I recognize there is a certain sense of superiority in the way the film has been shot, even as it pokes fun at itself.

A second matter is that what we have discovered in *Field of Dreams* is a pattern. It is not fortuitous. You find the same methods over and over in any number of films. You see this relationship between the father and the son in *Back to the Future*. A kid of the eighties goes back to the fifties to make sure that the father will not turn out to be the wimp, but the hero—the child—changes history by going back. The film changes history so it can happen the way it should be. I could go on and on: *Top Gun*, *Indiana Jones and the*

Last Crusade. Fathers, sons, grandfathers, children. Over and over again you see the same pattern, ways in which the past and the present are continually engaging in dialogue, though not in order to really understand the barriers between the two, but in order to reconcile differences that are irreconcilable, really, except if you change the present.

This connects with what I said about a conspiracy because I feel it refers to how the United States re-creates its community, how a community divided by the past is brought together by ridding itself of that past and reinterpreting it. I personally object to this because I think that this is not the way to confront the past and I think it is not the way to re-create community. Nor is it the way to bring magic back into our lives. And even less the way to enter into a dialogue with the dead. Nor the way to revive those who have been left on the margins of history and forgotten by it.

Let me finish by saying that I would like to historicize myself — putting into practice Dominick LaCapra's idea about the need to bring yourself in, to make your position clear. I would like to accentuate the place in history from which I speak. And my place in history, in fact, is such that I have changed since I made this video — just before I was about to return to Chile, which itself had just returned to democracy after almost seventeen years of dictatorship. I was resettling there. What I found when I went back to Chile — a Chile that was democratic, where the struggle was not against a tyrant — was a struggle about what you do with the tyrant's legacy. What do you do with the past? I found myself in a country that, strangely enough, instead of fighting tyranny was discussing openly and circuitously what to do with its own past. I found most of the Chileans very interested in resurrecting part of the past, some of the horrors that had been done, but not so much that we would destabilize the regime again and bring back the military one more time. In other words, if you investigate all the torture done to everybody, you are going to have to put the whole armed forces on trial. And the problem is that they've got the guns and we don't, so the past was in danger of repeating itself. Living this profound process, the fact that most of my countrymen were willing to resurrect part of the past but not all of it, was very painful. In this sense I was no better, we were no better, than people in America were. And somehow during those seventeen years I had always thought we were somehow superior, there was a space of salvation there in Chile where everything was perfect; but it wasn't. I had my own field of dreams — let's put it like that — and it turns out that if it was not a nightmare, it was certainly not reality. My community back home is as divided as yours was during the Vietnam War. And until we really confront that past we are not going to be able to create a different sort of country.

I will end on that note, stating that I am slightly bothered at this point by a certain attitude of mine, as if to say I know better than you do. I have become a bit more historical on the subject. On the other hand, I don't think

I have to apologize for having filmed this critique because it is a way of stopping the flow of history, of making an audience feel resistance to official history.

Question: My question is about your position as the narrator. I was struck by the fact that you looked so much like my father, and so when I saw you on the film I felt like I'm just getting another father here, only he's smarter. I'm wondering if you could envision some other narrative strategy so that other people were included.

Dorfman: It is a sort of paternal voice. First, from the merely technical point of view, unless we have enormous resources at our disposal there is really not very much we can do except to tell a counterstory with a narrator, I mean with a storyteller in a way. The second thing is that this is a father who is making fun of himself all the time. I'm playing around with myself. I think I'm slightly deconstructing myself, or rather Jon Beller, the director, is helping me to deconstruct myself. As soon as I become too authoritative there is a sort of perturbation of that.

But the real answer to this is that I really do not have much of an alternative. I am using the current, prevalent forms because I have seen alternative movies that are so deconstructive that nobody understands what the critic is saying. In other words, there is no rationality in it, no sort of master story being told. I hate that word *master*, but it's there. So somehow the idea is that I have accepted the genre of somebody talking his head off and telling everybody what the reality really is, laughing at the same time, but using it because to create an alternative that is so radical that people would not quite get the point might not work. Let's put it like that. It's an experiment. It's one experiment and very often experiments use all sorts of complicated ways of doing things.

Question: I think toward the end you raised the issue that this is more a problem of culture than some kind of problem endemic to America. Or this is a shared tendency and the community tends to be constructed through at least a partial process of forgetting. It seems this could be tied into the problem of confronting elements of one's past that one would like to construe as the other: you see yourself in the other, you appear different, and the other appears in you, and this is a violent or destabilizing action. This is the kind of problem that might unify what Dominick LaCapra said in his paper and what you said in terms of a more critical approach to history in the past.

Dorfman: My position is that the community that gathers around the fire, the hearth, of "Interventions" is a different community than the one that gathers around the playing field of the field of dreams. They are different communities, and if you look at it in those terms, the history of the United States and of the world is the constant clash of different communities. The difference between Chile and the United States in that sense is that our poverty gives us some hope in relation to the fact that we are only imposing this upon our poor people, whereas you are imposing this on the whole world. This form of storytelling has at its disposal such resources, such enormous power, such capacity, that you should really—I'm not lecturing you—be more responsible. In other words, it is terrible when you have such power and such lack of parental rights that the power demands. I recognize that somehow my voice is too large in that little film of mine. It sort of turns it into me against every Kevin Costner. And I disagree with that, it personalizes history, the antihistory of me, and, of course, I have no personal problem with Costner. What I think we should be doing is breaking open spaces so that other voices can come through. The problem is to find those spaces, and I would tell you that you've got those spaces. You've got the children and they're there and you have to find ways of making them participate and see their history, first deconstructed and then seen as happening all the time.

Question: If Americans laugh at mass culture, can they make sense of it?
Dorfman: Things are so serious that you have no alternative but to laugh. That is one of the most important things—to use a sense of humor all the time. It is one of the most subversive weapons that we all have at our disposal. Our kids probably use it continually, perhaps to your chagrin, and to mine at times, but I don't want to tell you what you've got to do. I would almost say you know what you've got to do. The real question is, Can we as a community do it? Can we find the little, tiny acts of courage? Mostly we don't want to do things that are going to end up denying us the possibility of teaching. First of all, I think that you know what to do and then I think that the youngsters that you are teaching know an enormous amount about history and about life. They have a wellspring of knowledge. I'm not idealizing them, but I do think, as Robert Coles and many others have proven, that people are really living, and the one thing they know about is themselves. They know about their community. Start from there.

Question: What about *Dances with Wolves*? In line with what you have said, I see it as an American myth in which Costner and the Indians ride off into the mountains. It is still a denial of a troubling past.
Dorfman: I agree with you. The first thing about these films is that they are contradictory. I think there are some wonderful things that happen in that film. The very fact that they happen, the very fact that you hear Native Americans talking in their own tongue, that's wonderful. But of course they disappear, out of history, fathers playing on the field of buffaloes.

So I love the fact that in the movie the indigenous peoples are speaking in their own tongue. But their culture is not really there. It's not there to perturb us because it's not really presented as a whole culture, which makes it safe. I would be interested in "Dances with Iraqis," because it takes real courage to deal with people who are a threat to you now—not people who are no longer a threat to you.

Question: What do you think of *Missing*?
Dorfman: I felt enormously happy that that film was made, and I'm a friend of Costa-Gavras. I haven't ever stopped thanking him for doing that film. That film did more for Chile than any other film. It was, however, the last gasp of a tide that was receding rather than the beginning of a tidal wave that was coming. There were no more films after that, or U.S. interventions, of that sort.

The film was extraordinarily brave in making connections. In fact, if you look at the film, it turns over, it is a reverse of *Field of Dreams*. It is the father being educated by the dead son, taking his place and having to face the fact that his system has created the destruction of his future, of the father's future, the system that he represents.

If you take the concept of John Sayles's *Eight Men Out*, and you put those people on that field of dreams, it is going to explode, because what John Sayles is saying is that if you're poor in America you're screwed, they're going to manipulate you and use you, no matter what. You don't even know what's happening there. And they can bring you back five hundred times from the dead and the pain will not go away.

Question: I teach a course on the sixties. Sixties movements presented a total denial of history; they made no attempt to understand the past. Is this characteristic of an America built on the immigration of peoples who left their own pasts behind?
Dorfman: In my book *The Empire's Old Clothes*, my basic theory has to do with this idea of rebirth and innocence—that the United States in order to carry out the sort of policies it carries out must become innocent again, over and over again. I'm taking that one step further in the new book I'm writing, which has to do with the fact that the media is the perfect way of doing this. It's not secondary to the fact that this is the only empire that has been built along with the mass media. But it's part of the way in which an empire thinks of itself. You can have a democratic empire, democratic inside or as democratic inside as you can possibly imagine in our world today, as long as you've got these forms of media. That's another sort of story, but I think you're basically right.

I may in fact be idealizing the sixties here, but it was a crack. I'm interested in those cracks, in those moments in which things don't work, because that's where knowledge comes from—in yourself as well. Of course, cracks are painful. When we were kids, you know, we jumped over the cracks because we knew what would happen if we touched them. We want to make believe they're not there.

Question: Are you denying the enjoyment of films? When I go to see a film like *Field of Dreams*, it is for pleasure.

Dorfman: We're all slightly schizophrenic and there is no other possibility but to be so. The moment when I stop enjoying a film, I stop having any connection with the people who are real people. I'm not going to situate myself outside, sneering at the film. I'm going to give myself the opportunity of looking at it, and going back and forth between enjoyment and critical distance.

There's a sense in which you've got to be able to enjoy the structures that are there or you're not going to be able to enter into adult life. You contextualize. Dominick LaCapra was extraordinarily eloquent in his paper when he set out the complexities of this back and forth. You've got to do it all the time. If you don't do it, you're going to shut yourself off from the people you want to reach. That's how knowledge works. And the system has become so overwhelming and taken over so many stages that you've got to find a situation in which—inside the world as it's constructed today—you can find forms of criticism that don't turn you into some sort of a monster and that don't prevent you from communicating with your culture.

Part IV
Political Culture and Historical Interpretation

American Foreign Policy and the Rhetoric of History and Morality

Frances FitzGerald

When President Bush made his speech to Congress at the end of the Gulf War, it occurred to me to wonder what the textbooks would say about the war in the Gulf five, ten, and twenty years hence. It was an idle thought. I was not seriously considering what the judgment of history would be on that war. It was just that, having done a book on U.S. history textbooks some time ago, I have something of a morbid fascination with the way the texts deal with the events we all have lived through.

My subject in this essay is neither textbooks nor the teaching of history in the classroom—at least not directly. What I want to discuss is the way we Americans teach ourselves about history in our public discussions of foreign policy. In our democracy there is a constant teaching and learning process going on outside the classroom in speeches, press conferences, talk shows, newspaper columns, and the like. Some of this talk is evanescent, but some of it makes a mark and endures in the writing and teaching of history. But political rhetoric about foreign policy and war has its own tradition, and that is my subject here.

What is striking at this particular moment in history is the absence of foreign policy rhetoric—the absence of a story about where we are going and what our role is in the world. With the breakup of the Soviet empire over the past few years, we have come to a watershed in our international relations as important as any since the end of the Second World War. The Bush administration has had a foreign policy—or it has had many foreign policies—and yet neither the Republicans nor the Democrats seem able to speak about our long-term interests and goals. This is true in general, but it

This essay was written in April 1991, shortly after President Bush's speech to Congress, but well before the Gulf War had moved from the sphere of journalism into the sphere of history.

is also true in the case of particular foreign policies. We have just had a war, and a very successful one from a military point of view. But what were our war aims, and what have we achieved with relation to our larger foreign policy goals? It has taken a top investigative reporter—Bob Woodward—to winkle out the answer to the first question.

In the past, when our presidents wanted to send troops into battle, they have put a good deal of effort into justifying their policies and persuading the American people that their sacrifice was worth while; and they have often appealed to history. The Gettysburg Address is of course the model of this kind of rhetoric. In the case of the Gulf War, however, George Bush resorted to another procedure. Administration officials laid out five or six reasons why it might be a good idea to go to war: maintaining oil prices, liberating Kuwait, destroying Iraq's chemical and nuclear weapons capability, and so on. Then they waited to see which reason got the most enthusiastic response, and when the answer came, they repeated it: Saddam Hussein was Hitler and had to be punished. This was a form of marketing strategy, and it worked—but then, as it turned out later, getting rid of Saddam Hussein was not George Bush's reason for going to war.

This approach must have come quite naturally to Bush and his aides, for these days such marketing strategies are quite routinely used in national political campaigns. Rather then tell us what they think, presidential candidates ask focus groups and opinion polls what the public would like to hear; then speech writers make phrases and ad people create images to illustrate them. In the 1988 campaign this procedure gave us Willie Horton, George Bush in a flag factory, and Michael Dukakis, incongruously, on the top of a tank. (This is, by the way, also quite normally the manner in which textbooks are written. The publishers find out in advance what the textbook purchasers think is politically acceptable.) There is a democratic aspect to this way of going about things. On the other hand, it tends to reduce political rhetoric to a lowest common denominator and it bespeaks a certain lack of leadership. Why, after all, should we elect people who don't know any better than we do what ought to be done?

There are, of course, a variety of possible explanations for this failure of rhetoric. In the case of political campaigns, the tendency has been to blame television with its ten-second sound bites—and to wonder about the length of the collective attention span. But television does not stop politicians from making speeches, and those of us who were willing to listen to a few of them during the presidential campaign in 1988 heard very little about the important change in the U.S.-Soviet relationship. Similarly, in the fall of 1990 we heard almost nothing from congressional candidates about the military buildup then going on in the Gulf. Was it the poor quality of the candidates? Is it that the president and the congressional leadership did not know how to react to the earth-shaking events in the Soviet Union, so quickly had they come? Surely not. George Bush was a foreign policy expert—certainly by comparison to his predecessor—and after his election he and his secretary of state, James Baker, dealt with the U.S.-Soviet relationship in nuanced, sophisticated fashion and gained support from Congress. What is more, Bush and Baker proved to be skillful diplomats when it came to creating an international coalition for the embargo against Iraq; and when it came to the question of military action, Bush was nothing if not decisive. So why this deafening silence in public discourse—a silence occasionally punctuated by quotations from Winston Churchill? The answer, I think, lies not in personalities—though George Bush is not much of an orator and not much on "the vision thing." Rather, it is a problem internal to the history of political discourse about foreign policy.

Since World War II we in this country have been preoccupied by communism in a way that most West Europeans have found difficult to understand. It is what we talked about in our public life—to the exclusion of all the other issues we quite routinely deal with, from the law of the sea to the economic challenge of Japan. But now that the end of the cold war has deprived us of our main topic of conversation, our politicians cannot figure out what will interest us any more. We are like a family whose infuriating neighbors have just moved away, leaving us nothing to complain about, dissect, and imagine. That is surely a part of the problem. But in my view the heart of the matter lies deeper still: it has to do with the extraordinary success of a nineteenth-century story about the role of the United States in the world—a story that had as much force in the elections of the 1880s as it did in those of 1980 and 1984. George Bush told a bit of the story in 1988, but it never was his story, so he told it half-heartedly. The great teller of it was Ronald Reagan. Reagan could tell it six ways to Sunday, for it came naturally to him, and after the Vietnam War and after the Iran hostage crisis, we seemed to have a particular need to hear it again. For most Americans, it was a pleasant, reassuring way to hear about their national history. I cannot think of another way to explain the fact that the Reagans lived in the White House for eight years.

If you go back and read the journalistic accounts of the 1980 campaign, you will see that they say very little about Reagan's views on foreign policy. All journalists knew that Reagan had a very slight grasp on the subject, and his rhetoric was so familiar to them they paid it small attention. I expect they thought he would lay off once the campaign was over. But he did not, and in 1981, the commentators were calling him—depending on their political persuasions—a right-wing ideologue or a defender of American values. I believe he was both—only his defense of American values had only superficially to do with the text of anticommunism and a good deal more to do with the subtext of the evil empire. Reagan, after all, was no more of an anticommunist or a free marketeer than, say, Margaret Thatcher or Helmut

Kohl. But he talked about foreign policy in a way that was different from any European politician. There are many examples I could use of his rhetoric (which, by the way, was essentially his own and not the invention of anonymous speech writers), but let us take for an example the way he spoke about Central America in his first term. You will remember, by the by, that until Reagan was allowed to meet Gorbachev he and his national security staffers concentrated their attentions on a number of very small countries— Grenada, Libya, Lebanon, Nicaragua, and El Salvador—while neglecting the largest ones and ignoring whole continents, such as Africa and South America, for years. Well, out of small countries large threats might appear.

In March 1981 President Reagan described the purpose of American military aid to El Salvador in this fashion:

> What we're doing . . . is [to] try to halt the infiltration into the Americas by terrorists, by outside interference and those who aren't just aiming at El Salvador but, I think, are aiming at the whole of Central and possibly later South America—and, I'm sure, eventually North America. But this is what we're doing, is trying to stop this destabilizing force of terrorism and guerrilla warfare and revolution from being exported in here, backed by the Soviet Union and Cuba and those others that we've named.

Two years later, the president revealed to a joint session of Congress the probable consequence of inaction in Central America:

> If we cannot defend ourselves there, we cannot expect to prevail elsewhere. Our credibility would collapse, our alliances would crumble, and the safety of our homeland would be put in jeopardy.

This is, of course, a prime example of what Professor Richard Hofstadter called the paranoid style in American politics. Reagan is telling us that we have a mortal enemy somewhere out there, but one that he cannot precisely name or identify. This enemy, he says, is backed by the Soviet Union—but it is not the Soviet Union (or Reagan would express concern about nuclear weapons and the Red Army). This enemy will appear in Central America, but it is clearly not Nicaragua or El Salvador per se, for how would countries with populations of three million and five million respectively threaten two continents? No, this enemy is a "force," not subject to the laws of history or geopolitics—invisible and potentially everywhere at once.

When Hofstadter spoke of "the paranoid style," he did not mean to imply that its practitioners were crazy. Reagan certainly was not crazy; indeed, he was the opposite of a paranoid personality—if the control group consists of Richard Nixon and Lyndon Johnson. No, Hofstadter was speaking of a tradition of populist dissent that came from such groups as the anti-Masonic movement, the Know-Nothing party, and elements of the Populist party in the nineteenth century, and from the John Birch Society and other groups during the twentieth century. Yet what I think Hofstadter did not realize was that even the logic of these groups was not crazy—or self-invented. In fact, it made perfect sense in the context of religious teaching. It makes perfect sense to those who live in a metaphysical universe in which the forces of good and the forces of evil are engaged in a constant struggle for the minds of men. This is the stuff of many religions, and the stuff of, among others, the dominant American religion of the nineteenth century—evangelical Protestantism.

Evangelical Protestantism is still an important strain in American religious life today, but in the nineteenth century a number of its elements were secularized—that is, transmuted from theology into national mythology, and, more diffusely, into a manner of conceiving the world. One of these elements you will recognize immediately, for it is the historical belief in American exceptionalism: the notion that although there is evil out there in the world, America is a nation guided by Providence and filled with grace. As President Reagan once put it, "America is great because she is good." Another is the notion of rugged individualism, and another the idea that history is unimportant given the potential for self-transformation, or for being "born again." There are others, and I think I could show that all of them influenced Reagan's view of the world. (His mother was, after all, a nineteenth-century evangelical.) But for the moment let us concentrate on two of these elements, the metaphysical battle, or what Hofstadter calls "the paranoid style," and the doctrine of American exceptionalism, for these have profoundly influenced the rhetoric of American foreign policy, and occasionally its substance, for over a century. Since World War II—in fact, since World War I in fundamentalist quarters—the counterideology of communism has fit most perfectly into the evangelical framework as the perfect opposite, the Other, the demon force.

Historians are never happy with the placement of starting points, but I think that if anyone were to identify the first major example of the paranoid style in postwar American foreign policy rhetoric, it would be, strangely enough, a 1947 speech of Dean Acheson's. That year President Truman and Secretary of State George Marshall had asked Congress to appropriate four hundred million dollars in aid to Greece and Turkey. What they found was that an influential group of congressmen from the West and Midwest were loathe to spend such a sum to help the Greek monarchy defeat the Greek communist movement and to help the Turkish government resist Soviet intimidation. In fact, as Truman discovered, these congressmen did not think of the defense of Europe from the Soviet Union as a priority for the United States. So Under Secretary of State Dean Acheson tried another tack. "Like apples in a barrel infected by one rotten one," he said, "the corruption of Greece would infect Iran and all to the east," including Africa by way of Asia Minor. Acheson had, as it turned out, found the lever. The congressmen voted aid to Greece and Turkey on the ground that it would stop the rot of communism all the way around the world.

There followed the Truman Doctrine committing the United States to support "free peoples who are resisting attempted subjugation by armed minorities or by outside pressures" around the world. Obviously, the United States was not capable of doing any such thing—it was like committing an army to advance in all directions at once. But Truman, Marshall, and Acheson had no intention of making the doctrine into operational policy. They had their priorities—which were in Europe—and just because the Chinese under Chiang Kai-shek might be a "free people," that was not for Truman sufficient reason to commit American ground troops to the folly of trying to rescue China from Mao Tse-tung. But, as George Orwell has told us, the corruption of language is a significant kind of corruption, and there was a price to be paid for promising what could not humanly be done. After Mao had ended his Long March, Senator Joseph McCarthy, in one of the purest examples of the paranoid style, attributed the "loss of China" to communist agents within Acheson's State Department, and witch-hunts ensued.

Under the pressure of McCarthyism, Acheson's "rotten apple" simile proved more applicable to his own speech than to the Greek civil war, for it infected the rhetoric of American foreign policy for years thereafter. In the 1950s and 1960s communism was quite routinely spoken of as a rot, a corruption, or a disease that spread mysteriously across national borders and through human societies, and whose progress was, of course, irreversible. In those years the American Congress could not seem to appropriate a dollar in foreign aid without proclaiming it crucial, vital, or critical in the global struggle; and American presidents could not take the most modest of initiatives without assuring Congress that it would save the world. The result was a general confusion among policymakers about priorities and a corruption of the relationship between them and the public at large. Inevitably, miscalculations occurred. In 1956 the Hungarians revolted in the hope that the Eisenhower administration would act on its promise to roll back the Soviet lines, and they were crushed by Soviet tanks. Between 1963 and 1965 the United States committed itself to a war in Vietnam that it had no strategy for winning.

The American commitment to Vietnam was, of course, something more than a miscalculation. Since it extended over a long period, the motivating forces can be discussed quite sensibly in a number of ways. But it is important to remember that the presidents who made the incremental commitments never did so in the name of saving the southern half of Vietnam from

Ho Chi Minh: they made them in the name of saving Southeast Asia, Oceania, and perhaps even the United States from communism. For Eisenhower, Vietnam was the first in a series of "dominoes": if it fell, then Cambodia would fall, then Thailand, then Malaysia, and so on. For Kennedy, Vietnam was "the keystone in the arch, the finger in the dike." For Johnson and his men, a victory in Vietnam would stop communism from spreading south and then east across the Pacific—or alternatively it would stop "wars of national liberation" around the world. In retrospect, these notions sound extremely far-fetched. But at the time our foreign-policy makers truly believed that South Vietnam was the keystone. They would not have sent 50,000 American troops to die in Vietnam for anything less. At the time the metaphors ruled.

Listen to President Nixon in April of 1970:

> We live in an age of anarchy both abroad and at home. We see mindless attacks on all the great institutions which have been created by free civilizations in the last 500 years. Even here in the United States, great universities are being systematically destroyed. Small nations all over the world find themselves under attack from within and from without.
>
> If, when the chips are down, the world's most powerful nation, the United States of America, acts like a pitiful, helpless giant, the forces of totalitarianism and anarchy will threaten free nations and free institutions throughout the world.

Nixon here was not speaking of a barbarian invasion of New England but of his own decision to send a small number of American troops to cross the Vietnamese border into Cambodia. It was an unpopular decision and one that required important historical and moral rhetoric—but this speech seems in retrospect to be madness. In this way of thinking there are no intermediate redoubts, no compromise positions—it is all or nothing. We are always on a slippery slope heading in one direction or another. National borders have no meaning, nor do the actual numbers of enemy troops, for no cost analysis is possible. Clearly we are not dealing with the real world here, but rather with a metaphysical landscape of good and evil. It is not metaphor anymore, but true eschatology—imagining the end times.

Nixon, of course, presented his eschatology in secularized language. Reagan, who was both less self-conscious and closer to the source, spoke of the Soviet Union as "the evil empire" and "the focus of evil in the world."

Let us turn now to the other element of transmuted evangelical theology—the doctrine of American exceptionalism. In the nineteenth century this doctrine was understood quite literally and used to justify American territorial acquisitions and other enterprises across the Caribbean and the Pacific. In the twentieth century it has quite often cropped up in secular form as a rationale for aid programs and even military undertakings. In 1965, for example, President Johnson pledged not only to stop communism in Indochina but also to bring peace, material progress, and human dignity to the Indochinese. "The American people have helped generously in times past in these works," he said in a typical appeal to historical precedents. "Now there must be a much more massive effort to improve the life of man in that conflict-torn corner of our world." These promises proved to be extremely troublesome. Not only did they lay Johnson open to the charge of hypocrisy, but their logic permitted elements within the peace movement to conclude that if the United States did not represent absolute good, it must represent absolute evil. This, too, was evangelical thinking. It occurs in all parts of the political spectrum, and, of course, when it is transmuted into politics it falls free of the constraints imposed by the rest of Christian doctrine.

In the nineteenth century evangelicals could be categorized as premillennialist or postmillennialist. The premillennialists saw degeneration, chaos, and Armageddon ahead before the return of Christ to earth; the postmillennialists believed that human society (viz., American society) would grow in virtue and righteousness to the point of perfection, when Christ would appear to inauguarate his millennial reign on earth. The doctrine of American exceptionalism derived from this rather more optimistic eschatology. In the twentieth century American politicians—like most other Americans—have tended to fall, figuratively speaking, into one or the other camp. Ronald Reagan is the great exception to this rule, for he fell into both.

You will remember that while Reagan spoke of the evil empire, Armageddon, and catastrophe stemming from Central America, he was on other occasions extraordinarily optimistic. He was optimistic not only about the survival of democracy and the free world, but also about the possibility for an end to the nuclear arms race, for perfect American security and peace in the world. His hopes for American security were focused on the Strategic Defense Initiative and the idea that we could build a perfect defensive shield against all nuclear weapons. In August 1985 he said that we were "moving forward with research on a project that offers us a way out of our nuclear dilemma—the one that has confounded mankind for four decades now." In his speeches, this shield was sometimes portrayed as a device that would protect the United States (and possibly its allies) from a Soviet attack. On other occasions Reagan promised to share the fruits of our research with the Soviets, so that the whole world would be safe from nuclear weapons. On these occasions Pentagon officials would register their objections to sharing the most sensitive American military research with the Soviets, and the defense secretary, Caspar Weinberger, would say that the Soviets should not feel threatened just because we possessed a shield as well as a nuclear sword. On one occasion—it was March 27, 1983—Weinberger said, "We have had and did have a monopoly of nuclear weapons for some years and never used them. And that is, I think, widely known to the Soviets that we would never launch a first strike."

Of course the Soviets knew nothing of the sort. Reagan later discovered for himself that they were terrified of American technological advances in the military field. Weinberger had rather forgotten the history of Hiroshima and Nagasaki, but the Soviets had not. This is American exceptionalism.

Reagan never gave up his dream of a perfect shield against nuclear weapons, but when he met Gorbachev he began to have another dream as well. It was that, thanks to the two of them, the United States and the Soviet Union would come not just to a working relationship but to a state of perfect peace and harmony. He spoke on a couple of occasions of the alliance they would make if the world were invaded by a force from outer space. According to *Washington Post* reporter Lou Cannon, the journalist who knew the Reagan White House the best, General Colin Powell, then head of the National Security Council staff, successfully dissuaded Reagan from speaking about this vision of his in public any more than that. "Here come the little green men again," Powell would say to himself every time Reagan brought up the subject.

But of course this is a fantasy that many of us have had. Reagan did, after all, represent us rather more than we would now like to admit.

Dreams of Armageddon or some other-worldly peace did not by and large guide our policy toward the Soviet Union after World War II, not even during the Reagan administration. On the whole Washington was cautious and conservative where the Soviet Union was concerned. All the same, it came as something of a shock when Henry Kissinger during the Nixon administration uttered the words "balance of power." The conception was hardly an original one. As Kissinger had taught at Harvard, balance-of-power politics had been the normal form of international relations in Europe at least since the Congress of Vienna in 1815. Yet as a description of U.S.-Soviet relations it was wholly novel in this country; Americans did not understand the history of foreign policy in these terms. To some degree, I think, Kissinger's reputation as a wizard was based on the fact that he dared to use the words "global balance of power" in public. Kissinger *might* have told us that, like Molière's *bourgeois gentilhomme*, who had been speaking prose all his life unbeknownst to himself, the United States had been engaged in balance-of-power politics with the Soviets since World War II. But he did not. Indeed, on occasion he seemed to suggest that this balance was his own invention. In his memoirs, for example, he tells us that he had proposed a "permanent exertion" to maintain the "global balance" and to avoid nuclear war, but that his grand design was thwarted. He then goes on to say that the American people may by their nature be incapable of maintaining any such long-term commitment, since throughout their history they have been caught up in cycles of "exuberant overextension and sulking isolationism," both conceived in moralistic terms. This, I think, is sour grapes. But had Kissinger been talking about the rhetoric of U.S. foreign policy, he would have been perfectly correct.

Since World War II many of our foreign-policy makers have understood that American power had its limits and that the United States was not the sole repository of virtue in an evil world. Yet the historical rhetoric of American exceptionalism has precluded any national consensus on the need for such fundamentals of international relations as alliances, international institutions, and even diplomacy. We have always had allies, yet often we prefer to think of them as vassals rather than partners with different, but quite legitimate, interests of their own. Or we prefer to ignore them and to act alone. We were instrumental in building the United Nations, the World Bank, and other useful institutions, yet from time to time we seem to believe that their sole purpose is to destroy us. As for our diplomats, we think of them as effete conciliators. Ronald Reagan actually called them striped-pants cookie-pushers in the 1980 campaign. Then, too, as former defense secretary James Schlesinger once said, we Americans prefer not to sully our moral purity with negotiations. In the realm of our relationships with Europe and the Third World, President Carter played the Kissinger role, speaking openly of the limits of power and using the word *interdependence*. But then, unlike Kissinger, he had to run for office. In 1980 the country rebelled at this kind of talk—and at the thought that the Vietnam War and the Iranian hostage crisis might actually demonstrate the truth of what he said. It rebelled not just by defeating Carter but also by electing a man who actually believed in American exceptionalism.

Reaganites called Reagan's first term a "revolution," but it was clearly a reaction and a reversion to type. In fact, the reaction was so determined that it created a purer example of the evangelical type than any other administration in this century. Reagan did not just talk American exceptionalism, he built his foreign policy around it. It is not to exaggerate too much to say that the Reagan administration had no foreign relations apart from Reagan's own personal relationships with Thatcher, Kohl, and Gorbachev. Otherwise it liked to act unilaterally. The trouble was that, marching ahead on its own particular crusade route, it would find itself in the thickets of Middle Eastern or Central American politics, lost and hopelessly confused. In this sense the Iran-contra affair was no aberration. In fact, Oliver North with his patriotic pieties and his farcical covert operations could be seen as the synedoche for the whole.

In the nineteenth century, when the United States was geopolitically isolated from the other great powers and unchallenged in its drive to the west, American exceptionalism could be preached without obvious contradiction and without too great a risk. But that time has long passed, and, given our experiences in this century, its survival—not to speak of its great revival in the Reagan years—is, on the face of it, puzzling. My guess is that the explanation has less to do with habit or tradition than it does with the perennial question of American identity. In the nineteenth century the evangelical Protestant theology of rebirth and self-transformation translated very well into the political project of molding former colonies with heterogeneous immigrant populations into a nation with its own distinct identity. That theology provided us with a powerful myth of origins. Well, today we are still a nation of immigrants and people on the move, a pluralistic society whose nature and culture is constantly contested and in flux. Who are "we?" What is "an American" like? These questions are partly historical and they are never settled, or not for very long. Any sociologist will tell you that when a community is divided or unsure of its cohesion, one way to keep it together is to project its own aggression upon the outside world. If "they" exist, then so do "we." I am not suggesting anything deterministic here. I am not suggesting that our internal conflicts translate directly into conflicts abroad. Rather, what I am suggesting is that those who wish to minimize or suppress internal contestation tend to project the aggression—or on the other hand to imagine a world in which there are no conflicts at all.

Possibly there is another explanation. Perhaps it is simply a matter of political habit. In any case, my purpose here is simply to point out how astonishingly successful this myth of origins has been in the public narrative of American history, and the extent to which it continues to influence the rhetoric of foreign policy. What the rhetoric of the Gulf War shows is that it persists almost regardless of circumstance and almost regardless of anyone's personal views.

When Iraq invaded Kuwait, President Bush at first condemned the invasion in much the same terms as his European counterparts did. He went on to say that the invasion threatened U.S. national security interests—not because of some evil miasma it had loosed upon the world but because Iraq threatened Saudi Arabia and the power balance in the Middle East. This was his first response. It was only after the pollsters and public relations people went to work that Bush told us that Saddam Hussein was Hitler, thus transforming the issue into the moral, historical language that has traditionally justified American actions abroad. When journalists then asked why it was that the Reagan and the Bush administrations had had perfectly normal relations with this Hitler for years, there was no answer from Baker or Bush.

On March 6, 1991, President Bush reported to a joint session of Congress on the conclusion of the war. In that speech he outlined four key goals to be pursued in the Middle East: shared security arrangements; control over the proliferation of weapons of mass destruction; progress toward a settlement of the Arab-Israeli conflict; and economic development for the region. All four were important, ambitious goals, whose achievement would not be at all easy. Bush then went on to speak about a "new world order" of justice and peace. While he was careful to say that "even a new world order cannot guarantee an era of perpetual peace," he was clearly speaking of a different order of phenomenon than the settlement of Middle Eastern conflicts. Toward the end of the speech Bush simply took off into the evangelical spheres, maintaining that the United States had "selflessly" confronted "evil for the sake of good" in a land far away and concluding:

> We went halfway around the world to do what is moral and just and right.
> And we fought hard and—with others—we won the war. And we lifted
> the yoke of aggression and tyranny from a small country that many
> Americans had never even heard of, and we ask nothing in return.

Now, there is nothing wrong with a little self-congratulation. But this, I submit, was dangerous talk. Soon thereafter the Iraqi Shiites and the Kurds rose up in arms, and in an echo of Hungary in 1956, they were brutally put down by Saddam Hussein. If they had believed that the United States would help them in their struggle against tyranny, then there had been a tragic misunderstanding. Bush's speech was aimed at an American audience, which was used to hearing such things about its own national history. But then even with the American audience, Bush had opened himself to charges of hypocrisy. If the war was a moral crusade, why didn't Bush get rid of this Hitler, Saddam Hussein? What about Iraqi civilian casualties? Why was the United States allied with other tyrannical governments in the region, and why did it do nothing about the human-rights abuses perpetrated by the Kuwaiti government? These were fair questions, and the Bush administration had no answers because the president had denied that we had any national interests in the Gulf.

We are not a cynical people. To the contrary, we tend to leave worldly wisdom to others. But over time the discrepancy between word and deed, rhetoric and policy, our civil religion and actual history has corrupted the relationship between foreign-policy makers and the rest of us. It has also made life extremely difficult for those who teach American history in the schools. After all, the doctrine of American exceptionalism is in essence the proposition that we have no history in the ordinary—or secular—sense of that word.

Now that the cold war is over, we have at least the occasion to rethink how we speak about our foreign policy and how we teach the diplomatic history of this country. In my view, students, among others, would find the history of our foreign relations a good deal more interesting, and perhaps also more inspiring, than the endless repetition of patriotic bromides. They would certainly have a better understanding of the world and our nation's role in it. And it is just possible that they would be better prepared to deal with the world of the twenty-first century.

Reflections on the Crisis in History

Edwin M. Yoder, Jr.

In 1981 or thereabouts (to echo Willa Cather's famous claim that the world broke in two "in 1922 or thereabouts") a new word began circulating in Washington. The word was *factoid*, and as its associations would suggest, a factoid was a statement that seemed factual but was not—for instance, that Franklin D. Roosevelt's New Deal was deeply influenced by Italian fascism, or that the eruption of Mount St. Helens had discharged more pollution into the atmosphere than all the automobiles in California.

The word accompanied the "Reagan revolution" of that year, and for good reason: it described the new president's amiable habit of making up his history as he went along, often to suit ideological need. And yet as he left office eight years later, Reagan, in a little-noticed farewell address, urged the schools to "teach history, based not on what's in fashion but on what's important." Otherwise, he warned, we might suffer "an eradication of the American memory that could result, ultimately, in an erosion of the American spirit." The admonition seemed at the time more impressive than the examples Reagan cited of what was historically important—his list included the Doolittle raid on Tokyo during World War II. But the sentiments are sound, as far as they go.

Unfortunately, Reagan was sometimes so heedless of his own counsel that "factoid" became a term tailor made for the anecdotes that often passed, for him, as history. Lars-Erik Nelson of the New York *Daily News* grew curious, for instance, about a story the president liked to tell. During the Second World War, the story went, a badly shot up B-24 bomber was headed down when the captain discovered that one member of his crew was too gravely hurt to bail out. "Son," he said, "we'll ride it down together." Reagan told the story with conviction, often with a catch in his throat, usually ending with the dramatic question, "Where do we get such young

201

men?" Few eyes remained dry. But Nelson discovered that the president was, in fact, recounting a scene from an old movie.

It was tempting to say that Ronald Reagan, with his propensity for factoids and for confusing old movies with history, was unusual. But was he really? If historical knowledge has become problematical in our time, the divergence between admonition and practice in Reagan's case might be taken to stand, symbolically, for a common default. We pay homage to history in principle; we affirm its centrality to the national identity. Yet we do not learn very much of it. What we do learn we apparently do not learn well. As some of the essays in this volume suggest, moreover, even those whose professional calling it is to discover and teach historical truth shy from the demanding challenge of judging what is primary and what is secondary.

The problem is no doubt in part a consequence of the collapse of the consensus of humanistic learning—the old certainties about what the curriculum should include. When I was a college student in the mid-1950s, these difficulties were little recognized. There were the usual quarrels—had the Southern states been justified in seceding after the election of Lincoln, for instance—but priorities were still confidently asserted. The two-semester course known as Contemporary Civilization in the West—a famous core survey designed at Columbia University during and just after the First World War—was required of every freshman, along with the courses in Chaucer, Milton, and Shakespeare, modern and classical languages, hard science, and mathematics. The liberal arts still claimed a firm foothold and the study of history, European and American in particular, was very much part of it. In her illuminating contribution to this book, Lynn Hunt of the University of Pennsylvania tells us that in the history departments of "elite" universities, where scholarly specialization is the rule, this is no longer the case. Western civ is often held in contempt, viewed as superficial for majors and pointless for nonmajors. Moreover, she writes:

> Like many people since World War II, historians have lost their confidence that the history leading up to the present has been a story of increasing freedom and progress. The confident teleologies about Western values, with their reliance on science, technology, and mass political participation, disintegrated in the aftermath of fascist rallies, death camps, and the atom bomb. The Vietnam War, the threat of ecological disaster, AIDS, and the new forms of state torture and terrorism have deepened further doubts about the meaning of modern Western history. By the 1980s, it was clear that Auschwitz and Hiroshima could not be dismissed as aberrations in an upward curve toward progress in human rights. . . . Historians have lost faith, along with their colleagues in other fields in the humanities, in any form of "master narrative," by which I mean a unifying teleological thread of interpretation.

The doubts Hunt describes are hardly limited to Western civ courses. American history appears to be taught badly or not at all. In a recent survey of secondary school students, Diane Ravitch found that

> two thirds of the sample of 17 years olds [whom she and a colleague had queried] did not know that the Civil War had occurred between 1850 and 1900, nearly 40 per cent did not know that the Brown decision held school segregation unconstitutional. . . . 70 per cent did not know that the purpose of Jim Crow laws was to enforce racial segregation; and . . . 30 per cent could not find Great Britain on a map of Europe.[1]

If ignorance were the only deficiency, we could go far to correct it by resolving to do once again, but better, what we did in former times—teach the meat and potatoes courses in history. But with the collapse of the liberal consensus and the faith that "progress" of some sort is the great theme of history, the conception of history itself has become problematical. A crisis of professional confidence is implicit in nearly every essay in this volume. It was my assignment, as a nonprofessional auditor and historical amateur, to react to these recitals of professional anguish. They sometimes reminded me of those hideous "reeducation" camps that were a feature of the Maoist revolution in China, places of penance where bourgeois thought-crimes were confessed and expiated. By all the evidence here, the great thought-crime in American academia, pre-sixties version, was a blind preoccupation with what used to be called, without undue self-consciousness, the ruling classes. It was taken for granted that they were the actors, the rainmakers, of the past. It is a much reiterated theme of these essays that one of the great tasks now before historians is to widen the tent, to include in the "master narrative" non-Westerners, former colonial peoples, women, blacks, "ordinary people." We are repeatedly told that the "canon" of conventional history has been Eurocentric; that it has been too much a "celebratory saga" of "male fantasies," stressing combat and dominance, as Professor Bonnie Smith asserts. She, for one, finds a residue of male aggressiveness embedded in the very terminology in which Ranke and other nineteenth-century scientizers of history discussed the importance of the archives—as if on a mission of rapine. She calls for the additional insights that are to be obtained by paying greater attention to "gender" roles:

> Even the most conservative historians will note that Nazis and fascists displayed misogynist tendencies. . . . The Nazi ideologue's power rested on his being distinct from the women around him, on redefining himself as a warrior and male after the shattering experiences of World War I. Hitler's first year in power saw major legislation working toward reestablishing gender clarity and the power of masculinity. . . . That legislation mandated

the removal of women from civil service and university jobs . . . and
provided subsidies for women who would stop working in order to have
families.

As I listened to these anguished confessions, musings, and admonitions
on the possibilities of alternative history, it was driven home to me how
deeply, just now, history as a subject and discipline is tormented by cultural
and political doubts and second thoughts. The crisis is obviously in some
sense political. But it would simplify, even vulgarize, a complex dilemma to
attribute it exclusively to the currently fashionable assault on the core cultural values of the West. There are traces of that; but such a diagnosis would
do violence to the subtlety of the problem. The doubts that assail professional historians cut deeper than leftist fashion. Indeed, they worry not only
people of the left but also historians whose political views are emphatically
centrist.

A process of disorientation is clearly well advanced. Speculatively, one
might guess that it follows a predictable pattern. First comes a political
revolution — the civil rights revolution, let us say, or decolonialization, or
the feminist agenda. With the revolution comes the now-famous "consciousness raising," whereby persons of normal sensitivity abruptly become
aware of new perspectives and new expectations that cannot be brushed
aside. The new consciousness soon penetrates the academy. Institutionally,
as we all know, the academy is normally very conservative. But it is, as we
also know, abnormally susceptible to new fashions in ideas, to the capri-
ciously rising and falling hemlines of the scholarly world. Soon, there arises
a demand for an accommodation of the "canon" of study to the new consciousness, and an entire generation of historians has soon grown restless,
with results so apparent in the preceding essays. These crosscurrents can no
more be ignored than the weather.

Even if we resolved to teach history more diligently, it would be hard in
this climate of doubt and unsettlement to shape a compelling story, a "master narrative," vivid and confident enough to capture the student imagination. It may be thrilling to shoot the rapids of controversy. But without a
strong story line, one is unlikely to win the uphill battle to engage the
young in history — or, indeed, to wean their parents from their own appall-
ing inability to differentiate between history and fantasy or to analyze a historical issue beyond the most childish level. My guess is that we must enjoy
some serenity of conviction about what is important if we are to teach history with conviction. And to make an impression it must be engaging, for
reasons suggested some thirty-five years ago by Hugh Trevor-Roper in his
inaugural lecture as Regius Professor of Modern History at Oxford. I was
present, and applauded, when Trevor-Roper said that "humane subjects . . .

can only bear a limited amount of specialization. They need professional methods, but always for the pursuit of lay ends." Oh, for the innocence of that worry, which was chiefly that overspecialization was the chief threat. No one was much worried, in the mid-fifties, that the "master narrative" might collapse altogether; the worry was only that it was threatened by the specialist's magnifying glass and tendency to segment the narrative into increasingly narrow spans of time and event.

In my own day as an undergraduate student of history, historians still spoke confidently of episodes, ideas, and personalities that remained comfortably familiar. There had been a Renaissance, we were told, a revival of classical learning and form following on the heels of the Middle Ages. Historians might debate when it appeared and whether it represented quite so sharp a turn as old textbooks suggested, but a Renaissance there had been. Historians spoke with confidence, too, of a Reformation, of a scientific revolution, of an Enlightenment, of the French Revolution, of the "origins" and "consequences" of epic struggles like the American Civil War and World War I. It was cheerfully assumed that one could hardly pretend to be educated—or fully civilized, in the root meaning of the word—without some substantial grasp of these pivotal historical events. The same held for the presumed importance of great figures—Augustine and Aquinas, Luther, Calvin, Louis XIV, Richelieu, Robespierre, Voltaire, Napoleon, Wellington, Metternich, Lincoln, Darwin, and Woodrow Wilson. And others, many others. Maybe in retrospect we were wrong to believe that the movers and shakers of history could possibly be so exclusively male, European, or of European origin. But the conviction of their enduring importance was entirely unself-conscious. We had heard of Toussaint and Nat Turner and other rebels; yet their historical impact was tangential, the one explaining Napoleon's abandonment of the Western Hemisphere, and his sale of Louisiana; the other explaining the deepening defensiveness of the embattled slaveocracy. In a portrait of one of my favorite history teachers of that period, I once tried to recapture the mood and ethos of that time:

In his deliberate and methodical way, J. R. Caldwell brought the past to life; at the least he made sense of it. As the last echo of the bell died, he would stub out his pre-class Raleigh 903 cigarette, prop a foot upon the handiest desk, and begin: "When the bell sounded, gentlemen, we were examining into . . . " Examining into! That was the trademark phrase of his teaching; it seemed novel and attractive to those of us for whom, at this stage, history remained an unmemorable muddle of dates, names, personages, treaties and other matter vaguely known and certainly of no practical consequence. History was something to be "examined into"—not a static or fixed pattern, not a lie agreed upon, but something for scrutiny? Here was something new.

I shall not urge the claim, here, that J. R. Caldwell was the most spectacular lecturer of his time; he was merely the most effective. If the subject was Napoleon—"a man on horseback," as he invariably called him—J. R. Caldwell gave you five reasons why Napoleon came to power; and when the proper time came, he gave you five reasons (all equally plausible) why he fell. . . . Like all historical accounts, J. R. Caldwell's account of modern history was of course an artifice, as a good parquet floor is an artifice. You knew that the design was imposed by human craft upon a good assortment of rough-hewn lumber. But there was no looseness about it, no ill-fitting joints. It would bear weight.

In Caldwell's classroom, it was assumed that history was an inquiry, yielding an artifice; that history would necessarily have a subjective bent and sometimes a nationalistic bias. But notwithstanding its parochial framework, "history" was still objectively there: a body of knowledge that one could grasp. One might argue over what it meant, who had been the heroes and villains. But there was a story line, a master narrative. That it might have struck a Nigerian or a Korean or an Eskimo as parochial did not trouble us.

Today, that situation obtains no longer. Earlier essays in this volume bear eloquent witness to the collapse of that earlier innocence about the story line. Worse, if Diane Ravitch's findings are typical, many young persons taking college degrees today, even very able ones, seem to know more about the deconstructionist controversy or the quarrel at Stanford over the great books than about how the United States or the larger world got from there to here, or from then to now.

The acceptance of this historyless condition, whatever its causes, seems something new. For at least three centuries a sense of history—as a process or body of learning or inquiry—has been considered basic to humanistic education. Sir Isaiah Berlin traces the origins of the tradition to the early eighteenth-century reflections of Giambattista Vico, the Neapolitan scholar and polymath. Vico, Sir Isaiah tells us, was the first notable student of history to assert that the story we weave from the past need not be regarded as a tissue of imprecise or derisory fable or myth but rather as the most reliable kind of knowledge accessible to the human mind. Since we have special access to our own thoughts and emotions, more exact and reliable than our access to the external world, we can infer what people who lived before us thought, what motivated them to act as they did. Vico's celebration of history was, by Sir Isaiah's account, a turning point in Western intellectual history. It represented a revolt against the Cartesian-rationalist view of knowledge, which held that the only reliable truths were intuitive, deductive, abstract, and self-evident. It was the beginning of an important empirical inquiry that orients us in the great stream of time.

Is history in that sense now "history" in the latest slang sense—something discarded, outdated, dispensed with? Have we reached the end of the age in which historical knowledge could be regarded as one of the higher forms of truth, and as a cornerstone of human identity? The quizzical titles of some recent books—Sir John Plumb's *The Death of the Past* comes to mind—suggest that possibility.

I began by recalling Lars-Erik Nelson's discovery that Ronald Reagan had been representing a movie as history. I wonder whether we might find some connection between that sort of romanticizing and the failure of nerve (if that is what it is) among professional historians. There has always been an intimate commerce between the imaginative and the historical—between poetry and truth, as Goethe might have put it. The great example is the more controversial Shakespeare history plays, *Richard III*, for instance. I have to plead guilty, myself, to liking Peter Brook's recent play *Amadeus*, in spite of the liberties it is known to have taken with Mozart's life and with the character of his rival Salieri. When one of the bastard forms of historical mimesis is artful enough, we tend to excuse the liberties it takes with fact. That is perhaps because such forms tap a tradition of historical recital in which the value of studying the past was thought to lie less in exactitude than in edifying example. President Reagan was frequently and severely rebuked for his tendency to confuse factoids with facts. But Reagan at his most romantic is no match for those—chiefly literary scholars—who now call themselves "new historicists," and who seem to be taking up the fallen standard of historical mythmaking where historians long ago abandoned it. Their curious works are worth a moment's (if only a moment's) glance, for they are symptomatic, also, of the uses of history in our time.

The word *historicism* itself has acquired a new meaning. "Historicism," a few short years ago, was a deterministic doctrine, associated with Hegel and Marx, holding that a brooding spirit—"History" with a capital H—provided the ultimate judgment over time and, in effect, punished or ratified human acts. It was the favored rationalization of merciless measures of social engineering by totalitarian regimes. It appealed to the unfathomable future; it looked for justification to a secularized adaptation of the *Eschatos*, the end of days.

Today, in the hands of the "new historicists," historicism has a more benign but equally dubious connotation. The new historicists are said to have discarded the naive view that history is "a set of fixed and knowable facts that furnish the background of a work of art." History may not be a set of fixed facts; but that does not mean that it is infinitely plastic. The leader of the new historicist school, Professor Stephen J. Greenblatt of the University of California, has proposed—for instance—that Shakespeare's *Tempest* should be read as a parable of colonialism.[2] Caliban, he claims, represents the anti-imperialist view. But what is known of the Elizabethan age and its attitudes toward exploration suggests that Shakespeare and his contemporaries were as innocent of ideological fixations about the settlement of new lands overseas as we would be about, say, the exploration of space. The brave new world whose marvels Miranda exclaims over was the frontier of its time, as space is of ours. One may doubt that *The Tempest*, however decoded, has much to say about colonialism, which, for that matter, is an "ism" of distinctly recent coinage. As is the exploitative purpose implied by the term.

Reviewing Greenblatt's work in the *New York Review of Books*, Anne Barton speaks of his "tendency to handle historical circumstances approximately." There is, for instance, his handling of a minor matter—how Christ Church, Oxford, obtained Cardinal Wolsey's hat. The hat is displayed in a case in the college library, and its provenance is explained by an accompanying card. But since the story on the card did not fit the new historicist version of the past, Greenblatt revised the story. It became a mere "approximation" of the known facts. Barton writes: "The elegance with which Greenblatt accommodates [the Cardinal's hat to the story he wants to tell about the Reformation] makes one almost regret having to disturb it with specificities."[3]

Is Greenblatt heedless of the line that separates the historical from the fabulous? Surely not. Does he assume that it is no longer important? Perhaps. And the view seems to be typical of the new historicism. Frank Kermode, commenting in the same publication[4] on yet another work of the new historicism, speaks of "the quest for novelty at the expense of the obvious," of "an habitual far-fetchedness," of "those hocus-pocus passages that enable the writer to say what he wants to say even though he knows better," of "the desire to astonish by novelty." "It is easy to say something new," Kermode says, "if you don't care whether it makes any sense."

Still another clue to the mentality of the new historicism may be found in a recent lecture by Professor J. Hillis Miller entitled "Hawthorne and History." Here, the word *history* is again massaged into unfamiliar shapes. Miller's subject is a familiar Hawthorne tale, "The Minister's Black Veil." In the story, a New England Congregationalist clergyman appears one day with a mysterious black veil of doubled crepe covering the upper part of his face. He never explains it; he never takes it off. He wears it to his dying day and he even insists on being buried in it. Miller notes that the idea might have been suggested by the report of an actual minister who, in Hawthorne's time, had done the same thing. The historical person had taken his veil in shame. But since no one within the four corners of the Hawthorne story is able to discover why the clergyman wears the veil, it becomes for Miller a symbol of impenetrability and thus underscores the indeterminacy of history. The "older assumption," Miller writes, was "that history is something solidly out there, external to language or other sign-systems":

What difference does it make [Miller then asks] whether a parable uses real history or pretended history as its analogical base? *Does not parable break down that distinction by showing historical events to be always already parabolic?* (italics added)[5]

The answer to Miller's question would obviously depend on what one meant by saying that historical events are "always already parabolic," but behind these mystifying words lurks the insinuation, at least as I read Miller's lecture, that history is so entirely indeterminate as to be radically subjective. In that case, there is no discoverable historical truth and invention or approximation do quite as well as the careful ascertainment or documentation of authentic past events. For those who delight in mind-twisting word games, such a formulation has a mischievous allure. Yet it is radically subversive of historicity. Perhaps that is Miller's intention. But if you believe, as I do, that history, elusive as it often is, nonetheless has discoverable contours, independent of the "parabolic" uses we make of it, then the pranks of the new historicism are mischievous and unacceptable. They trivialize what is demonstrably of human consequence. One can easily think of instances in which the distinction between the historical and the imaginary, or as Miller might put it, the historical and the "parabolic," made a great difference, and not merely in famous forgeries like the Donation of Constantine or the Protocols of the Elders of Zion. The "parabolic" representation of history made a cruel difference when Joseph Stalin used the Kirov murder to frame and judicially execute the Old Bolsheviks, and again when Stalin ordered the murder of a substantial segment of the Polish officer corps in the Katyn Forest in the early days of the Second World War and blamed the crime on the Germans. It made a difference for the State Department's "China hands," foully accused in the McCarthy time of complicity in what was fancifully called "the loss of China": the Maoist revolution of 1949. Perhaps you need to have lived, as many of the new historicists are too young to have lived, in a time when historical lies and inventions made a vast difference in human destiny to see that historical inquiry is not something to be trifled with or trivialized.

We are, to be sure, *homo ludens*—the playing animal—and perhaps I make too much of a game. What happens to history in the odd literary study or in Shakespeare or Hawthorne is clearly less consequential than what happened to it in the Stalin and McCarthyite purges—perhaps too inconsequential to bear comparison with those truly evil manipulations of the record that have been instrumental to great human tragedies in our century. But where to draw the line? It seems to me that the new historicism is entirely too complacent, content as it seems to be with "approximations" of the truth, and advertising, as Miller does, the dubious presumption that the historical is "always . . . parabolic."

I return, finally, to the superbly articulated concerns of professional historians that precede this essay. Perhaps Western parochialism is a danger. But there is also a danger, to judge by the evidence here, that history classrooms will come to resemble places of confession and atonement for thought-crimes more than places of balanced inquiry. In that case, history teaching will carry the baggage of excessive guilt and, accordingly, bear a very low charge of conviction. Western civilization may be parochial in the ways described by Lynn Hunt. But examining it and its part in shaping our minds and manners must nonetheless be a central concern if we expect students to develop a coherent sense of the processes of history and how we got where we are today. I am glad, myself, to have been exposed to at least a bit about such episodes, phenomena, and personalities as medievalism, scholasticism, Charlemagne, and other subjects of the old Columbia Western civilization course. I would guess that persons deprived of that benefit will always be a bit bewildered historically, no matter how much they eventually learn about colonialism in Africa or the marriage rituals of Eskimos. The latter things are surely worth knowing about; but it may be more important, in the first instance and in one's formative years, to study what happened, and why, at the Diet of Worms.

It is heartwarming to think that we have risen above what we take to be the moral blind spots of some earlier generation, to feel that our own "master narrative" is more just and inclusive. But there are dangers here, too. If it was among the vices of "whig" historiography that it incubated "teleological" history, history with the illusion of a clear and progressive tendency, another of its vices is surely the habit of patronizing the past, feeling morally superior to it, judging its crimes and follies by post hoc standards. It is tempting to feel a sense of moral superiority to the past, to the world that existed before the revolution of 1968, but we should also bear in mind that we live in the cruelest century of which we have record and have small warrant for smugness.

Likewise, the broadening of the "master narrative" to include the once excluded is surely desirable in principle—so long as the new historical canon is not determined by political fashion or by some sort of plebiscitary process. I have a nightmare vision of a California-like referendum—Proposition 2000, perhaps—in which by majority vote, in good democratic fashion, we shall determine which episodes, books, and heroes and heroines (and also which villains) are fit to figure in what is now the global civilization course. Or we vote to decide whether there really was a Renaissance, as once claimed, and whether the fifteenth-century version was prefigured by the twelfth-century version. This would be an Orwellian outcome in the determination of what is history and what is not.

I exaggerate to make a point, of course. Even in an age of political correctness, there will be no such referendum on history. But there is a legitimate link between history and popular will. Our own founding generation proposed to build a *novus ordo seclorum*, a "new order of the ages," situating the infant republic in the entire sweep of human history. Their Declaration of Independence had likewise appealed to real historic events, if sometimes (as in their reference to the alleged offenses of the king of England) to a tendentious version. The American revolutionaries thought they owed responsibility to history. Unlike dictators and tyrants, who often find it necessary to cover their historical tracks, they emphasized and appealed to history. Later, the Bill of Rights, and indeed the Constitution itself, would be creatures of history: this in the sense that you could not really understand their curiously exact provisions ("nor compelled in any criminal case to be a witness against himself"; "letters of marque and reprisal") unless you knew the history of the abuses of liberty it sought to shield us against. These examples could be multiplied; for as our most eloquent president said, we cannot escape history. History and democratic government go hand in hand; and our institutions are no more or less robust than our accumulated knowledge of the soil of time from which they sprang.

In some of the essays that appear in this volume, I detect an occasional subtle insinuation that the value of this or that course of study is to be gauged by the origins — racial, ethnic, sexual, or whatnot — of the designer or sponsor or author. Is that what we seek, even as we affirm inclusiveness as the paramount historian's virtue? Shall we swap one "privileged" perspective (to use the current jargon) for another, equally privileged? As teachers, writers, and journalists, we should take it as our mission to shape and communicate a plausible and reasonable "master narrative," and a humanizing history, whatever options we seize in deciding on its content. Content will always be debated, for time passes and perspectives change. Yet if we do not communicate some confident and compelling version of the common past, we fail at our paramount mission. If we seem to view civilization as a mere facade for a conspiracy against justice and the common folk, we shall do little but confuse and unsettle those who look to us for historical understanding.

NOTES

1. Diane Ravitch, "The Plight of History in American Schools," in *Historical Literacy*, ed. Paul Gagnon (New York, 1989), p. 52.

2. Stephen J. Greenblatt, *Learning to Curse* (New York, 1991).

3. Anne Barton, "The Perils of Historicism," *New York Review of Books*, March 28, 1991, pp. 53–56.

4. Frank Kermode, "The High Cost of New History," *New York Review of Books*, June 25, 1992, pp. 43–45.

5. J. Hillis Miller, *Hawthorne and History: Defacing It* (Cambridge, Mass., and Oxford, 1991), pp. 108, 111.

Contributors

James O. Anderson, professor of history of education and of history at the University of Illinois, Urbana, is coeditor, with V. P. Franklin, of *New Perspectives in Black Educational History* (1978) and author of *The Education of Blacks in the South* (1988).

William L. Barney received his doctorate from Columbia University and has published extensively in nineteenth-century U.S. history, especially in the era of the Civil War. He currently holds a Bowman-Gray Professorship from the University of North Carolina for excellence in undergraduate teaching. His most recent publication is *Battleground for the Union: The Era of Civil War and Reconstruction, 1848-1877* (1990).

Jonathan Beller is a doctoral candidate in the Graduate Program in Literature at Duke University. His dissertation is entitled "The Cinematic Mode of Production."

Ariel Dorfman is a Chilean citizen who was forced into exile after the 1973 coup that overthrew Salvador Allende. His numerous books—including novels, plays, and short stories—have been translated into more than thirty languages. Available in English are: *How to Read Donald Duck* (with Armand Mattelart, 1971), *The Empire's Old Clothes* (1983), *Widows* (1983), *The Last Song of Manuel Sendero* (1986), *Mascara* (1988), *Hard Rain* (1990), *My House Is on Fire* (1990), *Last Waltz in Santiago and Other Poems of Exile and Disappearance* (1988), and the plays, *Widows, Reader*, and *Death and the Maiden*. He is Research Professor of Literature and Latin American Studies at Duke University.

Frances FitzGerald is an author and journalist who lives in New York City. She has been a frequent contributor to the *New Yorker* and other periodicals. Her books include *Fire in the Lake: The Vietnamese and the Americans in Vietnam* (1972) (for which she was awarded a Pulitzer Prize) and *America Revised: History Schoolbooks in the Twentieth Century* (1979).

Alice J. Garrett is a doctoral student in educational leadership at the University of North Carolina at Chapel Hill. A classroom teacher for twenty-three years, she is now an assistant principal with the Johnston County schools in North Carolina.

Daniel Gordon taught in the core curriculum at the University of Chicago and at Stanford University before becoming an assistant professor of history and history and literature at Harvard University. He has written articles on the French Enlightenment and is preparing a book on the concept of sociability in prerevolutionary France.

Lynn Hunt is Annenberg Professor of History at the University of Pennsylvania. She is the author of three books on the French Revolution and the editor of *The New Cultural History* (1989). She is currently writing a Western civilization textbook.

Lloyd Kramer is an associate professor of history at the University of North Carolina at Chapel Hill, where his teaching includes courses on the history of Western civilization and on modern European intellectual history. He has received a students' award for excellence in undergraduate teaching, and is the author of *Threshold of a New World: Intellectuals and the Exile Experience in Paris, 1830-1848* (1988).

Dominick LaCapra is Bryce and Edith M. Bowmar Professor of Humanistic Studies at Cornell University, where he is also director of the Society for the Humanities. His books include *Rethinking Intellectual History: Texts, Contexts, Language* (1983), *History and Criticism* (1985), and *Soundings in Critical Theory* (1989), and he has edited *The Bounds of Race: Perspectives on Hegemony and Resistance* (1991).

Mary Beth Norton is the Mary Donlon Alger Professor of American History at Cornell University. She is the author of a number of books and articles on early American history, including *Liberty's Daughters: The Revolutionary Experience of American Women* (1980). Her current research, which should culminate in a book in 1995, focuses on gender in seventeenth-century English North America.

Donald Reid is Jan Joseph Hermans Professor of History at the University of North Carolina at Chapel Hill and recipient of the Tanner Award for excellence in undergraduate teaching there. He is the author of *The Miners of Decazeville: A Genealogy of Deindustrialization* (1985) and *Paris Sewers and*

Sewermen: Realities and Representations (1991).

Richard Roberts is associate professor of African history and director of the Center for African Studies at Stanford University. He has written widely on the economic and social history of West Africa, including *Warriors, Merchants, and Slaves: The State and the Economy in the Middle Niger Valley, 1700-1914* (1987) and most recently, with Kristin Mann, *Law and Colonialism in Africa* (1991).

Robert A. Rosenstone, professor of history at the California Institute of Technology, is author of *Crusade of the Left: The Lincoln Battalion in the Spanish Civil War* (1969), *Romantic Revolutionary: A Biography of John Reed* (1975), and *Mirror in the Shrine: American Encounters in Meiji Japan* (1988). A historical consultant on a number of dramatic and documentary films, including *Reds, The Good Fight,* and *Darrow,* Rosenstone created a film review section for the *American Historical Review* in 1989 and has served as editor of the section ever since. Currently he is working on a book about film and history that will be entitled *History in Images/History in Words.*

Bonnie G. Smith teaches history at Rutgers University and is finishing a book on gender and the rise of scientific history. She is the author of several books, including *Confessions of a Concierge: Madame Lucie's History of Twentieth-Century France* (1985) and *Changing Lives: Women in European History Since 1770* (1989).

Glenn Tetterton-Opheim has taught history and German at New Hanover High School in Wilmington, North Carolina, since 1980. He holds a bachelor of arts degree from East Carolina University, a master of arts in teaching from Duke University, and a master of arts degree from the University of California, Santa Barbara.

Edwin M. Yoder, Jr., is a Washington, D.C.-based author and syndicated columnist whose columns are distributed by the *Washington Post* Writers Group. The recipient of a Pulitzer Prize for editorial writing, he has also published several books, including *The Unmaking of a Whig and Other Essays in Self-Definition* (1990).

Index